Studies in Regional and Local History

General Editor Jane Whittle

David Hey, 1938–2016.

Histories of People and Landscape

Essays on the Sheffield Region in Memory of David Hey

Edited by R.W. Hoyle

University of Hertfordshire Press
Studies in Regional and Local History

Volume 20

First published in Great Britain in 2021 by
University of Hertfordshire Press
College Lane
Hatfield
Hertfordshire
AL10 9AB
UK

British Library Cataloguing in Publication Data
A catalogue record for this book is available from the British Library

ISBN 978-1-912260-39-3 hardback
ISBN 978-1-912260-40-9 paperback

Design by Arthouse Publishing Solutions
Printed in Great Britain by Charlesworth Press

Frontispiece photograph of David Hey courtesy of Pat Hey.

Contents

Figures

Tables

Contributors

John Beckett is Professor of English Regional History at the University of Nottingham, with a particular interest in rural history. He has published extensively on local history, including *Writing Local History* (Manchester, 2004). He was until recently chairman of the Thoroton Society of Nottinghamshire and chairman of the editorial board of *Midland History*. In 2016 he published a history of the University of Nottingham, where he has spent most of his career. He first met David Hey in 1977 and subsequently learnt a great deal from him, especially in reading the landscape.

John Broad taught at London Metropolitan University (1970–2009) and since then has been attached to the Cambridge Group for the History of Population and Social Structure. He first met David Hey at the British Agricultural History Society conference at Matlock in 1973. Since then he has served as secretary and president of that society. He is editor of *Records of Buckinghamshire* and chair of the Buckinghamshire Record Society's Executive Committee, and is currently completing a book on English rural housing since medieval times.

Alan G. Crosby is a professional local and regional historian based in Preston. He has taught for several universities, including Oxford, Cambridge, Liverpool and Central Lancashire, and has published many books and papers on aspects of local, social and landscape history, mostly relating to the north-western counties. Since 2001 he has been editor of *The Local Historian*. He particularly enjoyed many fruitful and stimulating discussions with David Hey during his presidency of the British Association for Local History (2008–16). In 2020 he received the honour of a festschrift: Marianne Howell *et al* (eds), *Lancashire Studies. Historical Essays in Honour of Alan Crosby* (Lancashire Local History Federation, 2020).

Peter Edwards is Emeritus Professor of Early Modern British Social and Economic History at the University of Roehampton, London. David Hey tutored him on the MA course in English Local History at Leicester and supervised his dissertation. Recently he has not only 'encroached' on David's home ground geographically, having long followed him as an historian of transport, though perversely ignoring the goods being carried in order to focus on the animals that provided the motive force.

Dorian Gerhold is an independent historian. His earliest research was as a local historian in Putney, south-west London, and he has since written about carriers and stage-coaches, industrial history, Westminster Hall, Old London Bridge, urban cartography and Chancery records. His *Carriers and Coachmasters* was the 2007 Transport Book of the Year. His working life was spent as a House of Commons Clerk from 1978 to 2012. He first met David Hey when working on carriers.

Richard Hoyle was successively Professor of History at Central Lancashire (1998–2000), Professor of Rural History at the University of Reading (2000–2014) and Professor of Local and Regional History at the University of London (2014–16). He is now Visiting Professor of Economic History at Reading. He served as editor of *Agricultural History Review* for 21 years, retiring in 2019. As he has described elsewhere, he first met David Hey on a train to the Agricultural History Society conference in 1985 and enjoyed his company over the following 30 years.

Melvyn Jones (1938–2021) taught at Sheffield Hallam University and its predecessors, Sheffield City Polytechnic and Sheffield City College of Education, for 30 years. He was a historical geographer and landscape historian. On his retirement in 1999 he was appointed Visiting Professor in Landscape History at Sheffield Hallam. He was the author or editor of more than 80 books during his career.

Charles Phythian-Adams spent his career at the department of English Local History at the University of Leicester, latterly as professor of English Local History. He was appointed there as a junior research fellow in late medieval urban history under W.G. Hoskins in 1965, and was soon joined by David Hey as his equivalent in rural history. Shared interests forged a long friendship, and in 1991 Charles edited David's splendid book *The Fiery Blades of Hallamshire: Sheffield and its Neighbourhood, 1600–1740* in the department's monograph series. In turn, David involved Charles in his substantial *Oxford Companion to Family and Local History* in 2008.

George Redmonds (1935–2018) was awarded his doctorate in 1970 on West Riding surnames, his thesis later appearing as the inaugural volume in the English surnames series. In 1974 he resigned from his post at Huddersfield Polytechnic to begin a freelance career in local history and names studies, lecturing world-wide. He has published a succession of books on surnames, including *Surnames, DNA and Family History* (2011), co-authored with David Hey and Turi King. Sixty years of research in Yorkshire surnames culminated in the publication in 2015 of his *Dictionary of Yorkshire Surnames*. His *Yorkshire Historical Dictionary* is now online at yorkshiredictionary.york.ac.uk and will appear in print in 2021. He and David were friends and academic collaborators for many years.

Ian D. Rotherham is Professor of Environmental Geography at Sheffield Hallam University and has written extensively on the ecology and history of ancient woodlands. Along with academic papers and books, he also writes and broadcasts for the popular media. He chairs a number of national and international research committees for bodies such as the International Union of Forest Research Organizations, the British Ecological Society and the European Society for Environmental History. He is a leading authority on countryside environmental history.

Nicola Verdon is Professor of Modern British History at Sheffield Hallam University. She has published widely on gender and labour in the British countryside in the nineteenth and twentieth centuries, including *Rural Women Workers in Nineteenth-Century England* (2002) and *Working the Land: A History of the Farmworker in England from 1850 to the Present Day* (2017). She served as secretary of the British Agricultural History Society from 2009 to 2016 and first met David at the Society's annual Spring conference in 1997.

The publication of this volume has been supported by generous subventions from the British Agricultural History Society, Hunter Archaeological Society and Yorkshire Archaeological and Historical Society, and donations from the contributors to this volume in memory of David Hey.

It is with great sadness that we record the death
of Professor Melvyn Jones on 14 January 2021
whilst this book was in press.

Volume 1: *A Hertfordshire demesne of Westminster Abbey: Profits, productivity and weather* by Derek Vincent Stern (edited and with an introduction by Christopher Thornton)

Volume 2: *From Hellgill to Bridge End: Aspects of economic and social change in the Upper Eden Valley, 1840–95* by Margaret Shepherd

Volume 3: *Cambridge and its Economic Region, 1450–1560* by John S. Lee

Volume 4: *Cultural Transition in the Chilterns and Essex Region, 350 AD to 650 AD* by John T. Baker

Volume 5: *A Pleasing Prospect: Society and culture in eighteenth-century Colchester* by Shani D'Cruze

Volume 6: *Agriculture and Rural Society after the Black Death: Common themes and regional variations* by Ben Dodds and Richard Britnell

Volume 7: *A Lost Frontier Revealed: Regional separation in the East Midlands* by Alan Fox

Volume 8: *Land and Family: Trends and local variations in the peasant land market on the Winchester bishopric estates, 1263–1415* by John Mullan and Richard Britnell

Volume 9: *Out of the Hay and into the Hops: Hop cultivation in Wealden Kent and hop marketing in Southwark, 1744–2000* by Celia Cordle

Volume 10: *A Prospering Society: Wiltshire in the later Middle Ages* by John Hare

Volume 11: *Bread and Ale for the Brethren: The provisioning of Norwich Cathedral Priory, 1260–1536* by Philip Slavin

Volume 12: *Poor Relief and Community in Hadleigh, Suffolk, 1547–1600* by Marjorie Keniston McIntosh

Volume 13: *Rethinking Ancient Woodland: The archaeology and history of woods in Norfolk* by Gerry Barnes and Tom Williamson

Volume 14: *Custom and Commercialisation in English Rural Society: Revisiting Tawney and Postan* edited by J.P. Bowen and A.T. Brown

Volume 15: *The World of the Small Farmer: Tenure, profit and politics in the early modern Somerset Levels* by Patricia Croot

Volume 16: *Communities in Contrast: Doncaster and its rural hinterland, c.1830–1870* by Sarah Holland

Volume 17: *Peasant Perspectives on the Medieval Landscape: A study of three communities* by Susan Kilby

Volume 18: *Shaping the Past: Theme, time and place in local history – essays in honour of David Dymond* by Evelyn Lord and Nicholas R. Amor

Volume 19: *Lichfield and the Lands of St Chad: Creating community in early medieval Mercia* by Andrew Sargent

Abbreviations

APC	*Acts of the Privy Council*
BL	British Library
BodL	Bodleian Library
BPP	British Parliamentary Papers
DA	Dudley Archives
DAJ	*Derbyshire Archaeological Journal*
DRO	Derbyshire Record Office
GPB	Gloucester Port Books
HALS	Hertfordshire Archives and Local Studies
HHA	Haddon Hall Archives
NA	Nottinghamshire Archives
NUMASC	Nottingham University Manuscript and Special Collections
ODNB	*Oxford Dictionary of National Biography*
RA	Rotherham Archives
SA	Sheffield Archives
TNA	The National Archives
TTS	*Transactions of the Thoroton Society*
VCH	Victoria County History
WYL	West Yorkshire Archives (Leeds)

Studies in Regional and Local History

General Editor's preface

Some regions benefit enormously from a dedicated local historian rooted in that area. Such historians not only carry out a rich range of research themselves, but educate and inspire others, creating 'hot-spots' of local historical knowledge. So it was with David Hey and the Sheffield region. David came from Penistone, just north west of Sheffield. His PhD was a study of Myddle in Shropshire, based on Gough's wonderful account of the parish written in 1700. But he soon returned to his roots with a post in Sheffield University's extra-mural department where he remained with great distinction for the remainder of his career. David's research spanned the history of families, industry, place-names and landscapes, with a particular focus on the period from 1500–1800. These interests are reflected in this collection which is a celebration of David's work, interests and friendships, and of the Sheffield region too. It is a region that is hard to define in simple terms, although it is familiar enough to those who have had the pleasure to live and work there. It encompasses not just the city of Sheffield itself, but most of the modern county of South Yorkshire (formerly part of the West Riding), and all of the historic region of Hallamshire. However, it also extends into the neighbouring parts of north Derbyshire and north Nottinghamshire, with which it shares strong social and economic links. It is appropriate therefore that this collection not only considers the various parts of this region and its key historical industry, steel, but also a chapter by John Broad on the history of settlements on county borders, as Sheffield is itself. The chapters emphasise the many facets of this varied region.

The first three chapters touch on the economic and political roles of the local gentry and aristocracy. Melvyn Jones' chapter takes us back to the medieval period when South Yorkshire was scattered with deer parks to satisfy the nobility and gentry's pleasure in hunting and consuming venison. Using a mixture of landscape history and archival research he traces both the location of parks and their disappearance from the landscape. Richard Hoyle asks why Sheffield did not become incorporated as a town, with its own urban government, until the nineteenth century and draws a comparison with Leeds, incorporated in 1626. He argues that the establishment of the Cutlers' company in 1624 was a solution to the problem of managing the industry rather than a response to the decline of the manorial interest of the earls of Shrewsbury. Peter Edwards investigates the more intimate life of the gentry, examining the wardship of Francis Wortley of Wortley Hall by his step-father William Cavendish of Hardwick Hall in the early seventeenth century. While the purchase of wards has been seen as damaging to their prospects, Edwards finds that Cavendish's wardship of Wortley benefitted both parties, allowing their two estates, located in similar areas, to be managed in unison.

Dorian Gerhold offers a masterful overview of the early development of steelmaking in seventeenth-century England, including the place of south Yorkshire within that development. His observations shed light on the adoption and transmission of new technology while also paying attention to the local context in which industrial development took place. Much of the Sheffield region remained non-industrial, however, and four further chapters pay attention to the history of the rural landscape and farming. Ian Rotherham examines the presence of woodland in the Derbyshire's Dark Peak, with particular reference to the Longshaw estate just outside Sheffield. He traces evidence of woodland from pre-Roman times to the present day, arguing that heathy moors were wood-pastures until Parliamentary enclosure in the eighteenth and nineteenth centuries. Trees were much more plentiful than they are now, as evidenced by 'shadow woods' where woodland plants such as bluebells remain even when the trees have disappeared. John Beckett turns his attention to Parliamentary enclosure in Nottinghamshire. He challenges earlier historians who concluded there was little popular opposition: Beckett shows that opposition was greatest where large areas of common grazing land were enclosed, as in the forest lands of north and west Nottinghamshire, rather than in the open-field villages of the clay lands. Alan Crosby examines the history of a single farming family, the Bagshaws of Hazelbadge in Derbyshire. This is a study of how generations of careful accumulation were undone in a few years by a single family member, but also how the family sought to protect itself by transferring its property to a more prudent brother in law. Nicola Verdon turns her attention to Derbyshire's more recent history, illuminating the campaign to increase food production during the First World War. Farmers were pressed to plough up pasture land for crops, but the process was not an easy one. Verdon shows how the policy was put into action at a local level, and the problems encountered with the supply of labour, the introduction of machinery, and farmers' attitudes.

The final two chapters are concerned with place-names. John Broad's wide-ranging chapter shows how untidy local administrative arrangements could be before the reforms at the end of the nineteenth century and the way in which boundary edge settlements were able to turn their liminal status to advantage. He then looks at the place-name 'Little London', showing how the places bearing that name are normally small, subordinate settlements and often on the edge of communities or in isolated locations. The late George Redmonds revisits the minor place-names of the Pennines, many of which he discussed with David Hey on country walks. He shows how surnames and minor place-names interacted, with hamlets or farms being named after the families who lived there, often as far back as the thirteenth and fourteenth centuries.

Through his many publications David Hey left us with a richer sense of how the Sheffield region's landscape and people developed over the centuries: this volume pays tribute by continuing his work and demonstrating the many different ways in which local history can be approached.

Jane Whittle
October 2020

David Hey, 1938–2016: a tribute

Charles Phythian-Adams

An address given at Dronfield Parish Church on the occasion of David Hey's funeral, 25 February 2016

Speaking of David as a friend of 50 years – five of them as colleagues – I think I can imagine how all of us here will have been similarly devastated by the ending of a life of such marvellous vitality, enormous good cheer and extraordinary productivity. Surely we thought: this man is unstoppable. He is always sunnily optimistic, purposefully and efficiently driven in his life's aims and energetic not only in constantly wielding a figurative pen but also when tramping at disconcerting speed across the rougher landscapes of Yorkshire or Derbyshire in pursuit of ancient ways or vernacular buildings, or conquering the fells and mountains of the Lake District each summer with his friends Barrie Blanksby, Tony Midgley and Tony Broadhead.

There was a quiet but indefatigable purpose about David and a strong sense of ongoing work to be added to the great store of his 30-plus books or contributions to books, including those commissioned by the National Archives. Yet another book by him – this time on local *England* no less – is in the press.[1] How many broadcasts he made I don't know. And the man was not far short of 80! Along the way, moreover, there were the many important positions he undertook at various times – as dean of the Faculty of Education at Sheffield University, or as president or chairman of the British Association for Local History, the British Agricultural History Society, the Sheffield and District Family History Society, the British Record Association and the Local Population Studies Society, let alone the South Yorkshire and North-East Derbyshire Ramblers Association (doubtless I've missed a few). He even served briefly as an elected member of the North-East Derbyshire District Council, until its processes disillusioned him.

Family and place were at the very heart of David's south-Yorkshire identity, as his highly personal *History of Penistone and district* (2002) so evocatively illustrates. His ancestral Yorkshire roots were traceable to medieval times, but about 1803 his great-great-grandfather, the ancestor of all the subsequent local branches of the Hey family, established himself in Thurlstone, towards the south-western corner of Yorkshire, within what David understood to have been an early medieval district known as Penisale. It was there that David's father – who led a hard, dangerous and ever unpredictable working life as a coal-miner – settled the family at the tiny hamlet of Catshaw in a cottage adapted from an eighteenth-century stone farmhouse. That,

---

1   *The grass roots of English history. Local societies in England before the industrial revolution* (London, 2016).

of course, was without modern facilities of any kind (although, thanks to his obviously highly capable mother, early photographs show our hero as well-scrubbed and warmly clothed). The family, in fact, included 'Grandma Hey' for a time, with David's Uncle Percy next door and David's mother's parents across the road, with his father's mother and his sister with *her* son eventually only a field or two away, and with all his 'numerous' cousins to boot within walking distance. From the age of two David attended Sunday School every week at the Independent Chapel in nearby Bullhouse. When he was nearly 11, however, the family moved to a council house in the small neighbouring market town of Penistone, and it was there between 1949 and 1956 that he was educated at its very enlightened grammar school, which, pursuant to the 1944 Education Act, made it possible for working-class children to be soundly taught and even to go on to university.

On leaving school David was young enough to be able to escape National Service, while obviously well enough qualified to take up the place he was now offered at what was soon to become the University of Keele, but which in his time was still the University College of North Staffordshire, otherwise envisioned as a 'people's university'. Here, between 1956 and 1960, he was to enjoy a four-year course, History with political institutions, which included a diploma in Education (and which released him from subsequently taking a PGCE). Those years must thus have represented David's first extended termly experiences of life away from his accustomed, but closely circumscribed, world in south Yorkshire. We don't know, indeed, whether by the age of 18 either he or his family was yet accustomed to venture regularly as far afield as Barnsley, some miles to the east of Penistone, let alone to Sheffield. It is certainly significant that on graduating he was drawn back immediately to his home country to work as a school teacher – to Ecclesfield Secondary Modern on the northern perimeter of Sheffield, then to Holmfirth Secondary Modern, a mere seven or so miles north-west of Penistone. During this time, too, having studied part-time for it, he was awarded an MA for a dissertation on the parish of Ecclesfield between 1672 and 1851 – with a rarely awarded Distinction – from the Department of English Local History at Leicester in 1967. Only then did he move out of Yorkshire and into Derbyshire to become a successful history lecturer at Matlock College of Education, but only until 1969. For it was then that he was appointed to a research fellowship in Agrarian History in the same Leicester department, his Leicester doctoral thesis on a uniquely documented Shropshire parish being approved in 1971.[2] He always took particular pride in working as a representative of the Leicester 'School' of English Local History, and kept close contact with the department.

Meanwhile, at Matlock, however, he had met a certain young lady with an impish sense of humour from Essex, called Pat, whom he married in 1971, and the two of them set up their first home on the outskirts of Leicester. Only when his fellowship expired in 1974, therefore, did David move to become lecturer in Local History, 'with special reference to south Yorkshire' in the Department of Extramural Studies at Sheffield University. From 1974 onwards the couple would live in Derbyshire, at Dronfield

---

2   David's doctoral thesis appeared as *An English rural community. Myddle under the Tudors and Stuarts* (Leicester, 1974).

Woodhouse. It is fair to say, of course, that none of David's many, many achievements over 46 years would have been even remotely possible without the constant loving support and efficiency of Pat, who, on top of her teaching, made such a warm home background for, domestically speaking, a somewhat traditionalist Yorkshire husband! Since the births of Emma in 1972 and of Jonny two years later, David's life was also immeasurably enhanced by huge pride in the children, the comfortable atmosphere of strong family life, and – especially – the prospect of succeeding generations of Heys.

David was pure Yorkshire. In his general and beautifully illustrated history of the county of 2005 he could justifiably claim 'I have ancestors from all three ridings, and know every part of Yorkshire on the ground'.[3] Above all, of course, David's broad and cheerful South Yorkshire accent proclaimed his regional identity throughout his life. He delighted in the subtle variations of local dialect, especially when a member of one of his audiences actually deduced that his accent stemmed from Penistone simply through comparison with someone else she knew from the same place. David recalled how his headmaster, when penning a supportive reference for his application to Keele, even 'urged the interviewing committee to make allowance for the fact that I was "rather a roughly spoken lad"'. If so, that certainly never stopped David's progress: in fact it lent authenticity and a conversational informality to his presentations on traditional local matters. He therefore fell on his feet when appointed to Sheffield, because there he found John Widdowson, a leading expert on dialect and eventually head of the Centre for English Tradition and Language; and, a few miles away, another dialect expert, Stanley Ellis of the University of Leeds.

David's doctoral supervisor had originally been the great W.G. Hoskins and, subsequently, Alan Everitt. Like the former, David naturally felt still connected through his background to an earlier regional cultural tradition and the surviving signs of it on the tongue and in a landscape with its own local building types. Joan Thirsk and Everitt, moreover, had elaborated the contexts of agriculture, rural industries and even religious tendencies as these might vary according to contrasted types of sub-region in ways on which David too would build. Also at Leicester he was fortunate to find two colleagues expert in the study of regional vernacular architecture – Peter Eden and Michael Laithwaite – who advised him in the field. From Sheffield, in turn, he profited likewise from the more locally focused expertise of Peter Ryder and others, as he did from David Crossley with regard to the Industrial Archaeology that was so relevant to his own detailed documentary studies of the local metal industries of Hallamshire. David was always punctiliously generous in acknowledging the help of others.

For David other things too spelled Yorkshire from his own experience or observation. Crucial to his thinking were the families – such as his own – which persisted in a locality for generation after generation, and transmitted customary ways across the centuries. Their mark was the persistence of their surnames. In the study of these he had benefited from the work of the English Surnames Survey, long pioneered systematically at Leicester by the deeply learned medievalist Richard McKinley. David himself would take forward the implications of such studies in his own work, most recently in *Surnames, DNA, and Family History*, which he co-authored with

---

3   *A history of Yorkshire, 'County of the Broad acres'* (Lancaster, 2005), p. viii.

two other Leicester scholars: the Yorkshire surname expert George Redmonds and Turi King, the geneticist who was involved in the analysis of the remains of Richard III. Not unconnected, therefore, were the localised clusters of such families or the networks of cousins like his own in limited districts with traditions peculiar to this part of the world. Here local economies were to be distinguished from more agriculturally focused regions of southern England because, in addition to farming, the former simultaneously developed pre-industrial craft industries such as those of the cutlers and the scissor- or nail-makers. Such a neighbourhood district – whatever its size – was sometimes characterised by contemporaries as a person's 'country', and for David these human areas came to comprise the basic building blocks of medieval and early modern regional identity and belonging.

David's own interests thus built up from the parochial concerns of Penistone to the special culture of all Hallamshire between 1660 and 1740, with Sheffield as its early manufacturing urban core (about which he wrote one of his most important books[4]), and so to a view of South Yorkshire as an entity in its own right even before local government reorganisation, and thence, wider yet, to Yorkshire as a whole. More than that still: in company with the archaeologist Barry Cunliffe he launched a now sadly discontinued series of immensely valuable volumes on all the regions of England.[5]

David was very astute in deciding to return to Yorkshire and to Adult Education as opposed to conventional university teaching and administration, for it gave him more freedom to explore, to research and to write. As he once stated, his work was 'a tribute to an era that is sadly past, when tutors in University extra-mural departments were able to teach whatever interested them and to inspire others to pursue their own research'. He himself, however, had caught that earlier tide. He was passionate and enthusiastic about not only communicating his discoveries to wider audiences but also involving them directly in the processes of local historical research as teams. Local History, he felt rightly, should not be confined to academics; it should inform local loyalties. The outcome of one such collaborative effort was perhaps his most original and fascinating book, *Packmen, carriers and packhorse roads*, for which a team reconstructed on foot the lost ancient pattern of routes and their markers across the wilderness moors of Derbyshire and South Yorkshire from the west and, in one case at least, as far east as the river port of Bawtry as the destination of these traders.[6] It was this engagement with the public that inspired him increasingly to concentrate on Family History and its essential connection to contemporary local conditions, for which he wrote a number of helpful guides. Following Hoskins, his genius lay in how to engage the general reader through linking family histories to local areas or particular regional developments, and by using buildings or landscape features to account for earlier ways of earning a living or to reflect periods of changing regional prosperity. And that is not to mention the compendious collaborative *Oxford Companion to Family*

---

4   *The fiery blades of Hallamshire. Sheffield and its neighbourhood, 1660–1740* (Leicester, 1991).

5   *A regional history of England* published by Longman. David contributed *Yorkshire from AD 1000* (1986).

6   *Packman, carriers and packhorse roads. Trade and communications in north Derbyshire and south Yorkshire* (Leicester, 1980) (which carried a dedication to W.G. Hoskins)

and Local History, which he initiated, largely wrote, and edited. His knowledge of his subject was encyclopaedic.[7]

David's great achievement, then, was to speak directly to both regional and specialist audiences and to provide each with the first reliable modern introduction to the continuous human history of Yorkshire from 1000 down to the present day, one that was built on decades of research into what lay beneath the surface of the largest county in England. In doing so he directly connected a deep past with the present in a way that has been rarely rivalled systematically by other historians except in other volumes of his splendid regional series.

David concluded his wide survey of his homeland on a wry note. Having recited the activities of past generations and their legacies in the landscape, he wrote: 'But Yorkshire no longer exists as an administrative unit, nor do its ancient Ridings. After a thousand years of history the county of Yorkshire was abolished on All Fools Day 1974'. Thanks to him, however, it certainly will not be forgotten, for David's writings represent the nationally influential work of the outstanding all-round local historian of his generation. It was fitting indeed that, only last year, he should have been honoured with the award of an honorary degree from the University of Sheffield, a rare and appropriate recognition of an extraordinary scholar.[8]

---

7   *The Oxford companion to local and family history* (1996); the second edition was the *Oxford companion to family and local history* (2008).

8   For formal obituaries see Christopher Dyer in *The Guardian*, 25 February 2016; John Beckett, 'Professor David Hey: an appreciation', *The Local Historian*, 46/2 (April 2016) (which includes a list of David's books); and John Chartres in *Yorkshire Archaeological Journal*, 88 (2016), pp. 252–3.

Chapter 1

Deer parks in South Yorkshire:
the documentary and landscape evidence

Melvyn Jones

Medieval deer parks were symbols of status and wealth, but they were much more besides. In South Yorkshire, as elsewhere, they were created by the nobility, knightly families and other lords of manors. A few were attached to monasteries.[1] There were also two royal deer parks: Conisbrough Park, formerly the property of the de Warenne family but which reverted to the crown in the fourteenth century, and Kimberworth Park, which became crown property for a period in the late fifteenth century. As all deer were deemed to belong to the crown, from the beginning of the thirteenth century landowners were supposed to obtain a licence from the king to create a park, although this appears not to have been necessary if the proposed park was not near a royal forest. The medieval parks at Conisbrough and Sheffield – both now lost from the landscape – predated the issuing of royal licences and so must have been of twelfth-century origin or even earlier. Thomas de Furnival, lord of the manor of Sheffield, when asked to explain before the *Quo Warranto* enquiry of 1281 by what right he held Sheffield deer park, said it had been in the possession of his family since the Norman Conquest.[2]

More commonly granted by the crown was the right of free warren, which gave a landowner the right to hunt certain animals – pheasant, partridge, hare, rabbit, badger, polecat and pine marten – within a prescribed area. This was often the forerunner to the creation of a deer park. Searches of parish histories, principally Hunter's two-volume *South Yorkshire*, reveal that more than 80 grants of free warren were made in the medieval period in South Yorkshire and that a deer park is known to have been subsequently created in nearly a third of the cases (Figure 1.1).[3]

---

1   Recent writing on medieval parks includes Rob Liddiard (ed.), *The medieval park: new perspectives* (Macclesfield, 2007); S. Mileson, *Parks in medieval England* (Oxford, 2009); and Rob Liddiard, 'Decline and disparkment: management trends in English deer parks, 1500–1750', *Agricultural History Review*, 67 (2019), pp. 175–202. For a regional study of parks in Yorkshire see Stephen Moorhouse, 'The medieval parks of Yorkshire: function, contents and chronology', in Liddiard, *Medieval park*, pp. 99–127.

2   J. Hunter, *Hallamshire. The history and topography of the parish of Sheffield in the county of York …* (London, 1819), p. 54.

3   J. Hunter, *South Yorkshire* (2 vols, 1828–31, repr. Wakefield, 1974); M. Jones, 'Deer in south Yorkshire: an historical perspective', in M. Jones, I.D. Rotherham and A.J. McCarthy (eds), *Deer or the New Woodlands?, The Journal of Practical Ecology and Conservation*, Special Publication 1, pp. 11–26. A complete list of the deer parks and rights of free warren (including dates and names of grantees) can be found there at pp. 23–6.

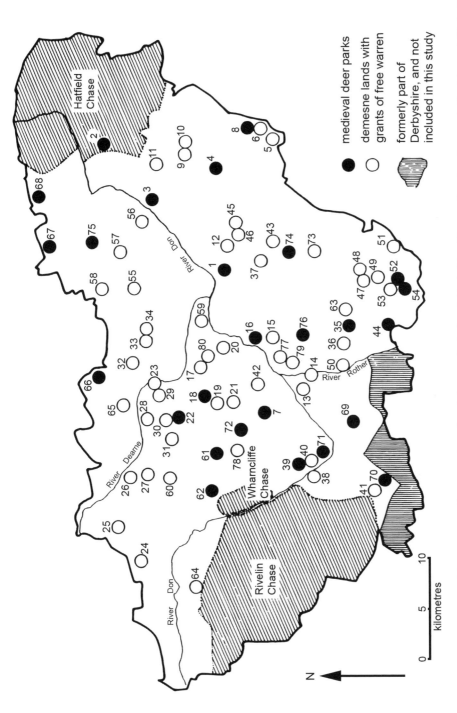

Figure 1.1. Location of rights of free warren, chases and medieval deer parks in South Yorkshire. The medieval parks are: 1. Conisbrough Park; 2. Hatfield Park; 3. Wheatley Park; 4. Rossington Park; 7. Kimberworth Park; 8. Austerfield Park; 13. Tinsley Park; 16. Thrybergh Park; 18. Rainbrough Park; 35. Aston Park; 39. Wadsley Park; 44. Northwood Park; 52. Thorpe Salvin Park (Worksop Abbey); 54. Thorpe Salvin Park (Sandford); 61. Tankersley Park; 62. Wortley Park; 66. Brierley Park; 67. Norton Park; 68. Fenwick Park; 69. Sheffield Park; 70. Ecclesall Park; 71. Shirecliffe Park; 72. Tinsley Park; 72. Hesley Park and Cowley Park; 74. Maltby Park; 75. Owston Park; 76. Whiston Park.

Most of the deer parks in South Yorkshire were created by the heads of the great Norman dynasties such as the de Warennes of Conisbrough Castle, who had parks at Conisbrough and Hatfield, the de Furnivals, who had a park at Sheffield and were also granted a licence to create a park at Whiston in 1316, and the de Buslis of Tickhill Castle, who had a park at Tinsley. They were also created by other local lords of Norman origin, such as the Fitzwilliams, Bosvilles, Chaworths and de Vavasors.

Religious houses were also granted rights of free warren and permission to create parks in South Yorkshire. A contemporary record states that Richard de Wombwell, prior of Nostell Priory in West Yorkshire from 1372 to 1385, was fond of hunting. Significantly, the priory was granted free warren on its lands in South Yorkshire at Swinton, Thurnscoe and Great Houghton (where there is still a wood called Little Park) during his term of office.[4] Besides Nostell Priory, other religious houses from outside the region, such as Rufford Abbey and Worksop Priory, both in Nottinghamshire, and Bolton Abbey in Craven, were granted free warren on their South Yorkshire properties. One of the properties of Bolton Abbey for which they had a grant of free warren in 1256–7 was at Wentworth Woodhouse, an antecedent of the surviving Wentworth Park (one of only two parks in South Yorkshire still containing deer, the other being Stainborough Park at Wentworth Castle). Monk Bretton Priory was granted free warren on its lands at Rainborough in Brampton Bierlow township at an unknown date and there is still a large wood there called Rainborough Park. Beauchief Abbey (then in Derbyshire) also had a small park attached to the abbey, which is still enshrined in the name Old Park Wood and the former medieval ponds that survive to the east of the abbey.

At least 27 parks were created in medieval South Yorkshire. Nationally the great age of park creation was the century and a half between 1200 and 1350, a period of growing population and agricultural prosperity. Landowners had surplus wealth and there were still sufficient areas of waste on which to create parks. In South Yorkshire the majority of grants of free warren, which, as already noted, were often the forerunners of the creation of deer parks, were made between 1250 and 1325 (44 grants). Significantly, no grants of free warren were made in the thirty years following the Black Death (1348–9), but then 21 were made between 1379 and 1400. The last known medieval royal licence to create a deer park was given in 1491–2, when Brian Sandford was granted permission to create a park at Thorpe Salvin. This grant is also notable for the fact that it was accompanied by a gift of 12 does from the king's park at Conisbrough 'towards the storing of his parc at Thorp'.[5] The latest known licence granted for emparkment in South Yorkshire was made to Nicholas Saunderson, second Viscount Castleton (*d.* 1640), in 1637 by King Charles I for a deer park at Sandbeck. The licence states that Castleton was given permission to make separate with pales, walls or hedges 500 acres or thereabouts of land, meadow, pasture, gorse, heath, wood, underwood, woodland tenements and hereditaments to make a park where deer and other wild animals might be grazed and kept.[6]

---

4   Hunter, *South Yorkshire*, vol. ii, p. 208.
5   Hunter, *South Yorkshire*, vol. i, p. 309.
6   A. Rodgers, 'Deer parks in the Maltby area', in M. Jones (ed.), *Aspects of Rotherham: discovering local history*, vol. iii (Barnsley, 1998), pp. 8–30.

Deer parks were still being created or restocked in South Yorkshire in the eighteenth century. John Spencer, of Cannon Hall, for example, remodelled his parkland in the 1760s, building a new boundary wall and a ha-ha to separate the park from the gardens. Once these works were completed he set about restocking his park with fallow deer. He recorded in his diary on 3 February 1762 that 'The Gamekeeper returned from Sprodborough with twenty bucks'. Two days later he noted that 'deer from Sir George Armytage's of Kirk Lees Hall' had been brought to his park and the next day he recorded that he had been to Gunthwaite and 'took the deer out of Gunthwaite Park & put them into my park'. By the end of the week he had a herd of 89 deer in his park at Cannon Hall,[7] a herd that survived into the 1940s.

I

The creation of a park, emparkment, involved enclosing an area of land with a fence to keep the deer and other game inside and predators (in the early days wolves) and poachers outside. The fence – the park pale – consisted either of cleft oak vertical pales with horizontal railings, often set on a bank, or a stone wall. Former park boundary walls and banks (the latter sometimes still surmounted with remnants of walls) can still be identified throughout South Yorkshire (Figure 1.2). The line of part of the pale at the former Wortley Old Park was named Pale Lane.[8] As parks could vary in size from under 100 acres to several thousand acres (Sheffield Park at its greatest extent covered nearly 2,500 acres and was eight miles in circumference), fencing was a major initial and recurring expense. For this reason the most economical shape for a deer park was a circle or a rectangle with rounded corners, as seen throughout South Yorkshire (Figure 1.3). Deer leaps were also constructed to entice wild deer into a park.[9] Rabbit warrens and fish ponds were characteristic features of medieval deer parks.

Sheffield Park and Kimberworth Park illustrate these general points. The park pale of Sheffield Park appears to have consisted in part, at least in the late medieval period, of a high cleft-oak paling fence. We know this from a surviving manorial account roll of 1441–2, which records a payment to John Legge and John Gotsone for repairing defects in the rails and paling around the park, Legge alone being employed for 122 days at this task. The cleft-oak paling fence was probably set on a bank, some remnants of which survive. A fragment of park wall was also recorded by Hunter at Newfield Green.[10] The park pale had, as already noted, three functions: to keep deer in and to keep predators and poachers out. The temptation was often too much for some, however. At the court leet of the manor of Sheffield in 1578 six local men

---

7   SA, Spencer Stanhope Muniments, 60633.

8   D. Hey, 'The parks at Tankersley and Wortley', *Yorkshire Archaeological Journal*, 47 (1974), p. 115.

9   Deer leaps were short sections of a park pale at a lower height than the rest of the boundary with a deep ditch on the inside. They enabled wild deer to enter a park but prevented the park herd from escaping.

10   A.H. Thomas, 'Some Hallamshire rolls of the fifteenth century', *Transactions of the Hunter Archaeological Society*, II (1924), p. 157; Hunter, *Hallamshire*, p. 332.

Figure 1.2. The former park boundary at Tinsley Park (above) and the boundary wall at Kimberworth Park (below).

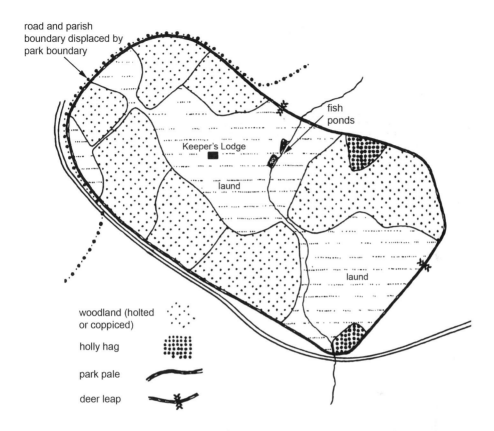

road and parish
boundary displaced by
park boundary

fish
ponds

Keeper's Lodge

laund

laund

woodland (holted
or coppiced)

holly hag

park pale

deer leap

Figure 1.3. The characteristic features of a South Yorkshire medieval deer park.

were each fined five shillings 'for huntinge the hare within my Lordes Parke … to the disturbance of my Lordes game there, & killed one deare & dyd hyte an other deare'.[11]

The existence, extent and boundaries of the park at Kimberworth – which was in existence by 1226 – were questioned in the Hundred Roll enquiry of 1276.[12] In 1276 the lord of the manor Robert de Vipont (who had died in 1265) and his heirs were accused of exceeding the bounds of the free warren in Kimberworth and of including within the deer park a portion of the king's highway.[13] In the *Quo Warranto* proceedings of 1292 Idonea de Leybourn, Robert de Vipont's daughter, was asked by what right she claimed the privilege of having a deer park. She was also charged with constructing a deer leap (*saltatorium*) to entice deer into her park to the disadvantage of the king, because deer

---

11   J.R. Wigfull, 'The court leet of the Manor of Sheffield', *Transactions of the Hunter Archaeological Society*, III (1929), pp. 143–54.

12   The Hundred Rolls were records of enquiries made on behalf of King Edward I about the privileges claimed by the nobility, clergy and others that diverted profits from the royal coffers into private hands.

13   Wigfull, 'Court leet', p. 154.

from the king's forest were likely to become part of the Kimberworth Park herd. The jury was satisfied that she had not created a park unlawfully but had inherited it from her father. On the matter of the deer leap the jury accepted that it was not to the detriment of the king because the nearest royal forest (Sherwood) was fifteen leagues away and the chases of the de Warenne family (Hatfield Chase, to the east of Doncaster) and of the de Furnivals (Rivelin Chase, to the west of Sheffield) were in between.[14]

Besides deer, other animals were kept in the late medieval parks of South Yorkshire, as intimated above, including hares, rabbits (introduced by the Normans) and game birds. Herds of cattle, flocks of sheep and pigs were also grazed within the pale. Another important feature of South Yorkshire's medieval deer parks, as elsewhere, were fish ponds, which provided an alternative to meat in Lent and on fast days. Within the boundaries of the former Kimberworth Park, in a narrow valley at the southern extremity of Gallery Bottom (one of the former coppice woods within the park), are the silted remains of three park ponds between 30 and 60 metres in length with stone-built sluices still in place in the earthern dam walls.[15]

Although there are records of parks without trees, South Yorkshire's medieval parks usually consisted of a mixture of woodland and open areas called launds or plains, which consisted of grassland or heath with scattered trees.[16] The park livestock could graze in the latter and find cover in the holts and coppices (when well grown). Many of the trees in the launds would have been pollarded – that is, cut at a height of at least six feet, leaving a massive lower trunk called a bolling from which a continuous crop of new growth sprouted out of reach of the grazing deer, sheep and cattle. In the launds the regeneration of trees was restricted because of continual grazing; new trees were able to grow only in the protection of thickets of hawthorn and holly. Some of the unpollarded trees might reach a great age and size and were much sought after for major building projects. A number of enormous trees in Sheffield Park were described in detail by John Evelyn in his book *Silva*, first published in 1670, by which time they were regarded as important economic assets for timber and for branchwood, which was used for charcoal making. Evelyn appears to have obtained his information from Edmund Morphy, one of the duke of Norfolk's woodwards. Evelyn said that in 1646 there were 100 trees in the park whose combined value was £1,000, and described one oak tree in the park whose trunk was 13 feet in diameter and another which was ten yards in circumference. On Conduit Plain within the park, Evelyn reported that there was one oak tree whose boughs were so far spreading that he estimated (giving all his calculations) that 251 horses could stand in its shade. Another oak, he wrote, when cut down, yielded 1,400 'wairs' and 20 cords from its branches.[17] Finally, he described an oak that, when felled and lying on its side, was

---

14   J. Guest, *Historic Notices of Rotherham* (Worksop, 1879), pp. 583–4.

15   M. Jones, 'The medieval park at Kimberworth', in Jones, *Aspects of Rotherham*, vol. ii (1996), p. 132.

16   The king's park keeper at Conisbrough Park in the second half of the fifteenth century was referred to in a document written in French as 'Laundier et Palisser de n[ot]re park de Connesburgh': Hunter, *South Yorkshire*, vol. i, p. 114.

17   A 'wair' was a plank two yards long; a cord was a stack of coppice poles eight feet long, four feet wide and four feet high.

so massive that two men on horseback on either side of it could not see the crown of the other's hat.[18]

The woods within deer parks were managed in different ways. Some were 'holted': that is, they consisted of single-stemmed trees grown for their timber, in the fashion of a modern plantation. Most parkland woods by the late medieval or Tudor period, however, were coppiced (cut down to ground level, usually every 20–25 years, and allowed to grow back from the stool). Coppices would be enclosed by a bank or wall to keep out the grazing animals during the early years of regrowth. There were also in South Yorkshire's deer parks separate woods or special compartments called holly hags within coppice woods in which the dominant tree was holly.[19] This was cut in winter as fodder for the deer and other park livestock. In Tankersley Park, for example, a lease of 1653 specified that the deer had also to be fed in winter 'with holley to be cutt therein'.[20] An engraving dating from the 1720s shows a walled wooded enclosure in the south-eastern corner of Tankersley Park that on late eighteenth-century maps is called the Far Hollings.[21] Bull Wood, which is also shown on the engraving, survives to this day and is full of holly. This was another holly hag (Figure 1.4).

II

The deer in most parks were fallow deer, which were not native to Britain and were probably introduced by the Normans. Fallow deer were much easier to contain within a park than the native red and roe deer because of their size and inability to breach high park boundaries. Locally both fallow and red deer were kept in parks. John Harrison's survey of the manor of Sheffield in 1637 remarked that Sheffield Park was said to be 'not meanly furnished with fallow Deare, the number of them at present is one Thousand'.[22] Nearly a century later, when Daniel Defoe rode through Tankersley Park, he commented that he had seen 'the largest red deer that, I believe, are in this part of Europe. One of the hinds, I think, was larger than my horse'.[23]

The function of a medieval park has been a matter of debate over the past two decades and more. It had long been assumed that they were primarily for hunting. For this reason they were often referred to simply as 'hunting parks' or 'hunting grounds'. More recently some writers have argued that they were basically deer farms.[24] In the most ritualised form of medieval hunting, *par force de chiens*, a single deer would be

---

18   J. Evelyn, *Silva or a Discourse of Forest Trees* (London, 1706 edn), pp. 229–30.

19   M. Jones, 'Woodland origins in a south Yorkshire parish', *Local Historian*, 16 (1994), pp. 73–82.

20   T.W. Hall, 'Tankersley Old Hall and Fanshawe Gate', in *Incunabula of Sheffield History* (Sheffield, 1937), p. 181.

21   For example, on William Fairbank's map of the manor of Tankersley of 1775 (private collection).

22   J.G. Ronksley (ed.), *An exact and perfect survey of the Manor of Sheffield and other lands by John Harrison, 1637* (Worksop, 1908), p. 3.

23   Daniel Defoe, *A tour through England and Wales divided into circuits or journies* (London, 1728, 2 vols, Everyman edn, London, c.1928), vol. ii, p. 185.

24   J. Birrell, 'Deer and deer farming in medieval England', *Agricultural History Review*, 40 (1992), pp. 112–26; Mileson, *Parks in medieval England*.

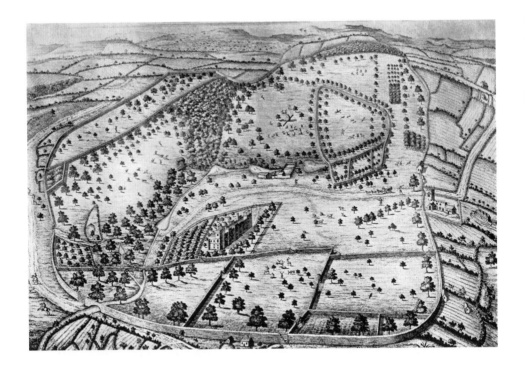

Figure 1.4. (a) An engraving of Tankersley Park dating from the 1720s (above) and (b) a map based on the engraving (below).

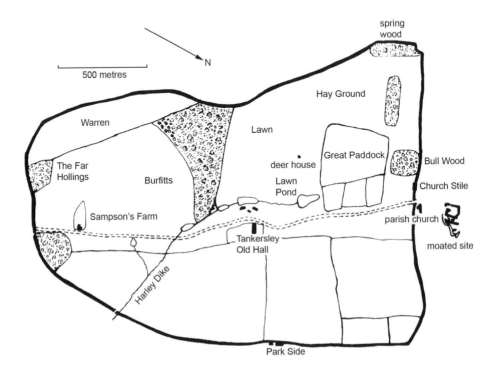

selected and chased for a long period, sometimes a whole day, by hounds, parkers and their assistants and the aristocratic party of hunters on horseback, until it collapsed from exhaustion, whereupon it was killed by the thrust of a sword through the heart. Many parks, however, were small, no more than 200 or 300 acres at most, and some as small as 50 acres, and their extent, topography and, often, close tree cover would not lend themselves to such a hunt. This type of hunt was only likely to have taken place in a large park or a royal forest or its private equivalent, the chase. A particularly extravagant hunt took place in Hatfield Chase in 1609. In that year Henry, Prince of Wales, and his royal party, having 'frighted' 500 deer 'out of the woods, grounds and closes adjoining', pursued them across Thorne Mere in a flotilla of nearly 100 boats.[25]

In the more restricted space of a park another hunting method, the 'drive' or 'bow and stable' method, where deer were driven into nets or towards a row of archers, was more likely to be used. Some writers have argued that this was the normal method of dispatching deer in parks.[26] Furthermore, most parkland deer were, as noted, fallow deer, which have poor stamina and tend to take flight as a herd rather than as single animals. An account has survived from the late sixteenth century of the bow and stable method of hunting taking place in the park at Ecclesall. The evidence comes from a set of depositions made in October 1587 by the sixth earl of Shrewsbury and others. The earl said that his father and grandfather (who died in 1538) had used 'Crosbowes to Kyll the Deare in Ecclesall …'. Another witness said the fourth earl had 'sett netts and long bowes to kyll dear' in Ecclesall Park.[27] In a law suit of 1527 Henry Savile was said to have been 'hunting at dere wythe houndes in hys parke at Tankersley'.[28]

The debate continues. Were medieval parks primarily created by royalty and the aristocracy for hunting or to be deer farms in which mainly fallow deer (which to early medieval eyes would have been exotic creatures) were carefully husbanded? Or did their function change gradually over time, with their once primary function, hunting, becoming over time one among several functions, then merely a subsidiary function and finally a disused function? If so, then for many owners their main function in the late medieval period would have been to provide a high-status meat for the table. The serving of venison took place in a specific social context. It was only eaten legitimately by the gentry and the aristocracy and then on special occasions. A good local example would be the funeral of the fifth earl of Shrewsbury in 1560. For the great dinner held in Sheffield Castle following the funeral, 50 fallow deer and 29 red deer were killed and roasted.[29] The fallow deer would have been culled from the herd in Sheffield Park and the red deer from Rivelin Chase, the earl's private forest. In fact, the two sides of this debate can be reconciled if we acknowledge that different areas within deer parks had different functions, a point to which we will return.

---

25   Hunter, *South Yorkshire*, vol. ii, p. 156.

26   M. Cartmill, *A view to a death in the morning: hunting and nature through history* (Cambridge, MA, 1993).

27   TNA, E 134/29 & 30 Eliz./Mich. 30.

28   John Lister (ed.), *Yorkshire Star Chamber proceedings*, vol. iv (Yorkshire Archaeological Society Record Series, LXX, 1927), p. 49.

29   C. Drury, 'The funeral of Francis Talbot, Earl of Shrewsbury at Sheffield, 1560', *Sheffield Miscellany*, 4 (1897), p. 140.

III

We also need to consider the argument that medieval parks were designed to be visually attractive and aesthetically pleasing. Park landscapes may have been intended to be viewed from high-level windows, from the roof leads or specially constructed balconies, or experienced by travelling through them on foot or horseback. Some writers, such as Christopher Taylor, contend that the entire medieval lordly landscape was planned with great precision.[30] From this there follows the question as to whether park landscapes were deliberately planned to be ornamental (as well as utilitarian) from the outset or, as perceptions and fashions changed, were reshaped in imitation and emulation of others. Some have expressed caution, suggesting that scholars are looking at medieval landscapes through their knowledge of the landscape design of later periods and are prone to read too much into what has been revealed by field archaeologists and the medieval documentary sources. Having said that, in the case of the medieval park at Sheffield there are several features and relationships that raise some intriguing, though in the end unanswerable, questions.

The establishment of a castle at the confluence of the rivers Don and Sheaf with a market town under its walls and extending up the ridge to the south-west, and with the baronial castle park ballooning away (to use Winchester's term)[31] to the east, south-east and south, across a river with ponds created beside it and with orchards at its entrance from the castle, has all the appearance of a deliberately planned landscape. Planning for protection, trade and pleasure are all evidenced here. Turning to Sheffield Park itself, it may be highly significant that in Harrison's survey of 1637 an area extending eastwards from the castle covering nearly 140 acres is called 'Ye Little Parke' (Figure 1.5). Little parks are familiar components of medieval parks throughout England. They were usually located adjacent to a castle, often running away from beneath the castle walls. Indeed, in Latin documents, as Liddiard has pointed out, they are often referred to as *parva parcum subtus castrum* ('the little park under the castle').[32] They are now considered to be 'pleasure parks' in contrast to the rest of the medieval park, usually referred to, as it was in Sheffield, as the 'Great Parke'. The little park was a place of retreat or entertainment where staged events could be organised, whereas the great park had the very different function of game larder and hunting ground. It might also be exploited for other resources, such as wood, timber, coal and ironstone.

In many medieval parks, the main residence, whether palace or castle, was moated. Moats and other expanses of water are now considered to have had an aesthetic as well as a military function. Bordering and running through Sheffield Park were three rivers, the Don, the Sheaf and the Porter, but it is not clear whether the ponds on the Sheaf within the park pale existed in medieval times and, if they did,

---

30   R. Liddiard, *Castles in context: power, symbolism and landscape, 1066 to 1500* (Macclesfield, 2005); C. Taylor, 'Medieval ornamental landscapes', *Landscapes*, 1 (2000), pp. 38–55.

31   A.J.L. Winchester, 'Baronial and manorial parks in medieval Cumbria', in Liddiard, *Medieval park*, p. 167.

32   Liddiard, *Castles in context*, p. 113.

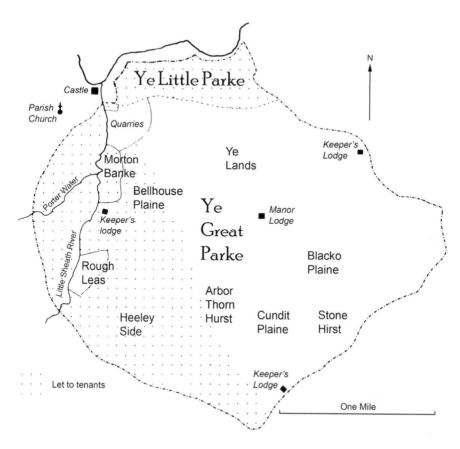

Figure 1.5. Sheffield deer park as described in John Harrison's survey of 1637, showing the location of the Little Park and the Great Park and the parts of the park (stippled) let to tenants.

whether they had a purely ornamental function, or an economic one as fishponds, or served for both. Waterfowl and other water birds were certainly kept in the park in the medieval period: in the manorial rolls of 1442–43 there is a record of four swans being brought to Sheffield, a gift from Lord de Willoughby.

In the late medieval and immediate post-medieval period there is certainly evidence of planned ornamental additions to Sheffield Park: the Manor Lodge, first recorded in 1479–80, was converted from a simple lodge into a comfortable country residence in the late fifteenth and sixteenth centuries. (The surviving Turret House at Manor Lodge, now generally believed to be a 'standing' or 'prospect house', is shown in Figure 1.6.) The Hall in the Ponds, possibly a banqueting house in the Great Park, was built in the early sixteenth century. At some unknown date an avenue of walnut trees was planted along the route between the Castle and the Manor Lodge – a deliberate act of beautification. It was recorded in 1715 that '30 old walnut trees at ye Mannor' had been sold to Jonathan Hall, a Sheffield joiner; given that walnut trees can live for more than 200 years they could have been late medieval plantings. Joseph Hunter was in no doubt that the Manor Lodge was deliberately constructed

Figure 1.6. The Turret House at the Manor Lodge, at a high vantage point in Sheffield Park.

and expanded where it was because of the views of the park and the countryside beyond that could be enjoyed in every direction:

> The fir-crowned heights of Norton, the sweet vale of Beauchief, the purple moors of Totley, and the barren hills of the Peak, the thick woods of Wharncliffe and Wentworth, the widening vale of the Don, and the hills of Laughton and Hansworth, each distinguished by its spire, are all comprehended within the view from this elevation.[33]

33   Hunter, *Hallamshire*, p. 332.

IV

The decline and disparkment of parks in England from the beginning of the sixteenth century until the mid-eighteenth century is the subject of a recent wide-ranging discussion by Liddiard.[34] In his paper he questions, among other things, whether the increasing sub-division, contraction and disappearance of medieval parkland and the substitution of a wide range of non-deer-related economic activities within the confines of medieval parks were post-medieval phenomena or simply a continuation of trends that began in the late medieval period. The latter is certainly true in the case of South Yorkshire's largest medieval park, Sheffield Park. A manorial roll for 1441–2 gives a detailed glimpse into the functioning of the park in the mid-fifteenth century, by which time it had become a multi-functional space for its owner and tenants.[35] By this date substantial parts of the park were let to tenants. There were leased grazing pastures and hay meadows and a 'mine of sea-coal'. Income was also derived from allowing holly trees to be cropped (for fodder), from the pannage of pigs, from the sale of timber of felled trees and a parcel of coppice, from charcoal made from the branches of trees where they were being cleared to make a new pasture, and from cinders (from burnt coal) sold to the dyers of Chesterfield. The park also supplied firewood for the castle, timber for building repairs at the castle stables and brushwood and stakes to repair the dam and weir of the fulling mill. Quarries in the park supplied both wall stone and stone tiles for house building and repairs to the manorial corn mill and fulling mill.

Gilbert, the seventh earl of Shrewsbury, died in 1616 and after that date the lords of the manor rarely visited Sheffield. In 1637, when John Harrison completed his survey of the manor, 971 acres (nearly 40 per cent) of the former 2,461-acre deer park was let to tenants. By 1693 the park wall had been reduced from eight miles to three miles in circumference.[36] A century later the deer had gone and the western part of the deer park had been built over.

Between the late fifteenth and mid-eighteenth centuries many of South Yorkshire's medieval deer parks were reduced in size, changed their function (and hence their appearance) or disappeared altogether. When a landlord was an absentee (as was the case with the owners of Sheffield Park from 1616) or where his house lay some distance away from his park there was an increased possibility that the park might disappear altogether. There were at least 27 medieval deer parks in South Yorkshire, yet John Speed's map of the West Riding of Yorkshire published in 1610 shows only ten surviving deer parks (at Wortley, Tankersley, Brierley, Sheffield, Kimberworth, Thrybergh, Conisbrough, Treeton, Aston and Austerfield). Speed omitted a number of parks that were still in existence in the early seventeenth century, such as the very small ones at Gunthwaite and Maltby,[37] but also substantial ones, as at Tinsley (396 acres) and Ecclesall (300 acres), both of which had been converted into compartmented

---

34   Liddiard, 'Decline and disparkment'.
35   Thomas, 'Some Hallamshire rolls', pp. 65–79, 142–56, 225–46, 341–60 on which the following is based.
36   SA, Arundel Castle Muniments S127.
37   Rodgers, 'Deer parks in the Maltby area'.

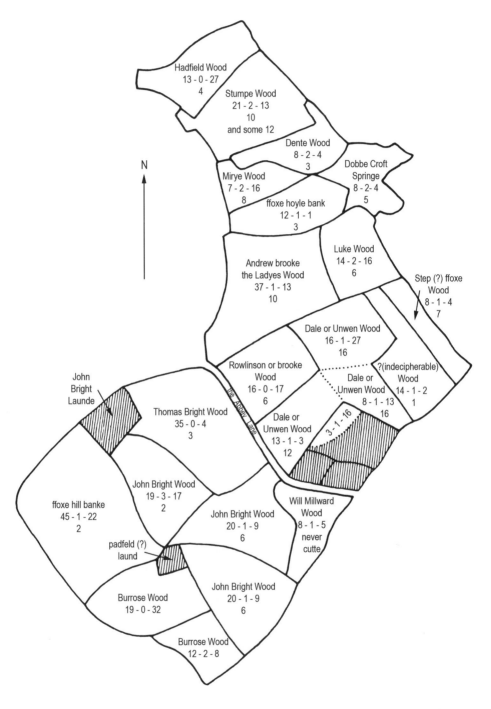

Figure 1.7. Redrawing of a mid-seventeenth-century map of the former Ecclesall Park after its conversion into a compartmented coppice wood. Each compartment is named and its acreage and the age of the coppice are given. Note the two named launds. *Source*: Wentworth Woodhouse Muniments, WWM MP 46.

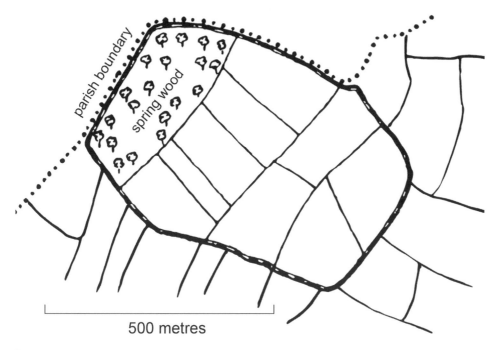

500 metres

Figure 1.8. The dissolution of Aston Park into the farming landscape.

coppice woods during or by the end of the seventeenth century. Ecclesall Park, for example, had been created by Sir Robert de Ecclesall in 1319 and was still a place where bow and stable hunting of fallow deer was taking place in the late sixteenth century. Less than a century later it was a compartmented coppice wood made up of more than 20 'spring' (coppice) woods ranging in age (since they were last coppiced) from between two and 16 years (Figure 1.7). Other well-wooded parks also simply became large coppice woods. Cowley Park and Hesley Park, for example, became coppice woods of 163 and 135 acres respectively. A large part of the former Shirecliffe Park survived into the twentieth century in the form of a large wood called Shirecliffe Old Park, which in Harrison's 1637 survey of the manor of Sheffield was described as 'A spring wood called Shirtcliffe parke' of 143 acres.[38] Tinsley Park by 1657 was a compartmented wood that was let by its owner, the second earl of Strafford, to the ironmaster Lionel Copley for felling for charcoal making. It extended over 413 acres and comprised ten coppice woods and three holts.[39] Rainborough Park at Brampton became a coppice wood and the shape of the modern wood, a long rectangle with rounded corners, still suggests that it was once a fenced enclosure for deer.

Some parks were broken up and used for a mixture of activities. Kimberworth Park, for example, which still had a mixed herd of deer, both red deer and fallow, in

---

38 Ronksley, *An exact and perfect survey*, p. 228.
39 SA, Wentworth Woodhouse Muniments, D778.

the 1630s,[40] also had a coal mine within its medieval pale in the late sixteenth century. By 1649 Park Gate Farm, covering 141 acres, had been carved out of the park and by 1671 the remainder of the park (nearly 100 acres) had been leased to Copley. By 1732 the whole of the former park had been divided into farmland.

Thrybergh Park was reduced in size by Sir John Reresby in the seventeenth century through the sale of woodland and farmland to pay his debts, but it survived as a much smaller park than its medieval predecessor. Other medieval parks were wholly converted to farmland. South Yorkshire examples include Aston Park, Brierley Old Park and Conisbrough Park. The outline of a small park at Aston still survives in the agricultural landscape as a rectangle with rounded corners (Figure 1.8). This small park appears on John Speed's map of 1610 and seems to be the one created by Osbert de Arches, who had been granted a right of free warren in 1256–7. The park became part of a farm called Old Park Farm.

Brierley Old Park, north-east of Barnsley, was created by Geffrey de Nevile following the grant of a right of free warren in 1279–80. It is not known when disparkment took place, but this probably occurred, in part at least, in the sixteenth century, although the park appears on John Speed's map of 1610. The last owner to live at Brierley died in 1513. In 1580 the manor of Brierley, including the park, was purchased by the sixth earl of Shrewsbury. The estate passed to the Savile family in 1617. It is now largely farmland but most of the long eastern and western sides of its perimeter still survive as ghost features in the form of curving field boundaries visible on large-scale Ordnance Survey maps (Figure 1.9). Lying in the southern half of the former park is a moated site called the Hall Steads; in the northern part is a farmhouse that incorporates parts of the former manor house that was substantially repaired in 1632. Hunter, writing in 1831, suggested that the Hall Steads might have originally been for defence and security and 'the manour for refreshment and pleasure, like the Castle and Manor Lodge in Sheffield Park'.[41]

Conisbrough Park was a large park attached to the castle at Conisbrough, the former royal estate at Conisbrough having been granted by King William to William de Warenne after the Norman Conquest. As noted earlier, the park appears to have been in existence from at least the twelfth century. In the fourteenth century it became crown property once again (as did the former de Warenne deer park and chase at Hatfield). Today it is difficult to exactly delineate the boundaries of the park, although its general location and extent can be identified from the surviving park-related place-names, some medieval, others post-medieval, that dot the farming landscape in the area of the former park.

While substantial numbers of medieval deer parks were disappearing, others took on a new lease of life and a few new parks were created. The concept of the park was changing. Its primary function altered from being a game preserve and a valuable source of wood and timber to being the adornment of a country house. New residences were built within existing parks and the park boundaries extended.

---

40 Hunter, *South Yorkshire*, vol. ii, p. 303; SA, Arundel Castle Muniments, S131; M. Jones, 'The medieval park at Kimberworth', in Jones, *Aspects of Rotherham*, vol. ii, pp. 115–35.

41 Hunter, *South Yorkshire*, vol. ii, p. 407.

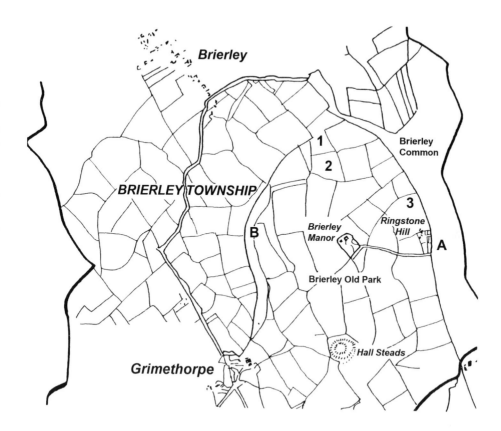

Figure 1.9. Ghost features in the landscape indicating the boundaries of Brierley Park. A and B indicate the long western and eastern pales and 1, 2 and 3 indicate fields with names incorporating the word 'park'.

The parks surrounding the new country houses in the post-medieval period were essentially still deer parks, although grazing cattle were a much more common sight than in the medieval period, with both the deer and the cattle being an aesthetic backdrop to the house as much as a source of food. Wentworth Woodhouse, the eighteenth-century residence of the marquises of Rockingham and in the nineteenth and twentieth centuries of their successors, the earls Fitzwilliam, provides the clearest South Yorkshire example of this change.[42] A park at Wentworth Woodhouse is not shown on the printed seventeenth-century maps of John Speed (1610) and Joan Bleau (*c.*1648). In 1732 Thomas Wentworth (later the first marquis) embarked on the building of his magnificent Palladian mansion and the improvement of the surrounding

42   M. Jones, 'Rents, remarks and observations: the first marquis of Rockingham's rent roll book', in Jones, *Aspects of Rotherham*, vol. i (1995), pp. 113–28.

park, or, as he put it in a letter to his son, to 'beautifye the country and do the work ordered by God himself'. He extended the surrounding park, which, as shown on a contemporary engraving,[43] already had a herd of deer and a magnificent 'deer shed', until it was more than nine miles in circumference, planted woodlands and created 'a Serpentine river'. The sixth earl Fitzwilliam in the second half of the nineteenth century also added a herd of buffaloes to the red and fallow deer that grazed in the park. The red deer were brought from what remained of Tankersley Park in the 1850s. This had been successfully converted from deer park to farmland to an ironstone mining ground for neighbouring ironworks.[44]

V

It is clear that the history of the deer parks in South Yorkshire, as elsewhere, is a complex one. The creation of nearly 30 deer parks and three chases in the region over a 500-year period suggests the importance of the hunt to the king, lords and gentry in that period and the importance of the park-based deer herd for sport and as a venison larder. Park creation continued throughout the medieval period to its very end, with the last medieval park being created in 1491–2, but changes were already taking place. Although the keeping of deer was still perhaps the most important activity in almost every park, this activity generally co-existed with other uses. In the case of the region's largest park at Sheffield, it was already much reduced in size by the mid-fifteenth century through the use of hundreds of acres as leased meadow and grazing land and the exploitation of coal and quarried stone. Yet there is still evidence of deer hunting in the region's parks by both the *par force de chiens* and the bow and stable methods in the sixteenth century. By the early seventeenth century many deer parks had either been sub-divided into coppice woodlands or much reduced in size through sale or renting, and this process continued throughout the century. However, two parks, at Wentworth and Sandbeck, were of post-medieval origin. Where deer remained in parks after the end of the Middle Ages their function was largely ornamental. The parks themselves, once mixed areas of wood and open pasture, had taken on their modern form of open grassland.

---

43   BodL, Gough Maps, 35, fo. 48.

44   Hey, 'The parks at Tankersley and Wortley'; M. Jones, 'Ironstone mining at Tankersley in the nineteenth century for Elsecar and Milton ironworks', in B. Elliott (ed.), *Aspects of Barnsley: discovering local history* (7 vols, Barnsley, 1993–2002), vol. iii, pp. 80–115.

Chapter 2

The Sheffield cutlers and the earls of Shrewsbury: a new interpretation

Richard Hoyle

Sheffield was fortunate to have had David Hey as its historian, and equally David was lucky to have been able to live and work in a town and district with which he had such empathy and understanding. In this foray into Sheffield history I want to question David's interpretation of a key aspect of the town's history, not simply to annoy or provoke argument (although I am sure that David would have enjoyed the latter) but because I think that the history of the town is susceptible to an alternative reading and one which is less flattering to its manorial lords than the conventional narrative. As these questions are poorly documented, much of the argument has to rely on the close reading of familiar documents and on what was happening elsewhere.

I

Sheffield was one of those northern industrial towns that remained essentially a manorial borough into the nineteenth century: we might count Manchester and Bradford as others with a similar history. Sheffield secured improvement commissioners in 1818 and parliamentary incorporation in 1832, but incorporation only in 1843. Many second-rank towns secured incorporation much earlier, especially in the rash of incorporations in the mid-1550s, when Sheffield secured only a grant of its church lands to trustees who became known as the Church Burgesses (a point of some significance to which we will return).[1] So in the year that the Church Burgesses received their letters patent, 1554, full grants of incorporation were given to (among others) Aylesbury, Banbury, Buckingham, Chippenham and Droitwich, but what was offered Sheffield fell far short of the corporate self-government established in these southern towns. Sheffield developed in a different direction, with a statute establishing the Cutlers' Company in 1624: but at much the same time, in 1626, Leeds secured a charter of incorporation. Sheffield historians have read the 1624 statute as the benign work of manorial lords who recognised that, as they had largely withdrawn from the town, their influence over it and capacity to control the town's cutlery trade had also diminished, and so a different form of government was needed. And yet it seems more likely that the lords inhibited – and continued to inhibit – the corporate growth of Sheffield and that the 1624 statute was an answer to a different problem.

---

1   For the incorporations granted in these years, Robert Tittler, 'The incorporation of boroughs, 1540–1558', *History*, 62 (1977), pp. 24–42. Tittler includes Sheffield among the towns receiving incorporations (p. 42), but, as we shall see, the town did not receive a full incorporation.

Medieval and sixteenth-century Sheffield was dominated by its castle, the size of which has only recently become clear as a result of recent excavations on its site.[2] This is the essential leap of imagination that it is necessary to make: Sheffield grew up in the shadow of a baronial castle. The castle was demolished at the end of the 1640s but was apparently still maintained in a habitable state in the 1630s.[3] It had the usual adjuncts of a park containing a lodge – Manor Lodge – which may have served as a seigneurial house in a more modern style and acceptable size in the sixteenth century, and, in addition, what may have been a banqueting house, the Hall in the Ponds. It follows from this that Sheffield had resident lords until around the end of the sixteenth century and possibly a little later.

The medieval lords were the de Furnivals. William sixth Lord Furnival died in 1383: the manor then passed by descent through his daughter to her daughter, who married John Talbot. He took the title of Lord Furnival but more importantly was created earl of Shrewsbury in 1442. The descent of the manor was then in the line of the Talbot earls of Shrewsbury. The earls that chiefly concern us here are George, sixth earl (*d.* 1590), and Gilbert, his son, seventh earl (*d.* 1616). After the seventh earl's death the title passed to his younger brother, Edward, eighth earl, who died the following year. It then passed to collateral heirs. On Gilbert's death the majority of the estates passed to his three daughters as co-heirs. Of the three, only the youngest, Alethea, who married the earl of Arundel, had any issue. In 1627, when the elder daughters were almost certainly beyond child-bearing age, a settlement entailed the estates on the son of Alethea and her husband and thereafter the descent of the manor was in the line of the Howards, earls of Arundel and, after 1660, once again dukes of Norfolk.

George, sixth earl of Shrewsbury, died at Manor Lodge, but had built, in the last decade of his life, a new house at Worksop. It was here that the seventh earl greeted James I on his way to claim the English throne in 1603.[4] For the earls of Shrewsbury, though, Sheffield remained their town. Successive earls and their wives and children were buried in Sheffield parish church. The seventh earl was the last of the line to be buried there. The scale and traditional character of his funeral may be seen as a recognition that the old ways had come to an end. He may well have attempted to give the Talbot name a more permanent memorial in Sheffield by making provision in his will for the foundation of a hospital (almshouses), although his bequest was not implemented until much later in the century.[5]

It was David Hey's judgement that after the death of the seventh earl in 1616 the manor was managed by stewards, and this is surely correct: it is unlikely that any of his daughters or their husbands were often seen in Sheffield. The castle was demolished

---

2   J. Moreland and T. Hadley, *Sheffield Castle: archaeology, archives, regeneration, 1927–2018* (York, 2020).

3   Rachel Askew, 'Sheffield Castle and the aftermath of the English civil war', *Northern History*, 54 (2017), p. 190.

4   For Worksop see Mark Girouard, *Robert Smythson and the Elizabethan country house* (New Haven, CT, 1983), pp. 110–15.

5   *ODNB*; G.R. Batho, 'Gilbert Talbot, seventh earl of Shrewsbury (1553–1616): the "Great and Glorious earl"?', *DAJ*, 93 (1973), pp. 23–32.

at the end of the 1640s.[6] Manor Lodge was kept in repair and paid the hearth tax on 57 hearths in 1672, but it was allowed to fall into ruin thereafter and was demolished in or about 1708.[7] Thereafter the dukes used Worksop as their northern house, rebuilding it after the Elizabethan house was destroyed by fire in 1761. One reason for their move to Worksop may have been that Sheffield had ceased to be a pleasant place to live. In 1608 Sir John Bentley told the seventh earl that he hoped to see him at either Wingfield or in Sheffield, 'where I look to be half choked with town smoke'. That smoke probably came as much from the cutlers' forges as from domestic chimneys.[8]

Thomas Furnival had secured a grant of a market charter for Sheffield in 1296, although it is clear that the market predated the grant and the charter merely regularised what was already happening.[9] The following year Furnival made a grant to all the free tenants of the town of Sheffield and their heirs that made three concessions. The first confirmed their tenancies in fee farm, paying in total a fee farm rent of £3 8s 9¼d, a sum later called the Burgery rents. Second, he gave an undertaking that the court baron would meet three-weekly, which had been the practice in the past, and that amercements would be set by a jury of tenants and should not be arbitrary. Third, the tenants of Sheffield were to be toll free within Hallamshire. This fell far short of being a charter of borough privileges and so the town remained unincorporated.[10] This charter, though, stands apart from later developments in the town.

By the end of the fifteenth century civic institutions had developed in the form of a town trust that held property for public ends. The earliest reference to it appears to be a charter of 1498, which granted property in Sheffield to the vicar and other feoffees to pay for obits and other masses in the parish church. The grantor also made provision that if his feoffees failed to perform his will then the property should be to the use of the freeholders of Sheffield 'called the Burgesses', and they were to use the profits of the premises for the repair of roads within a mile of Sheffield and other meritorious acts for the health of the soul of the granter.[11] By the time of the making of the chantry certificates in 1547–8 the town trust had lands that generated £16 10s for the salaries of three stipendiary priests in the parish church and £12 8d for obits in the parish church. A petition to the queen of 1553–4 to recover the £16 10s claims that the trustees accepted responsibility for the wages of the priests only after the voluntary gifts that had supported them dried up around 1539–40.

---

6   Askew, 'Sheffield Castle'.

7   David Hey, *The fiery blades of Hallamshire: Sheffield and its neighbourhood, 1660–1740* (Leicester, 1991), p. 22.

8   David Hey, *A history of Sheffield* (Lancaster, 2005), p. 33.

9   Samantha Letters with Mario Fernandes, Derek Keene and Olwen Myhill, *Gazetteer of markets and fairs in England and Wales to 1516*, 2 vols, List and Index Society, 32–33 (Kew, 2003), pt 2, p. 404; Barbara English, *Yorkshire Hundred and quo warranto rolls, 1274–1294*, Yorkshire Archaeological Society Record Series, 151 (Leeds, 1996), p. 278 (proceedings in 1293–4).

10 The charter is printed in J. Hunter, *Hallamshire. The history and topography of the parish of Sheffield in the county of York …* (London, 1819), p. 39, and J.D. Leader, *The records of the Burgery of Sheffield commonly called the Town Trust* (London, 1897), App. pp. 1–3 (with translation).

11 Leader, *Burgery*, p. xxvii.

In fact this was the only part of the town trust's income that was used for religious ends. What appears to have happened on the confiscation of the chantries in 1549 is that £17 9s 4d, being £17 for the salaries of the priests and 9s 4d for an obit, was forfeited. The crown, however, continued to pay the £17 to the three priests as pensions, so there was no immediate advantage to the crown. An annual income of £9 10s remained in the hands of the trustees of the town lands, suggesting that in 1545 or a little later they had an annual income of slightly under £27.[12]

The town managed to secure the return of the confiscated income early in Mary's reign. On her accession or soon after Robert Swift and William Taylor, on behalf of all the inhabitants of the parish of Sheffield, petitioned the queen asking for the restoration of this sum to the town, in return for which they would free the crown of the pensions paid to the three priests and re-employ them to serve the town.[13] Swift, it should be noted, was the earl of Shrewsbury's steward. The identity of William Taylor is unknown, but a man of that name was a tenant of the town's estate in the later 1560s.[14] The petition was successful and letters patent were issued in June 1554.[15] From this point on there were two town trusts in Sheffield. The first was the original trust, which came to be called the Town Burgesses Trust.[16] It lacked any formal constitution until 1682, when it was regulated by a Commission of Charitable Uses that vested the property in the hands of 13 trustees. Vacancies were to be filled by new members drawn from the inhabitants of the town and appointed by them. The funds of the trust were to be applied to essentially secular ends: the repair of bridges, the cleaning and keeping in order for the common use of the inhabitants of a pool called Barker's Pond and the repairing of causeways and highways. By the early nineteenth century none of these purposes were a call on the funds of the charity. The Charity Commissioners noted that, instead, the income was applied to purposes that in an incorporated town would be funded out of the corporation's income, including the provision of a town clerk, and gas-lighting, paving and widening the streets. No rates were raised for these purposes until 1818, when a Police Act was passed, but the costs of securing the act were supplied by the Town Burgesses.

The Church Burgesses established in 1554 were established as a corporation called the 'Twelve Capital Burgesses and Commonalty of the town and parish of Sheffield'. They formed the second town trust. Vacancies amongst the burgesses

---

12 W. Page, *The certificates of the commissioners appointed to survey the chantries … in the county of York*, 2 vols, Surtees Soc. 91–22 (Durham, 1894–5), II, p. 400; Leader, *Sheffield Burgery*, pp. xxvii–ix.

13 The petition is printed in Hunter, *Hallamshire*, p. 133.

14 There were two generations of Robert Swift: the elder, d. 1561 and the younger, d. 1558. G.R. Batho, *A calendar of the Shrewsbury and Talbot papers in the Lambeth Palace Library and the College of Arms* (London, 1971), p. 433. For Taylor, Leader, *Sheffield Burgery*, pp. 14–15.

15 The patent is published (in Latin) in Hunter, *Hallamshire*, pp. 133–5 and in English abstract in *Calendar of Patent Rolls, Mary*, I, pp. 170-2. The patent says that it was made at the request of the earl of Shrewsbury as well as the burgesses; so far as the earl is concerned, this may be true, although it may also be common form.

16 Hey, *Fiery blades*, pp. 202–8 and Leader, *Sheffield Burgery*. Also BPP, 1828, 374. *Commissioners of Inquiry into Charities in England and Wales, nineteenth report*, pp. 378–81 and 624–30.

were to be filled by co-option, so this was a perpetual oligarchy. It had a seal. It was charged with paying the salaries of the three clergy and devoting any surplus to the repairs of the church, bridges and highways, and to the poor. The Church Burgesses had an income of £1,400 in about 1828, the major part of which was spent on the salary of the clergy, the employment of a church organist and bellows blower, vergers and other church officials.[17]

None of this amounted to the incorporation of the town. Sheffield remained, formally and practically, an urban manor, albeit one with two public trusts. In this respect it did not advance beyond the arrangements made in 1554 until 1818: its institutional development was retarded.

The other feature that we might expect to find in an increasingly populous town is a grammar school.[18] It would be surprising if the stipendiary priests were not expected to do some teaching, but nothing says that this was the case. The Marian grant made no provision for teaching but their accounts suggest that the church burgesses maintained a school and school master.[19] A grammar school was established only by letters patent of 1604 and followed on a bequest by one Thomas Smith made the previous year. Smith gave a rent of £20 for the salary of a headmaster and £10 for that of an usher, the pair to be nominated by the minister and 12 parishioners of the parish. In 1606 an assessment of the town raised £108 18s 3d towards the cost of building a school. The land on which it stood was donated by the church burgesses, from among whom the governors were drawn.

II

Let us turn to the question of incorporation. In its fullest form, incorporation confers the right to hold land, levy taxes, make and enforce bylaws, sue and be sued. All of this was symbolised by the possession of a seal. Corporations might elect officers (although what is meant by election varies from place to place and time to time: at its simplest it is merely co-option by the existing trustees or feoffees). Where an urban corporation was granted the right to have a mayor or alderman, they might also have the status of Justices of the Peace. So, at Leeds, the charter of incorporation of June 1626 created a 'free borough' as 'a body corporate and politic'. The borough had the right to possess property, to plead and by impleaded at law and to have a common seal. There was to be an alderman, nine principal burgesses and 20 assistants. The first holders of these posts, as was normal, were named in the charter. The alderman and nine principal burgesses were to act as justices of the peace in the borough, which was defined as the whole of the parish of Leeds. The corporation was to appoint junior officers, including a coroner, a clerk of the market and constables. There was a particular emphasis in the charter on the regulation of the textile industries in the

---

17   *Commissioners of Inquiry into Charities in England and Wales, nineteenth report*, pp. 581–3, 631–40.

18   *Ibid.*, p. 576.

19   John Roach, *A regional study of Yorkshire schools, 1500–1820* (Lewiston, NY, 1998), pp. 116–17.

parish and the maintenance of standards in the manufacture of cloth.[20] This is the institutional form that Sheffield lacked until the nineteenth century.

There is a tendency to see incorporation as an uncontested, neutral and even natural outcome. It was an answer to the aspirations of towns by giving them a formal standing. It was also an answer to some of the problems they faced, including that of holding property and regulating production. What is insufficiently appreciated is that incorporation was not there for the asking. The power to grant incorporation rested with the crown and was used sparingly and with discretion. There is good evidence that not all towns that sought incorporation received it. Many were perhaps deterred from asking, knowing that, for every request they made, there would be objections and counter arguments. Moreover, there is evidence that the securing of a charter could be costly, not only in terms of the fees incurred but in terms of the wining and dining of friends and even outright bribery.

Incorporation was not seen as improving the efficiency of government but as being antithetical to monarchical and aristocratic government. Early in Elizabeth's reign, Lord Keeper Bacon expressed the view that there were already too many incorporations in existence.[21] County magistrates were liable to oppose requests for incorporation because it meant that a corporate town would slip out of their grasp.[22] A late example of the hostility directed at corporations comes from the '*Advice*' that the earl of Newcastle offered Charles II in the months before his return to the throne:

> For corporations I see no reason why there should be so many, for why should tanners and shoemakers not be contented to be governed by the same way that lords, gentleman and good yeomen and freeholders are, which is by the known laws of the kingdom, by the judges and justices of peace. But these townsmen must be exempted by their charter. The truth is that every corporation is a petty free state, against monarchy, and they have done your majesty more mischief in these late disorders, with their lecturers, than anything else hath done.

Newcastle went on to say that corporate towns spent too much of their income on feasting and debauchery.[23]

There was therefore a tendency to look on the incorporated town with suspicion. But, where a town was a manorial borough, incorporation meant escaping the grasp of the manorial lord and his officers. We can see tensions over incorporation as finally being a naked power struggle, as at Aylesbury, where

---

20   G.C.F. Forster. 'The foundations: from the earliest times to c. 1700', in D. Fraser (ed.), *A history of modern Leeds* (Manchester, 1980), pp. 12–13. The charter is printed in translation in James Wardell, *The municipal history of the borough of Leeds* (London, 1856), pp. xxxi–xliii.

21   J. Craig, *Reformation, politics and polemics. The growth of Protestantism in East Anglian market towns, 1500–1610* (Cambridge, 2001), p. 86, n. 81.

22   A point developed at length in an unpublished paper of mine, 'Incorporation and the Monarchical Republic', on which this section draws.

23   Thomas P. Slaughter (ed.), *Ideology and politics on the eve of the Restoration: Newcastle's advice to Charles II* (Philadelphia, PA, 1984), pp. 40–1 (spelling and punctuation both modernised).

the town's manorial lords finally overturned the town's charter.[24] By the end of the Middle Ages Aylesbury had developed institutions of self-government. In 1499 we have a reference to the Twenty-two and Twelve of Aylesbury, which suggests some form of bi-cameral and hierarchical government in the town, but the fact that they were petitioning their lord in a dispute over access to the town's court rolls suggests a tense relationship with him.

The manorial rights were inherited by Sir Thomas Pakington in the mid-1540s. He began to chip away at the inhabitants' rights, bringing a suit against them for their self-government by an allegedly forged custumal. They riposted by appealing to the crown and secured a charter in January 1554, having claimed that they had supported Mary in her accession the previous year. The charter gave the inhabitants a bailiff (a de facto mayor), ten aldermen, 12 capital burgesses and a range of borough officers, together with a weekly market and two days of fairs. The charter cut across Pakington's rights and was never accepted by him or his heirs, and it seems likely that the town was never able to exercise the range of rights given it by the charter. It was able to exploit the weakness of Sir John Pakington in the 1650s (when he was a sequestered royalist) to secure some of the manorial rights, but this was reversed by a private act of 1664 and the charter cancelled. The one element of the 1554 charter that was exercised was the right to elect two MPs, but, at some periods at least, the Pakingtons rather than the town controlled the elections.

More locally and of much greater relevance for this paper, Chesterfield offers a supreme example of aristocratic opposition to a town's corporate standing.[25] The sixth earl of Shrewsbury considered Chesterfield to be *his* town. The burgesses had secured a lease of the guild lands in the town but in 1562 were bullied into assigning the lease to Shrewsbury in return for a rent change and the lease of a market hall that the earl had built in the town. Apparently under pressure from the earl's continued interference in the borough, in 1566 the burgesses drew up a detailed statement of their customs and tried to give this a greater surety by having it exemplified in Chancery. This claimed a more elaborate system of government than had been outlined in an earlier custumal (of 1480), including an alderman elected annually, 12 brethren and 12 common councillors. A variety of other rights were claimed that made Chesterfield into a corporation by prescription. This drew down the wrath of the earl: the leading inhabitants were summoned to Sheffield to be confronted by a display of noble temper. In 1568 he forced them into a composition in which they were forced to disown not only the rights they claimed in their custumal of 1566 but those achieved by the time of their custumal of 1480. In effect, they surrendered their claim to be a corporation: where they had had an alderman, they were forced to admit that they had

---

24   For what follows, see VCH *Bucks.*, III, pp. 8–10; P.W. Hasler (ed.), *The history of Parliament. The Commons, 1558–1603*, 3 vols (London, 1981), vol. i, pp. 118–19; Tittler, 'Incorporation of boroughs', pp. 29–30.

25   For what follows, P. Riden, *Tudor and Stuart Chesterfield*, History of Chesterfield, II (i) (Chesterfield, 1984), pp. 56–72. The leading documents, including the 1598 charter, are printed in P. Riden and J. Blair (eds), *Records of the borough of Chesterfield and related documents, 1204–1835*, History of Chesterfield, V (Chesterfield, 1980), pp. 63–85.

no right to choose their own officer and the earl imposed his bailiff as the town's ruler on his behalf. Moreover, this settlement with the earl left the town without any income of its own. This was not a situation the town could accept, but they had to bide their time until after the sixth earl's death in 1590, and in 1598 they secured a charter of incorporation from the crown, much to the annoyance of the seventh earl. We can assume that the sixth earl of Shrewsbury would have been every bit as hostile to any proposal that Sheffield should seek incorporation.

It is in this light that we should look again at the establishment of the town trustees in 1554. There is no sign that before this date the town had a custumal or a civic organisation. It had feoffees who held land for the maintenance of communal ends and for obits. This is a much more rudimentary form of government than that which had already evolved at Chesterfield. The request made to the queen in 1553 was a modest one: it merely asked for the restoration of the rents. The patent created a much more elaborate arrangement than the petition sought, but it stopped well short of being an incorporation of the town. The outcome of this episode, then, is that Sheffield remained an unincorporated manorial borough but with two town trusts, one based on the letters patent of 1554 and the other informally constituted, and the lineal descendent of the pre-Reformation arrangements in the town. And until 1604 the town continued to lack a formally constituted school. Even this may overstate the town's independence from an overbearing earl. We have already shown that the Robert Swift in whose name the town petitioned the queen in 1553 was the earl's steward for his Yorkshire estates. For a succession of years after 1574 the accounts of the Burgery (the town trustees) are said to have been taken before the lord's bailiff, William Dickinson. This followed immediately on litigation that appears to have been about the lord's claim to the wastes of the town. Twenty years later Dickinson wrote to the earl reporting that two of the feoffees had died and suggesting replacements.[26] At this time Sheffield may well have been a more closely supervised town than it appears at first sight.

III

And so we turn to the cutlers.[27] The trade of knife-making was established in Sheffield long before the sixteenth century. A Robert le Coteler was recorded in the lay subsidy roll of 1297. The scale of the medieval industry cannot be established for certain, but what is clear from the references gathered by Hey is that its product, 'thwhitel', a short pointed knife with a wooden handle used for eating, was widely employed. By 1540

---

26 Leader, *Sheffield Burgery*, pp. 34 (1574), 35 (1576) and following years to 1585 (p. 48). C. Jamison, *A calendar of the Shrewsbury and Talbot papers, in Lambeth Palace Library and the College of Arms*, vol. i, *Shrewsbury MSS in Lambeth Palace Library* (1966), p. 86.

27 The following is based on David Hey's writings, chiefly 'The origins and early growth of the Hallamshire cutlery and allied trades', in John Chartres and David Hey (eds), *English rural society, 1500–1800. Essays in honour of Joan Thirsk* (Cambridge, 1990), pp. 343–67 and 'The establishment of the Cutlers' Company', in D. Hey and C. Binfield (eds), *Mesters to masters. A history of the Company of Cutlers in Hallamshire* (Oxford, 1997), pp. 12–25.

the topographer John Leland reported that 'there be many good smiths and cuttelars in Halamshire', Hallamshire being the parishes of Sheffield, Ecclesall and Bradfield. (At a later date Handsworth was treated as a part of the lordship.)

Cutlery making was not limited to Hallamshire. Hey pointed to other areas that had communities of cutlers, notably Thaxted (Essex), where a substantial industry is revealed by the Poll Tax of 1379. Sheffield had a number of advantages over any English rival, however. There was the availability of local ironstone and coal. By the sixteenth century Sheffield was importing Spanish steel with which to edge the tools, then German steel and finally Swedish steel. No locally made steel was available until after 1640.[28] The real advantage that Sheffield possessed (and which its domestic rivals lacked) was the power of water in streams coming off the surrounding hills used to power grinding mills. The smithies, using imported steel for the edge of the tool, were relatively simple, consisting of a hearth and bellows, an anvil and a water trough into which the tool would be plunged to harden it. The tool's edge would then be sharpened at a water-powered grinding mill. Each mill would contain several stones on a single rotating shaft so a number of cutlers could work alongside each other finishing their knives.

Hey thought that the quality of Sheffield cutlery improved over the late sixteenth century. He saw the development of the Sheffield trades as being encouraged by George, sixth earl of Shrewsbury (*d.* 1590). Certainly he was involved in the trade: he may well have been responsible for bringing to Sheffield iron workers of French descent to establish blast furnaces and water-powered forges on his estates. His steward, William Dickinson, is found importing steel through Bawtry to Sheffield, suggesting that the earl, in part at least, controlled the trade through the supply of raw materials. But he also had a further financial interest in the trade through the rent of the grinding mills. A rental of 1581 shows the manor then had 15 grinding wheels shared by 23 tenants. A survey of the manor in 1637 found 29 mills, each mill containing several wheels. The surveyor explained that the wheels were 'employed for the grinding of knives by four or five hundred master workmen'.[29]

So the involvement of the sixth earl of Shrewsbury in the trade is not to be doubted. He had interests in coalmining and in rent from the sites for the grinding wheels, and he may have supplied the iron and steel. There is doubtless more about this to be discovered. Hey testified to his role in nurturing the trade, even if he was vague as to exactly what the earl contributed to its development.[30] The sixth earl certainly provided an institutional framework, consisting of ordnances issued by the manorial court and the registration there of cutlers' marks. The first bylaws are dated 1565. Fuller ordnances were issued in 1590 and again in 1614. However, in 1624 the Cutlers' Company was incorporated by act of parliament. There had been an earlier attempt to do this in 1621 and perhaps (a speculation, as I shall explain) in 1614. The established narrative is that Gilbert, the seventh earl, recognised that

---

28 See Dorian Gerhold's contribution to this book, at p. 65 below.

29 Hey, 'Origins and early growth', p. 353; J.G. Ronksley (trans. and ed.), *An exact and perfect survey and view of the manor of Sheffield with other lands by John Harrison, 1637* (1908), pp. 3, 31–2.

30 Hey, 'Establishment of the Cutlers' Company', p. 16.

his daughters and son in law were unlikely to be either a presence in Sheffield after his death or a patron of the cutlers in the way that he and his father had been and so, as a parting gift, he cut them free of the manorial regime under which they had operated for the previous half-century and perhaps more. Yet this interpretation is not entirely convincing. It supposes that the earls had the best interests of Sheffield at heart (which, to a non-Sheffielder, seems unlikely) and that they were willing to give up their power for the benefit of the town. And it supposes that their power was entirely personal and could not be exercised through a bailiff or steward.

One senses that there is more to this than immediately meets the eye. There are several possibilities. The first is, as Hey and others have supposed, that the earls really did encourage the cutlers' trade. They might have concluded that they could no longer assist the cutlers once the estate had passed into the hands of the co-heiresses and so let them take their own institutional form. A second reading of developments is to see the cutlers as a form of guild. Supervision by the earls increasingly became insufficient and, whether they liked it or not, both the earl and the cutlers finally had no option but to look for alternative forms of supervision. A third option is that the cutlers themselves increasingly resented manorial control and looked for instruments of self-government rather than government under the earl, or with the consent of the earl.

IV

The 1565 orders were a relatively short document made 'by the whole consent of the cutler makers of knives and cutler occupation within the lordship of halamshire and liberties and bordes of the same'.[31] They were made 'for maintenance of the common wealth of cutlers craft and cutler occupation according to the ancient customs and ordnances by men of the said occupation there dwelling made and heretofore used'. The orders therefore claimed to be grounded in ancient custom, but this was no more than common form and should not necessarily be taken at face value. The ordinances were to be enforced by 12 men of the said craft 'elected, chosen or sworn' by the earl of Shrewsbury and his council. Fines were to be paid to the earl.

This introduces a paradox. The customs were those of the cutlers. But the cutlers – it seems – had no power to enforce their customs. Under the ordinance, enforcement was to be by the earl empanelling a jury of 12 men who were to search for and present misdemeanours, with fines paid to the lord. This might be read as the cutlers entering into an alliance with the earl whereby he provided a mechanism for enforcement in return for the profits. It might equally be read as the earl extending his control over the cutlers. Whichever, the ordinances placed the cutlers in a subordinate position, unable to choose their own searchers, unable to keep their fines and in an arrangement that existed only as long as the earl was satisfied by it. The earl gave the customs an institutional form and provided a means of enforcement. This, then, is the paradox. We are asked to believe that the customs were old (or else they could not be customs). But they could not have been customs if the earl was their guarantor and

---

31 R.E. Leader, *History of the Company of Cutlers of Hallamshire*, 2 vols (Sheffield, 1905–6), vol. i, pp. 1–2.

could withhold them as he chose. The final clause suggests that the arrangements were an experiment: 'provided always that it shall be lawful for the said earl at all time and times hereafter upon further and better experience of the proof of the premises to revoke the same or any part or article thereof at his will and pleasure'.

So what were the customs? The ordinances consist of eight clauses, the last being the clause that empowered the earl to revoke some or all of them.[32] The first clause defined two periods in which the cutlers were not to work: for the 14 days following 15 August (the Feast of the Assumption of our Lady) and from Christmas (the Feast of the Nativity) to 23 January, making six weeks in all when they were to 'apply and work other hand labours'. This, it might be suggested, was to free up labour for the peak demands of the agrarian calendar: harvest in August and ploughing and sowing in January. It was also a levelling down: if some could not devote time to craft work, then no one should work. In clause four the same holiday dates were applied to the owners of the grinding mills. Clauses two and three were orthodox rules about recruitment into the industry. In clause two it was ordered that no one was to set up in the cutlers' trade and hire a man to help him unless he had served an apprenticeship or learnt the trade from his father. In clause 3 it is instructed that no one was to take an apprentice for a term of less than seven years. The final three clauses define the bounds of the trade. No cutler or hefter of knives was to supply chapmen with unhefted blades – that is, blades without handles. The next clause forbade blacksmiths to make or sell blades. The final clause forbade cutlers to heft blades themselves.

These are the sort of bylaws that we might expect to find in any guild: controlling the admission to the trade, the demarcations between occupations, periods when the occupations took a holiday. But then there is what these rules do *not* say. There is nothing about the registration of marks, although we know this was being done from about the same date. There is nothing about maintaining quality by inspection and no comment is made about marketing. There is absolutely no indication that the trade had its own officers. And where in a guild one would expect fines levied on its members to be paid into a general fund, here fines were to be paid to the earl. And of course the orders remained in force only at his will, which could be withdrawn. The cutlers were therefore subordinate to the earl. On the other hand, the ordinances gave the cutlers an embryonic institutional form under the manorial government of the lordship of Hallamshire.

The 1590 ordinances, made right at the end of Earl George's life, were much more elaborate, consisting of 17 numbered clauses.[33] They were made by the 'whole fellowship and company of cutlers and makers of knives within the lordship of Hallamshire', whose names were given in a schedule. But the orders were also made by the 'assent' of the earl, 'for the better relief and commodity of the poorer sort of the

---

32 They are not numbered in the printed text. There is a dating clause after clause 6, suggesting that the last three clauses may be additions.

33 Leader, *Company of Cutlers*, vol. ii, pp. 2–4. The orders do not survive except in an eighteenth-century copy. This names George earl of Shrewsbury in the heading, but says that they were signed by Gilbert earl of Shrewsbury. There were evidently some personal subscriptions on the back of the original.

said fellowship'. This does suggest that the earl had his own agenda in putting his name to these orders. That this was so is confirmed further in the final clause (clause 17), which gave the earl the power to revoke the orders 'if [they] do not bring unto the poorest sort of the said mystery and occupation of cutlers such help and benefit as is thereby looked for'. The appearance is that the orders had a social purpose in rebalancing the trade in favour of its poorer members.

The enforcement of the orders, we are told in the first and subsequent clauses, was to be undertaken by presentments made by 12 cutlers. It is only towards the end, in clause 16, that we discover who these people were and how they were to enter into office. Every year at the 'Great Court' held at Sheffield in Easter week[34], the earl or his learned steward were to appoint 12 men 'of the science or mystery of cutlers' who were to be sworn to search and enquire upon all offences committed contrary to the ordinances. Any fines they levied were to be estreated among the other fines of the court and collected by the court's officers. It seems to have been envisaged that the 12 men would remain in post throughout the year. They might be called upon by the foreman of the jury to determine any matters that arose touching the ordinances (clause 14). They were given the power to amend or add to the ordinances (clause 15). (This suggests that they maintained a register in which their deliberations could be recorded.) What we have here is a proto-guild lacking formal powers of self-government but which had to shelter under the manorial court: it only existed by the patronage of the earl of Shrewsbury. It did not elect its own officers; these were chosen for it by the earl or his officers (which does not rule out the possibility that in fact the earl accepted a list of cutlers presented to him or that each jury of 12 nominated its successors). Because the ordinances could not formally bind people to their observance, personal subscription was needed. This was achieved by having the cutlers sign the document to show their subscription (as intended in the heading): apprentices, when they set up independently, were to add their names (clause 12). This is, then, an elaborate structure to establish authority, potentially coercive authority, where none existed. But the whole structure belonged to and could be amended or even terminated by the earl.

The individual clauses are a mix of elaborations of the corresponding clauses in the 1565 ordinances and new clauses. So clause 1 dealt with the holiday periods, although it laid down slightly different dates. Clause 2 forbade any person to set up or use the 'science or craft of a cutler or knife maker', or procure anyone to teach him the 'science' unless the person setting up in the trade or teaching the trade had been an apprentice for seven years or had been sufficiently instructed and taught 'the said mystery and science' by their father. Clause 3 instructed that no cutler was to have more than one apprentice at a time but could take a second apprentice when his current apprentice was in their final year. No apprentice was to be taken for a term of less than seven years. Clause 4 imposes the same holiday periods on the owners of grinding wheels as on the cutlers. Clause 5 is new. It forbids the owners of grinding mills within the lordship from allowing any persons from outside the lordship to use their mills. Clause 6 perhaps reiterates what has been said before:

---

34   For the Great Court see Ronksley (ed.), *Exact and perfect survey*, pp. 2, 43.

No person nor persons using the said art, mystery or craft of cutlers within the said lordship and liberties of Hallamshire [shall] neither set up nor work upon the said craft or science except they have been sufficiently learned [in] the said art and science *within the lordship* … .[35]

Clause 7 is new. No one was to use a mark other than the one assigned him in the lord's court. This put in writing what had been practice for at least a quarter century. Clause 8 is also new, and forbade any cutler or hefter of knives to do any work for any chapman, 'hardwareman' or dagger maker, or any other person living outside the Lordship. This is repeated in a different way in clause 9: no one was to sell any knife blades to be hefted outside the lordship. These clauses all serve to keep business within the lordship, stop any person from outside taking advantage of the grinding mills in the lordship and prevent the export from the lordship of knives to be finished elsewhere.

The ordinances then turn to questions of employment. Clause 10 says that no cutler was to employ a journeyman under the age of 21 years (i.e. the normal age for the end of an apprenticeship) unless permitted to do so by the jury of 12 men. Nor were cutlers to employ anyone who had not been either an apprentice or taught the skills of the trade by their father. Clause 11 orders that anyone who had not been an apprentice or who was insufficiently learned in the craft should only set up in and exercise the craft if they paid an admission fine of £5 to the 12 men, half of which was to go to the earl and the remainder to be distributed to the relief of the poorest sort of the occupation. This 'social fund' was to be distributed by the 12 men. Clause 12 continues the regulation of apprentices. They were to be brought before the jury of 12 men (although a quorum of two would suffice) in the first year of their apprenticeship to have their indentures sealed. An apprentice finishing their term was to show his indenture to the jury of 12 men and sign the acts and ordinances of the cutlers before setting up as a cutler. Clause 13 laid down a fine of 6s 8d on any cutler who refused to serve on the jury. In clause 14 the same fine was laid on any juror who failed to attend its meetings. The remaining three clauses concern the appointment and workings of the jury of 12 men and we have already considered them.

It may be seen how the 1590 ordinances are a much more elaborate and developed document for the management of the cutlers. Some of the clauses carry forward by-laws laid down in the 1565 ordinances, but the emphasis on the control of access to the trade through the close regulation of apprenticeship, the payment by outsiders of a substantial fine for admission and the determination to keep the trade within the lordship rather than allowing unfinished goods to be brought into (or transported out of) Hallamshire is new. The sense is that the ordinances reflect a feeling that the number of cutlers had grown too large and that it had been too easy for people to set up as cutlers, with the result that there was now a problem of poor (or under-employed) cutlers. The rules therefore address a social problem. It might be argued that the purpose of the revised and extended ordinances was to ensure the maintenance of standards among the knife makers, but the overwhelming impulse behind the ordinances is, to my mind, the need to control access to the trade. The

---

35   My italics.

orders do not lay down any mechanism for the inspection of knives: quality is to be maintained through controls on training, either through apprenticeship or by a son's service to his father, if a cutler.

In the absence of any other information, it seems likely that the ordinances of 1590 remained in force until 1614, a significant year. As David Hey put it,

> Earl Gilbert foresaw the need for the cutlers to assume responsibility for their own affairs. Two years before he died [1614] a book was purchased to enter the marks of 182 cutlers then working within Hallamshire. Seventeen Derbyshire cutlers who lived immediately beyond Hallamshire in other lordships were accepted into membership. The jury of sixteen [sic] cutlers (which had been in existence since 1590) was empowered to issue future marks and to raise and spend money although the lord continued to enjoy the manorial perquisite of receiving the fines.[36]

There is quite a lot in this short statement to unpick and query. We know that there were ordinances agreed on 10 September 1614 but we do not have their text. All that survives is a heading in 'The Great Book of the Cutlers' that tells us that the orders were 'agreed amongst the cutlers of Hallamshire' and were established by the assent of Gilbert earl of Shrewsbury.[37] The little we know about the contents of these ordinances comes from the lists of fines levied in 1615 and 1616 by the cutlers' jury.

'The Great Book of the Company of Cutlers' was started in the latter part of 1614. It had the names of the Cutlers' jury of 1614 entered together with a list of 185 cutlers' marks, the list of presentments and fines levied by the 1614 jury (in 1615 one assumes) and the 1615 jury (dated 4 April 1616). We have accounts for the expenditure of the jury. The book contains a declaration made on 22 November 1614 by 17 Derbyshire cutlers consenting to the orders made on 10 September and agreeing to conform to them. They all signed or made their marks, thus continuing the personal subscription that formed a part of the 1590 orders. Nothing further was added to the Great Book for some years except for apprenticeship indentures from 1618 onwards (but these were perhaps entered at the end of the apprenticeship rather than when the indentures were entered into). It was not thought necessary to enter the 1614 ordinances into the book – or perhaps this was intended but never completed – even though this was the governing document under which the jury men were operating. The book then picks up again after the 1624 act.

The purchase and commencement of a register book marks the beginning of a new administrative regime. But the regime was shortlived, having apparently petered out after the fines levied in April 1616. The sole evidence for the 1614 orders being

---

36 Hey, 'Establishment of the Cutler's Company', pp. 16–17 and, for similar comments, *Fiery blades*, pp. 7, 18, 56.

37 Leader, *Company of Cutlers*, vol. ii, p. 4. The 'Great Book' remains in the custody of the Cutlers Company at Cutler's Hall, Ms C6/1. Much of its contents are printed in Leader, *Company of Cutlers*. I am grateful for their archivist, Joan Unwin, for supplying images and advising me on the manuscript.

Table 2.1
Fines levied by the cutlers in 1615 and 1616.

	1614 jury	1615 jury (dated 4 April 1616)	Fine (each offence)
Making of knives without any steel contrary to sixth article	2	5	40s
Using the science of a cutler within the liberty, not having served an apprenticeship, contrary to third article	1		40s
Using two marks on knives, contrary to seventh article	7	1	10s
Damasking of low price knives using silver wire contrary to a branch of the sixth article	2		40s
Grinding knives for people using the cutlers trade who had not served seven years at the same contrary to the third article	2		40s
Lending tools (to a cutler with less than seven years' service)	1		40s
Failing to attend jury when summoned contrary to the tenth article: three offences at 6s 8d levied on a single person	1		20s
Working in forbidden time contrary to the first article	1	3	40s
Setting people on work who were not allowed [i.e. had not served an apprenticeship] contrary to the fourth article	1		40s
Working contrary to orders		1	40s
Taking an apprentice contrary to the second article		1	40s

implemented comes from the two lists of fines. Taken together, they are capable of telling us something about the preoccupations that led to the issue of the ordinances (Table 2.1). The important developments that the fines reveal are: first, that the 1614 orders included at least some inspection of the knives being made, as individual cutlers are fined for making sub-standard wares; and, second, the fines, with some exceptions, remained with the cutlers. This implies a separation from the manorial court. The cutlers no longer had the court to enforce their will.

More can be learnt about the cutlers' organisation in these two years if we look at the accounts contained in the Great Book.[38] In 1614–15 they admitted three men by composition, taking fines from them. In 1615–16 they allowed two men to take apprentices in unusual circumstances. In the first instance a boy changed master after his first master left the district. In the second a poor boy was allowed to be apprenticed while his master had another apprentice. Both of these instances could be claimed to have fulfilled charitable ends, but in both the masters paid handsomely: 50s and 13s 4d, respectively. As for what the jury did and the costs it incurred, much of the expenditure in the first year was on start-up costs, including 3s 8d for engrossing the orders and making copies of them (40s in total), on the purchase of the register

---

38   printed, Leader, *Company of Cutlers*, vol. ii, pp. 28–9.

book and the box to keep it in (5s 6d) and entering the accounts and other documents (6s). But the jury also met on ten occasions between 20 November 1614 and 3 May 1615. On each occasion the cutlers paid for the jurors' dinners at 5d or 6d a head, so that the year's major expense – £2 17s out of £5 9s – was on hospitality. One result of this was that the jurors overspent by 9s, which was left to the incoming jurors to find.

The jurors met on five occasions between 19 August 1615 and 3 April 1616 at a cost of £1 16s 6d. They paid 3s 8d for the collection of amercements and 2s 2d for having their accounts entered into the Great Book. This left them with a small balance to spend on charitable ends: 3s for a poor cutler, 12d for a cutler who was sick, in all 6s 6d out of an income of £3 3s 4d. The cost of dining took a disproportionate part of the income, perhaps an instance of exactly the behaviour that the earl of Newcastle so roundly condemned 35 or so years later.

It was one thing for the cutlers to make presentments: it was quite another for the jury to be able to enforce its will on the cutlers as a whole. It would appear that the cutlers were able to levy the fines for a time (and they paid someone to collect them), but the cessation of record keeping suggests that these new arrangements quickly went into abeyance. It would come as no surprise if there was not a law suit or counsel's opinion that held that the cutlers could not fine non-members. Their actions had no basis in law: they were no more than a voluntary society. They could perhaps enforce a degree of discipline over cutlers who had subscribed their names, but it is impossible to see how they could regulate cutlers in the lordship as a whole who did not accept their authority. Moreover, and this is equally important, neither they nor the manorial government of the lordship of Hallamshire could bind cutlers living outside its boundaries. In 1590 an attempt had been made to deny out-lordship cutlers access to the lordship. Now a small group of Derbyshire cutlers agreed to place themselves under the jurisdiction of the cutlers operating under the 1614 ordinances, but the suspicion must be that many outside the boundaries preferred not to and rejected the cutlers' authority.[39]

This is where we have to part company with David Hey's interpretation of events. The problem was not that the earl recognised that after his death there would be no benign lord of the manor to guide developments, nor that the time had come to cast the cutlers free because they had reached sufficient maturity to regulate their own affairs. The problem was that treating the cutlers as a branch of manorial government no longer created a body with the authority to regulate the cutlers, in terms of either controlling who could be a cutler or the standards of the goods they produced.

The question therefore resolves itself into a different one to that considered by previous historians. It is not about the fortunes of the earls of Shrewsbury. It is a much more elementary question of how you created new regulatory bodies in early modern England. The answer, as will be shown, was either by letters patent or by act of

---

39   It might be no more than chance, but there is a close coincidence in date between the evident collapse of arrangements in Hallamshire and the Case of the Merchant Tailors of Ipswich (Michaelmas Term 1615). Here Sir Edward Coke ruled in King's Bench that a guild or corporation could not remove the right of a person to work at a lawful trade. He held that restrictions on the right to earn a living could be made only by parliament. See Christopher W. Brooks, *Law, politics and society in early modern England* (Cambridge, 2008), p. 386.

parliament. Before turning to the 1624 act that established the cutlers as a corporate body, let us note that there was a previous attempt to secure legislation in 1621. It is not an unreasonable speculation that there was a still earlier attempt to do this in 1614. It will be recalled that neither the 1614 parliament nor the 1621 parliament, for different reasons, produced any legislation, so someone who hoped to secure legislation in 1614 would, in effect, have had to wait a decade before their ambitions became law. It is possible that the cutlers promoted a bill in the 1614 parliament and, having failed to secure an act, attempted to implement something akin to what they had sought in their bill. So, while an obscure episode, the signs are that the project quickly failed – and we can guess why.

V

We know nothing about the management of the cutlers between 1616 and 1621. In the latter year a bill was moved in parliament to establish them as a corporation with regulatory powers. As noted, no legislation came out of this parliament, but a similar, if not identical, bill was brought forwards in 1624 and passed into law.[40] This established the Cutlers' Company, which survives to the present day.

It seems likely that the arrangements for the cutlers established in 1614 did indeed break down in 1616 or shortly after, and that for a period there was little or no regulation of the industry. The preamble to the 1624 act (which is the same as that to the 1621 bill) justified the need for the act in those terms. The cutlers of the lordship of Hallamshire, it said, had been very successful and had secured a great reputation for their skill and dexterity in the trade. They had been able to maintain their families and set many poor men on work. But more recently some people using the same trade in and about the lordship and living within six miles of it had refused to be subject to any order, ordinance and search.

> Every workman in the said lordship and liberty and within six miles compass thereof have taken liberty to themselves to receive, entertain and take as many apprentices and for what term of years, more or less, as he thinketh fit, whereby and by the multitude of workers the whole trade and the exact skill formerly exercised therein is like in a short time to be overthrown, by means of which want of government, order and search, the same workmen holding themselves free and exempted from all search and correction are thereby emboldened and do make much deceitful and unworkmanly wares, and so sell and put the same to sale in divers parts of the kingdom to the great deceit of His Majesty's subjects and scandal of the cutlers in the lordship and liberty and disgrace and hindrance of the sale of cutlery and iron and steel wares there made, and to the great impoverishing, ruin and overthrow of multitudes of poor people, which offenders, not being subject to any oversight, survey or authority do pass unpunished for their offences, abuses and misdemeanours.

---

40   W. Notestein, F.H. Relf and H. Simpson (eds), *The Commons Debates, 1621*, 7 vols (New Haven, CT, 1935), vol. vii, pp. 179–84; the text of the act, albeit abbreviated, can be found in Leader, *History of the Company of Cutlers*, pp. 7–8.

Having identified the problem, the act laid down the remedies. It created a corporation to be called the 'Master, wardens, assistants and commonalty of the company of cutlers of the lordship of Hallamshire in the county of York'. Its members were to be all persons making 'knives, blades, scissors, sheers, sickles, cutlery wares and all other wares and manufactures made or wrought of iron and steel dwelling within the lordship and liberty of Hallamshire or within six miles compass of the same'. Its jurisdiction therefore extended over cutlers living *outside* the liberty and, being inclusive, it removed any need for personal subscription. The company was to have a master elected annually, two wardens, six searchers and 24 assistants. The master and other officers were empowered to make bylaws and impose penalties on those who broke them. The right to take apprentices was closely defined. No cutler was to have more than one apprentice at a time (besides his own son or sons) until the apprentice had served for five years, when a new apprentice could be indentured. No apprentice was to serve for less than seven years or have his term expire before he reached the age of 21. A master was allowed to take an apprentice only if he had himself served an apprenticeship or had been 'so long instructed by his father, and be the owner of his work himself' (so an independent master and not a journeyman). He had to be over the age of 21. Any breach attracted a penalty of 40s a month. No person was to make knives or other edged tools without adding steel to them at a penalty of 10s for every offence. Any wares lacking steel were liable to be seized. No cutler was to use any mark other than the one assigned him by the master. Apprenticeship, the use of steel by the cutlers and the regulation of marks were, as we saw (Table 2.1), the preoccupations of the cutlers under the 1614 orders.

We are not concerned here with the history of the Cutlers after the 1624 act or how easy they found it to impose the terms of the statute on the trade. The signs are, though, that they established a necessary discipline over the practitioners of the craft, including those who did not live or work within the lordship of Hallamshire. This followed on most of a decade when things had gone awry. Future admission to the trade was by apprenticeship or equivalent experience obtained by working with a father. Much more rigorous quality control was instituted, and poor-quality or defective work could be traced back to its maker by his mark. By the end of the 1630s the Company had the resources to build its first hall and was admitting 50 or 60 freemen per annum and registering a similar number of apprentices.[41]

VI

While an account that bases its interpretation on the fortunes of the earls of Shrewsbury and their withdrawal from Sheffield has long been current, a different, and to our mind preferable, interpretation can be grounded on the inadequacy of rules, whose authority was finally derived from the jurisdiction of the lordship of Hallamshire, to regulate the cutlers. There may have been problems securing the compliance of cutlers dwelling in the lordship, but the Hallamshire cutlers could certainly do nothing about cutlers dwelling outside the lordship except forbid their own members

---

41   Hey, *Fiery blades*, p. 57.

to have any dealings with them. After 1614 regulation appears to have been based on personal subscription of cutlers within the lordship. A small group of cutlers from Derbyshire joined, but one suspects that a larger number from outside the lordship saw no reason to accept the supervision – and standards – of the Hallamshire cutlers, preferring to trade in their own way. The answer to this was an act of parliament that placed all the cutlers under a single jurisdiction.

Was statute the only way that this could have been done? It is at this moment that we might usefully consider the fortunes of Leeds, which, as we mentioned earlier, was incorporated by letters patent in 1626.[42] Sir John Savile (1555/6–1630), MP for Yorkshire in successive parliaments, appears to have had a hand in both the passage of the Cutlers' bill through the 1624 parliament and the negotiating of the Leeds patent. He was named in the patent as the first alderman of the new borough, and of course Leeds adopted the Savile owl as its symbol. Here we have an individual who was familiar with developments in both towns.[43]

Leeds was a new town founded in 1207 by Maurice Paynel,[44] who established 30 burgage plots on Briggate under a bailiff. There was a market from this date. Like Sheffield, Leeds sat at the centre of a multi-township parish. But there are three important differences between the two towns. The first was that Leeds became a manor of the Duchy of Lancaster. It never had the overbearing presence of a resident lord. Second, its economy was based on the clothing industry rather than the metal trades, the structures of which were very different. Third, by the beginning of the seventeenth century Leeds had an elite of wealthy clothiers.[45] At the moment we know nothing about how the cutlery trade was organised or the extent to which the individuals promoting the orders of 1614 and the act of 1624 were cutlers or merchants dealing in cutlery. There is no sign, however, that Sheffield had a figure akin to John Harrison of Leeds (1579–1656), who devoted much of his wealth to the benefit of the town, building a moot hall in 1615–16 and leading a campaign to make Leeds a staple town in 1619. He bought land to the north of the town and laid out a new street on it, giving the ground rents to the support of the poor. Perhaps most importantly, he financed the building of a new church, dedicated to St John the Evangelist and consecrated in 1634. Harrison served as alderman after Savile and again in 1634–5. He and his circle dominated the new incorporated borough until the First Civil War, when their

---

42 The letters patent are conveniently published in translation in Wardell, *Municipal history of …
Leeds*, pp. xxi–xliiii.

43 For Savile, see A. Thrush (ed.), *The history of Parliament. The Commons, 1604–29*, 6 vols (Cambridge, 2010), vol. vi, pp. 223-35 and *ODNB*. He sat for Yorkshire in the parliaments of 1597, 1604, 1614, 1624 and 1625, but not at all in the parliament of 1621.

44 For Leeds, see Forster, 'The foundations', and J.W. Kirby (ed.), *The manor and borough of Leeds, 1425–1662: an edition of documents*, Publications of the Thoresby Society, 57 (Leeds, 1981), which has a sizeable introduction.

45 J.W. Kirby, 'A Leeds elite. The principal burgesses of the first Leeds Incorporation', *Northern History*, 20 (1984), pp. 88–106. For Harrison see *ODNB*. For tensions in the town in the early 1620s and interesting material on Harrison, M. Bullett, '"Son of thunder or good shepherd". Contesting the parish pulpit in early seventeenth-century Leeds', *Northern History*, 55 (2018), pp. 161–77.

power was shattered. In short, Leeds had a much more developed civic culture than Sheffield in the 1620s.

There is a further important similarity between the Cutlers' act and the Leeds charter. Both sought to regulate industry in the town and in its the rural hinterland. Both justified their act or charter with claims that a successful industry was being undermined by falling standards and deception in the making of their staple products. In Sheffield it was knives without steel. In Leeds it was fraudulent practices in the making of cloth and inferior dyeing. In Leeds, as at Sheffield, new structures of government were needed to stamp out abuses in the trade. The Leeds charter not only made the town of Leeds a corporate borough but extended its jurisdiction over the whole parish. All the inhabitants of the parish became members of the 'body politic and corporate'. The borough was to have an alderman elected annually, nine principal burgesses and 20 assistants. Together they were to form the common council, which was empowered to make bylaws to regulate the making and dyeing of cloth. In addition, the aldermen, recorder and principal burgesses were to be JPs.[46]

The overt purpose of Leeds's charter was to exercise a tighter grip over the clothing trade in the town and parish. We might see this as being the means by which the leading clothiers strengthened their hand over their employees, lesser clothiers and dyers who were prepared to cut corners and produce sub-standard products that were damaging to the reputation of the town. This was well understood at the time and the grant of the charter was opposed, with a counter-petition being submitted to the crown.[47] The new governors proceeded to issue ordinances 'for the ordering and well governing of the tradesmen and inhabitants within the borough' in 1629–30. While the question of apprenticeship is not addressed in the borough charter (unlike the Cutlers' act), the ordinances laid down detailed regulations. In this there is a strong resemblance to the cutlers. Shortly afterwards the borough established a guild for clothworkers, although this seems not to have been a success.[48]

The Leeds letters patent and the Cutlers' act reflect similar preoccupations. Why did one choose one form of legal instrument and the other a different one? It seems unlikely that in the 1620s the heirs of the earls of Shrewsbury would have objected to a charter given that their interest in the town was now largely fiscal. We have no evidence that they argued against or attempted to amend the Cutlers' act. The choice may be one of strategy alone, a distinction without a difference.

It is worth noting that the cutlers were not the only occupational group that sought legislation as an answer to their problems.[49] There was a movement among the nail makers and metalworkers in Staffordshire, Worcestershire and Shropshire

---

46 But the patent did not make Leeds into a parliamentary borough although this had been canvassed in 1620: Thrush (ed.), *The Commons, 1604–29*, vol. vi, p. 222.

47 *Ibid.*, p. 166, n. 17.

48 Kirby, *Manor and borough of Leeds*, pp. lxvii–lxx, 211–30.

49 The following is chiefly based on W.H.B. Court, *The rise of the Midland industries, 1600–1838* (London, 1938), pp. 61–2. Court was doubtful of the 1584–5 reference, but see David Dean, *Law making and society in late Elizabethan England. The parliament of England, 1584–1601* (Cambridge, 1996), p. 146 for evidence that a bill was brought forwards in that year. See also p. 69 below.

from at least 1584–5 that made repeated attempts to secure an act to protect their interests. This is – for the moment at least – an obscure group. It is not known how it was funded or organised, or who sponsored its appeals to parliament. And, while we do not yet know who led the cutlers' campaign for incorporation, the Black Country movement was unquestionably subaltern and had among its aims the regulation of the relationship between nailer and master. The 1584–5 bill appears to have been concerned with apprenticeship. A bill promoted in 1604 aimed to prevent 'deceits' in the trade of blacksmiths and nailers but also the oppressions practised among them. We know that there was a bill moved in the parliament of 1610. The bill moved in the parliament of 1621 was

> for the reformation of sundry abuses committed by diverse evil disposed persons that engross and get into their own hands great store of victuals and other commodities and exchange the same at unreasonable rates with poor handicraftsmen that work in iron and steel within the several counties of Stafford, Salop, Wigorn and Warwick. And also for the better government of the said craftsmen in that none of them hereafter shall keep above two [ap]prentices at one time and one to serve three years before the taking of the second and they to serve seven years before they shall be free to work of themselves in the said handicraft.[50]

The metalworkers evidently believed that a statute could solve their problems and improve their lives. Unfortunately none of their bills made any progress in parliament, so their hopes were repeatedly dashed.

The cutlers were centred on Sheffield and so their act could quite define a relatively tight area over which they sought jurisdiction. The nailers' bills, so far as we have them, did not seek to establish any organisation to regulate the trade, but the nailers were more widely spread, their area falling between several county jurisdictions. Nonetheless, the nailers provide a sort of parallel with the cutlers. Their concerns were not entirely the same, but in their concern to control entry into the trade through apprenticeship there is an element of congruence.

VII

In short, it has to be questioned whether the cutlers' incorporation by statute in 1624 (itself delayed from 1621) was simply or solely a response to the withdrawal from Sheffield of the Talbot heirs. It is really about the much larger issue of how you manage a rural craft industry, in the sense of both controlling entry into the trade and maintaining standards among its practitioners. As I have suggested, the problem was not unique to Sheffield and Hallamshire. The solution was specific: a different strategy to deal with similar problems was arrived at in Leeds. As is so often the case, bringing new light to bear on an old problem raises new questions. Who, for instance, organised (and funded) the campaign for the cutlers' statute? David, I think, would have enjoyed that thought and thought it a good outcome.

---

50   Notestein *et al.*, *Debates 1621*, vol. vi, pp. 141–2.

Chapter 3

Lord William Cavendish of Hardwick Hall (Derbyshire) and the wardship of Sir Francis Wortley of Wortley Hall (West Riding), 1604–1612

Peter Edwards

In feudal England landowners holding directly from the king held their land in return for services, especially the obligation to fight and provide soldiers in wartime. So, when a minor who, because of his age, was unable to render these services succeeded a tenant-in-chief, the monarch took control of the land and the disposal of the heir's hand in marriage.[1] These rights, which we call wardship, survived until the Civil Wars of the mid-seventeenth century.[2] By the beginning of the sixteenth century, however, what had begun as a means of maintaining the vitality of the link between land and military service had degenerated into a money-making exercise. Although medieval monarchs had obtained revenue by selling their right of wardship and marriage, Henry VII was the first to exploit the system efficiently. He developed its fiscal potential through a new body, the Court of Wards and Liveries, which achieved official status under his successor in 1540. Ironically, as Bell points out, 'the legal rights of livery and wardship continued, and were systematically extended, when the feudal structure, which had given them purpose and been their excuse, had ceased to exist'.[3]

Putting the guardianship of a ward and his or her marriage up for sale clearly prioritised income over the interests of the individual concerned.[4] Throughout the sixteenth and early seventeenth centuries, for instance, the family of the ward, who might be expected to act honourably, secured the guardianship of only a minority of wards. The situation improved after 1610, reflecting the impact of Robert Cecil's *Instructions*, which not only allowed the ward's family a month's grace to purchase the custody of the ward but also preferred nominated friends of the deceased over

---

1 H.E. Bell, *An introduction to the history and records of the Court of Wards and Liveries* (Cambridge, 1953), pp. 1–2.

2 *Ibid.*, p. 1; Joel Hurstfeld, *The Queen's wards. Wardship and marriage under Elizabeth I* (London, 1958), F. Heal and C. Holmes, *The gentry in England and Wales, 1500–1700* (London, 1994), p. 144; L. Stone, *The crisis of the aristocracy, 1558–1641* (Oxford, 1965), p. 670; J.T. Cliffe, *The world of the country house in seventeenth-century England* (New Haven, CT, 1999), p. 108. Feudal tenures and so wardship were abolished by the Long Parliament in February 1646 and definitively by the Tenures Abolition Act of 1660 (12 Charles II, c. 24).

3 Bell, *Introduction*, pp. 2, 13–15, 114.

4 *Ibid.*, p. 114.

strangers when awarding the guardianship. Nonetheless, Bell's calculations for the years 1611–14 reveal that more than half of the wards were still being assigned to outsiders.[5] Of course, it depended on what one was willing to pay and the number and identity of other interested parties. Under Burghley's management fines were normally set at one and a half times the value of the lands, based on surveys taken by feodaries, the Court's officers in the counties, but under his son the rate rose to at least three times the annual value.[6] Even if, as in Francis Wortley's case, the mother obtained the wardship, that did not necessarily mean that she would perform her duties any more conscientiously than a stranger would. Numerous examples indicate that mothers who remarried were 'dangerously ready' to surrender control to their child's step-father, who might exploit the ward's estate in his own interest. In practice, it was difficult for a wife to oppose the wishes of her new husband.[7]

This essay explores the inner workings of wardship by assessing – so far as it is possible – the relationship between Lord William Cavendish and his ward, Francis Wortley. Sir Richard Wortley, Francis's father, died on 25 July 1603 leaving a widow, Elizabeth, three sons and five daughters. Sir Richard's death may have been anticipated. An indenture between Sir Richard and his son Francis, made on 20 December 1602, names his heirs and makes provision for his widow after his death.[8] Less than a year after Richard died Elizabeth Wortley married William Cavendish, a union that produced a son. Cavendish had already acquired the wardship of Francis Wortley in what was probably a move orchestrated with his mother. At the time, Cavendish (1551–1626) was a widower with his own children by his first wife. He was created Baron Cavendish in 1605 and earl of Devonshire in 1618.[9] Of course, the central question to be considered is whether Cavendish sought to exploit his stepson's estate or was he a benign figure, concerned to protect the interests of his wife and her children, a substitute for their deceased father?

Ideally, documentation would exist for all the parties concerned, notably for Francis Wortley himself and for his step-father and mother. Unfortunately, the Wortley archives contain little material for the period up to and including the period covered by this essay.[10] Francis Wortley, as a minor, has left no personal archive covering the years of his wardship but nothing exists for his mother either, even though she possessed a good deal of money and property. Lady Elizabeth paid her children's allowances,

---

5   *Ibid.*, pp. 115–17. The percentage for the years 1611–14 was 45.7 per cent; in the years 1587–90 it had been 32.4 per cent.

6   *Ibid.*, pp. 58–9.

7   Stone, *Crisis*, p. 604.

8   TNA, WARD 7/45/32.

9   For Cavendish see *ODNB* sub William Cavendish, first earl of Devonshire (an ill-informed account that gets his marriages wrong) or P.W. Hasler (ed.), *The history of Parliament. The Commons, 1558–1603*, 3 vols (London, 1981), vol. i, pp. 568–9. The most recent account, although not a biography, is Peter Edwards, *Horses and the aristocratic lifestyle in early modern England: William Cavendish, first earl of Devonshire (1551–1626) and his horses* (Woodbridge, 2018).

10   C.R. Andrews, *The story of Wortley ironworks*, 3rd edn (Nottingham, 1975); R.A. Mott, 'The early history of Wortley Forges', *Historical Metallurgy Journal*, 5 (1971), pp. 63–70.

as well as some of their ordinary, daily expenses such as clothing, out of her own income. These accounts have not survived, nor have the letters that passed between her and her children.[11] If, essentially, therefore, we are left with a one-sided viewpoint, the one portrayed in the Cavendish accounts remaining at Chatsworth, it does provide a very detailed perspective, given that the entries list expenditure on items down to 1d. From this information we can assess how conscientiously Cavendish carried out his responsibility to care for his step-children and husband the estate of his ward. Of relevance to this essay are two disbursement books: H23 covers the period January 1599 to March 1607 and H29 begins in February 1608 and ends in July 1623. There is, therefore, a gap of almost a year between the two sets of accounts and no record of 'casual' income – that is, income derived from the sale of items from the estate. On the other hand, a rental book for the years 1597–1612 (H22) not only supplies information on Cavendish's estate income and leasing policy but also offers valuable insights into the exploitation of his demesne. Finally, William Senior's surveys and maps of the Cavendish manors – as well as surveys of the Wortley manors of Babworth (near East Retford) with its members, Bollom, Clarborough, Heyton and Tyln, in Nottinghamshire and Beighton and its members, Birley Hackenthorpe, Socall and Waterthorpe, in Derbyshire, provide further evidence of the topography and leasing policy on the two estates.[12]

I

William Cavendish was the second son of Sir William Cavendish by his third wife, Elizabeth Barley (née Hardwick). Commonly known as Bess of Hardwick, she later married George Talbot, sixth earl of Shrewsbury. Our William married Elizabeth Wortley (née Boughton), Francis's mother, on 2 July 1604, having paid 15s 0d for a licence four days earlier.[13] In Trinity Term 1604 Mr Crooke, a London lawyer, received £3 'for penning assurances between my Master & my Lady Worteleye', presumably a reference to the marriage settlement, which included an allowance of £200 a year.[14] Mr Griffiths, another lawyer, received a further £2 for the drawing up and engrossing of tripartite indentures for Elizabeth's jointure.[15] For the wedding Elizabeth wore a

---

11   This is galling because she was well provided for by her husbands, whether as a settlement or a jointure. For the jointure from Sir Richard Wortley: TNA, WARD 7/45/32. It comprised the manors of Beighton in Derbyshire and Babworth in Nottinghamshire; for the marriage settlement with William Cavendish: H23, fos 133v–134r.

12   Chatsworth Archives, H22, H23, H29 (hereafter cited by their shelf number alone); D.V. Fowkes and G.R. Potter (eds), *William Senior's survey of the estates of the first and second earls of Devonshire, c. 1600–28*, Derbyshire Record Society, vol. 13 (Chesterfield, 1988).

13   H23, fo. 133r.

14   H23, fo. 133v; P. Riden (ed.), *The household accounts of William Cavendish, Lord Cavendish of Hardwick, 1597–1607*, Derbyshire Record Society, vols 40–42 (Chesterfield, 2016), vol. iii, p. 142, fn. 2. H29 fo. 221 records the payment of £100 to Lady Elizabeth 'for her part allowance due at our Ladie Daie nest'.

15   H23, fo. 134r, 184v.

gown that, with jewels and pearls, cost £420. One and a quarter ounces of seed pearl for the veil added £6 10s and the wedding ring set with a diamond a further £21.[16] The ceremony, at which the rector, Dr King, officiated, took place at St Andrew's, Holborn, the parish in which Cavendish was then living. Cavendish probably knew King through the latter's north Midland connections, King being archdeacon of Nottingham from 1590 to 1611, when he resigned the office on his elevation as bishop of London.[17]

At the time of his father's death Francis, Sir Richard's eldest son and heir, was only 12 years old – his birthday fell on 15 August – so the question of his upbringing and marriage came under the jurisdiction of the Court of Wards and Liveries.[18] In the event, in Trinity Term 1604 the court assigned his wardship to his mother, apparently for a fine of £1,000 – that is, at the top end of the going rate for the wardship of heirs of Yorkshire's upper gentry.[19] Cavendish loaned Elizabeth the money. It cost him a further £1 6s 8d to enrol the grant of wardship and secure a debenture for Francis's allowance. Then Mr Crooke oversaw the drawing up of a tripartite indenture and a pair of indentures for his marriage, which safeguarded Francis's reversionary interest in the estate and his marriage. Similarly, Mr Dyott, Cavendish's lawyer, gave advice on the drawing up of two pairs of indentures: one for assigning Francis's wardship to Cavendish and the other for Elizabeth's security for £1,100 (for the fine to the Court of Wards and Liveries).[20] For his work sealing the assignment and for drawing up the deeds Mr Yelverton received £3 the following (Michaelmas) term.[21]

Other expenses included the annual rent due to the Court of Wards and Liveries. For Wortley's Derbyshire manors Cavendish paid the county feodary, Mr John Bullock of Darley Abbey, between £13 8s and £13 13s 4d a year, while Mr Francis Bussey, the Nottinghamshire feodary, received sums of between £4 4s 0d and £4 18s 7d. Cavendish's accounts do not indicate the fee paid for the Yorkshire manors, which his ward inherited on his father's death and which Cavendish managed on his behalf.[22] Cavendish normally paid in half yearly instalments at Lady Day and Michaelmas, but he occasionally fell into arrears. On 23 October 1604 he gave Mr Bullock double the amount for the year, having

---

16 H23, fo. 133v.

17 For King, see *ODNB*.

18 For Sir Francis see A. Thrush (ed.), *The history of Parliament. The Commons, 1604–29*, 6 vols (Cambridge, 2010), vol. vi, pp. 845–8.

19 J.T. Cliffe, *The Yorkshire gentry from the Reformation to the Civil War* (London, 1969), pp. 132–3; Francis's father, Sir Richard Wortley, left a personal estate valued at £1,181 in 1603: *Ibid.*, p. 381.

20 H23, fos 133v, 134r.

21 H23, fo. 142v.

22 H23, fos 136r, 139v, 146v, 171v, 173v, 178v, 198r, 202v; H29, fos 44, 92, 112, 144, 158, 184, 216, 241, 261, 267, 276. Sir Richard Wortley's IPM notes that he granted as a 'reasonable jointure' to Lady Elizabeth the manors of Beighton and Hackenthorpe in Derbyshire and the manors of Babworth, Bollom, and one-third of Tyln, Hayton and Clarborough in Nottinghamshire, and all other property in the two counties: TNA, WARD 7/45/32. If so, this raises the question: where would the rental income of the Wortley manors in Yorkshire be recorded if not in Cavendish's rentals? After all, he did administer them and incorporate them into his overall scheme of estate management, even if they feature only intermittently in his disbursement books.

Table 3.1
Rentals of Babworth, Bollom, Hayton and Tyln, and Beighton, Birley and Hackenthorpe, 1603–12.

Date	Babworth &c.	Beighton &c.
1603–4	£110 17s 10d[1]	£184 0s 6d
1604–5		
1605–6	£131 7s 1d	£276 11s 5d
1606–7	£119 14s 6d	£321 11s 3d
1607–8	£120 12s 2d	£334 6s 6d
1608–9		
1609–10	£125 2s 10d	£353 14s 2d[2]
1610–11	£105 13s 10d	£366 9s 10d
1611–12	£97 3s 8d	£376 11s 6d

Source: H22/Babworth, Beighton + dates.

Notes:

1   Half year sum ×2. Also offered at Babworth £8 5s 4d for New Park; £5 8d for Free Warren and £9 for letting Broom Close & the Old Warren.

2   Half year sum ×2.

just acquired the custody of Francis, and on 21 October 1609 he paid Mr Bussey £9 6s 8d for two years' rent.[23] Normally, his servants took the money to the feodaries' homes in their respective counties, but on one occasion Henry Travice paid Mr Bullock in London, even though the acquittance was issued in Derbyshire.[24] Cavendish's final payments were made in 1612, the year that Francis reached the age of 21 and gained control of his estate.[25] To set against the cost of purchasing the wardship of Francis and looking after the family, Table 3.1 indicates the income derived from the annual rents paid in the manors of Babworth and Beighton. They reveal a considerable increase in the annual rental income in the former manor but some decline in the latter. As is shown below, Cavendish integrated the Wortley land into the overall management of his estate and may have increased the yield by sound practice and improvement, even if some fluctuation in the acreage of the demesnes kept in hand has to be borne in mind. Income from these two manors alone outweighed the cost of purchasing the wardship and demonstrated the value of controlling a ward's landed property.

II

The rapid growth of England's population in the late sixteenth and early seventeenth centuries caused the price of agricultural land and its products to rise, prompting

---

23   H23, fo. 136r; H29, fo. 112.
24   H23, fo. 174r.
25   H29, fo. 276.

many landowners to commission surveys to ascertain the actual value of their estates.[26] Maps often accompanied these surveys. By 1600 improvements in surveying and cartographical technology meant that surveyors could produce maps and surveys that were more accurate than hitherto.[27] Cavendish commissioned dozens of surveys and at least 65 maps from William Senior, assisted by his son, John, in the years 1609–19 and 1626–8.[28] It is likely that Senior obtained the commission because he had surveyed the Wortley estate of Lady Elizabeth's former husband in 1600 and she had recommended him to Cavendish.[29] In 1604, at Cavendish's request, Gilbert Dickenson resurveyed the manors of Beighton and Babworth. He valued the annual income of the former manor at £469 9s 1d, of which £134 19s 6d was due in rent, and the rents and profits of the latter manor at £137 7s 10d.[30]

The disbursement books reveal how carefully Cavendish audited his accounts. He added up the sums on each page or checked the totals of sections of his receivers' accounts, signing the ledger when he had done so. He inserted glosses in the margin and pointed out discrepancies in the arithmetic. Thus, when his receiver totted up expenditure under the various categories for the nine months April to December 1597 at £5,193 8s 8½d, Cavendish wrote 'I say Fyue Thowsand one huudreth forescore thirteen pounds eight shillings eight pence' and signed the page.[31] He also questioned some of the entries. When Fretwell presented his account in August 1606 it included a payment of £2 9s 9d that Edmonds had spent on 40 yards of flaxen cloth and 13 yards of hurden cloth. When he read the entries Cavendish bracketed the items together in the margin, adding the words 'call for this cloth'.[32]

Cavendish was just as scrupulous in the management of his ward's estate. Thus, in October 1604, shortly after his marriage to Lady Elizabeth and at a crucial time in the year financially, he sent his officers Humphrey Edmunds and William Launt to ride to Birley, a member of Beighton manor, and elsewhere (presumably on the Wortley estate) to view the ground, the first of a succession of visits.[33] In August 1609, for instance, Robert Parker, Cavendish's chief estate steward, with the two Mr Mannerings and two servants, spent £3 19s inspecting the Wortley estate.[34] In September 1610 it cost 13s 4d for Parker, who was accompanied by Messrs Bellamy and Bladen, to undertake

---

26   Edwards, *Horses and the aristocratic lifestyle*, p. 8.

27   For an outline account of developments, see P.D.A. Harvey, 'English estate maps: their early history and their use as historical evidence', in David Buisseret (ed.), *Rural images. Estate maps in the old and new worlds* (Chicago, IL, 1996), pp. 27–61.

28   Fowkes and Potter, *William Senior's survey*, pp. xii, xvi–xxiv.

29   *Ibid.*, pp. 3–10.

30   *Ibid.*, pp. 1, 2.

31   H10A, fo. 21r.

32   H23, fo. 189v.

33   H23, fo. 136r.

34   H29, fo. 79: as at least one of the Mr Mannerings was an Exchequer official, their presence may well have involved an assessment of the Wortley estate with regard to the subsidy. For Cavendish's dealings with Mr Mannering in relation to his subsidy payments: H23, fos 87v, 199v; H29, fos 218, 227.

another tour of inspection. Four months later William Champion rode to Hull to fetch William Senior to survey the grounds at Hayton.[35] Apart from gaining an overview of the Wortley estate, Cavendish's officers involved themselves in the detailed management of it. In December 1605 Parker was working alongside Broomhead and Wood in and about Swinton, Pontefract, Carlton and townships thereabout, helping to buy sheep and drive them to Haddlesey. In June 1606 Roger Fretwell travelled to Babworth to see the wool weighed at the shearing there and elsewhere, while in February 1608 Parker drove sheep from Ewden near Wortley to Woodthorpe, Northope and Stainsby. In May 1610 Parker supervised tillage and sowing of land at Babworth; in March 1612 he sold peas at Beighton; and the following month he received money for barley sold at Babworth. In 1613 he stayed at Beighton while accounting for the movement of sheep around the estate, and in November he and Fretwell rode to Babworth to view husbandry, cattle and corn there.[36]

The 1604 survey of the Wortley estate commissioned by Cavendish reveals that most of the tenants at Babworth and Beighton held their properties for 21 years, although George Clay leased a farm at Beighton for the lives of himself and his wife in return for services performed and to be performed for Sir Richard Wortley and his wife. Only one entry records both the entry fine and annual rent, revealing that Thomas Newbold leased 51 acres and 20 perches in Waterthorpe, for which he had paid an entry fine of 100 marks and was paying an annual rent of £10 in 1604.[37] The Cavendish rentals also indicate that parcels of the Wortley demesne were being leased by the year or even the half-year at a rack rent: the Martinmas 1606 half-year rental of Babworth shows that the Hall and Hall Close at Babworth were being leased for a half-year for £3. Between 1604 and 1610 – that is, the years Cavendish did not keep it in hand – that property had three tenants. Cavendish also rack-rented marginal land there by the year, leasing the light soil brecks and the heavy clay lands to Mr Francis Barker for £20 13s 4d in the years 1604–6. Subsequently he detached the brecks, letting them for £6 per annum to William Aston, Robert Oker, Richard Southworth and Robert Wright, along with the new park, for £12 per annum.[38] Rack-renting obviously gave the tenant no incentive to improve the land. At Welham Moorgate, land lying alongside the River Idle, which was probably poorly drained and waterlogged, was let to halves, a form of sharecropping, which gave the tenant an incentive to improve the land. [39] Forms of tenancy were therefore flexible and reflected local circumstances.

Cavendish's officers dealt with the tenants concerning all aspects of their tenancies. In June 1605 Parker and Edmunds accounted for the 18s 4d it had cost

---

35   H29, fo. 192.

36   In order: H23, fos 169r, 175v; H29, fos 5–6, 129, 248, 250, 339, 341.

37   The 1604 survey was drawn up by Gilbert Dickenson: Fowkes and Potter, *William Senior's survey*, pp. 2–3.

38   H22, Babworth + date.

39   H22, heading Babworth + date. For farming to halves, see E. Griffiths and M. Overton, *Farming to halves: the hidden history of sharefarming in England from medieval to modern times* (London, 2009), pp. 13–16.

them when they toured the Wortley estate for almost a fortnight, letting grounds at Beighton, Newall, Wortley and elsewhere. Perkin had spent 8d to join them at Newhall and Edmunds had paid a further 3s 6d dealing with two millers at Beighton and Wortley.[40] When the officers rode to the Wortley estates in Nottinghamshire, East Retford was a convenient base from which to conduct business. In September 1605 Parker stayed in the town for two days while he viewed the sheep and let the grounds. A year later he and Roger Fretwell spent 7s 3d during three days at Retford letting the warren at Babworth and other grounds there.[41] In December 1609 Parker's bill includes expenditure at Beighton as well as in the East Retford area. He spent 2s 6d on two days at Beighton collecting rents and examining an officer's accounts. In Nottinghamshire he spent 4s 6d at Babworth and East Retford receiving rents and bargaining for land to be sown to halves, presumably with Thomas Redman and Robert Pernell, the tenants listed in the rental. In April 1611 Parker rode to Beighton to let the mill and other grounds, take a bond for the miller's arrears and receive some rents, and supervise the housing of William Ludlam, the warrener, who had moved with the warren from Babworth to Beighton. In February 1612 Fretwell rode to Bollom to speak to witnesses about sealing a lease on the ground and making an entry. In June he and Parker were sealing leases there.[42]

III

William Cavendish was neither a politician nor a courtier by nature. Austere and parsimonious, his main concerns were the extension and exploitation of his estate and his investment in overseas ventures.[43] He kept a good deal of his demesne in hand, therefore. Cavendish operated primarily as a grazier, a trend that developed on demesnes in the late sixteenth century as wool prices fell.[44] As Stone observed, most large-scale demesne farmers focused on 'sheep and cattle ranching' on enclosed pastures, fattening up stock for the expanding meat market, especially in London.[45] In 1611 Lord William Howard of Naworth (Cumberland) had 1,100 cattle and 3,000 sheep grazing on his estate when the year's accounts were drawn up at Martinmas.[46] While Cavendish did maintain herds of cattle and flocks of sheep,

---

40 H23, fo. 153v.

41 H29, fos 156v, 172r.

42 H29, 120, 197, 247, 252.

43 Edwards, *Horses and the aristocratic lifestyle*, p. 6.

44 Stone, *Crisis*, pp. 297–9.

45 *Ibid.*, pp. 297–9; J. Thirsk (ed.), *The agrarian history of England and Wales, IV, 1500–1640* (Cambridge, 1967), p. 509; F.J. Fisher, 'The development of the London food market, 1540–1640', in P.J. Corfield and N.B. Harte (eds.), *London and the English economy 1500–1700* (London, 1990), pp. 61–79; Edwards, *Horses and the aristocratic lifestyle*, p. 17.

46 G. Ornsby, *Selections from the household books of Lord William Howard of Naworth Castle*, Surtees Society, 68 (Durham, 1878), p. 416.

unlike the Spencers of Althorp (Northants.), he mostly bought in animals.[47] Taking advantage of the autumnal sale of sheep from northern farms, he purchased wethers at such fairs as Atherton in Lancashire and Appletreewick, Northallerton and Rotherham in Yorkshire. He obtained some of his store cattle locally at Chesterfield and Mansfield but also at the Yorkshire fairs of Pontefract, Rotherham, Wakefield and York.[48] Some of the cattle were fattened for the household or used for the draught, but many of them as with the sheep bought at northern fairs were driven further south by his officers. Among Cavendish's men was George Brooke of Carlton, a manor on the Wortley estate.[49] A substantial drover and dealer, he was very active in the conduct of Cavendish's grazing business. In April 1613, for example, Cavendish told Gervase Watts to go to Carlton to ask Brooke when he was going to London with the oxen.[50] For Cavendish, the acquisition of estates in south-eastern and eastern England allowed him more effectively to finish off animals for consumption in the capital. In 1610 he leased Sopwell Priory (Hertfordshire) as a base for his London enterprise, but two years later he shifted it to Hundon in Suffolk, where the animals could graze on one of his three parks. In 1618 he switched the focus to Sawtry in Huntingdonshire. In April 1618 Brooke, who bought cattle and sheep with money loaned by Cavendish, rented the Westley pasture there from him.[51]

Cliffe notes that demesne farming in several parts of Yorkshire, including the Pennine region of the West Riding, focused on livestock husbandry. Some of the wealthier gentry there produced meat and wool for the market on a large scale, at least until a further slump in wool prices from about 1610.[52] Even so, the meat market continued to expand and sheep still provided wool, if only as a by-product. Agriculturally, therefore, the acquisition of Wortley manors enabled Cavendish to expand his grazing activities as his officers integrated them into the annual movement of his cattle and sheep onto, through and beyond the combined estate. They also produced additional hay and fodder crops for the livestock and corn for the household and for sale. Integration started straight away and was particularly notable in the management of Cavendish's flocks of sheep. In October 1604 Cavendish bought 565 sheep from his mother for £5 a score and sent them to Babworth. The rental of the manor of Beighton for the following year (1605–6) indicates that a part of Blackcliffe at Beighton and the intake at Birley were being grazed with sheep. In 1609–10 50 sheep were over-wintered in Babworth and the following year the winter pasture of the intake hosted 60 wethers.[53] Sheep commonly moved around both estates over the course of a year. In March 1607

---

47 Edwards, *Horses and the aristocratic lifestyle*, p. 37.
48 *Ibid.*, pp. 38–9.
49 *Ibid.*, pp. 41–2, 46, 47–8, 148.
50 H29, fo. 293.
51 Edwards, *Horses and the aristocratic lifestyle*, pp. 37–49; pp. 48–9 for the lease of the Westley Pasture.
52 Cliffe, *Yorkshire gentry*, pp. 50–1.
53 H23, fos 136v, 138r; H22, heading Beighton + dates.

two Beighton men drove 98 sheep to Swinton for onward transit to Haddlesey.[54] A detailed bill submitted by Parker in 1608 describes the degree of integration, which in this instance involved the movement of sheep from a Wortley property at Ewden to Woodthorpe, Northope and Stainsby on Cavendish's estate. Cavendish also earned an income from the sale of the wool: he had a designated storeroom called the woolhouse at Chatsworth. In March 1606 Parker rode to Babworth to weigh the wool and then transport it to Retford. Two months later he was selling wool at Beighton.[55] The processes and costs are illustrated by an entry in the accounts in June 1613 when Hides, the overseer of the manor of Woodthorpe, supervised the shearing of 100 sheep there: he paid 2s 7d for clipping, 2d for pitch and grease, 2d for tar, 1s 8d for washing the fleeces and 10d for the shearers' meals.[56]

Store cattle were also driven around the combined estate for feeding on various pastures, with the Wortley manor of Beighton prominent. In May and June 1605 the 12 beasts that Parker had bought for £45 were grazing in the Maynes at Beighton. That year the Nether and Upper Maynes, together with the Castlesides, were set aside for fat oxen. In the winter of 1612–13 160 oxen were feeding at Beighton.[57] Cavendish also bought in oxen for the draught. Contemporary writers were still comparing the respective merits of horses and oxen,[58] but for a grazier such as Cavendish, oxen served a dual purpose: for power and for sale as meat. In May 1610 Parker acquired eight draught bullocks for use at Babworth, paying £26 13s 8d, plus 1s 5d in costs to buy them and 8d to drive them home. At Babworth they grazed on the eddish of Lane Close and then on the grass in the Old Warren and Broom Close. At Whitsun in 1611 22 draught oxen were being fed on hay and the eddish at Tyln and Babworth.[59] In August the previous year Parker had paid £70 6s 6d for 16 draught oxen at Wakefield fair 'for yinninge of harveste' at Beighton. He spent a further 1s 4d in toll, 4s 9d at Wortley &c., 4s for a night's grazing at Wombell and 6d for driving them to the manor. The following Spring two Woodthorpe men came for 14 of the oxen.[60]

The possession of the small tithes at Babworth and Beighton, as elsewhere on the estate, provided Cavendish with a variety of livestock – lambs, geese and pigs – as well as animal products such as eggs and wool. In addition, Cavendish possessed seigneurial dovecotes in both townships. In 1610–11 the one at Beighton produced 119 pairs of pigeons and the following year 130 pairs, all of which were sent to Cavendish's household at Hardwick. Five more pairs were cooked at Beighton when Mrs Susan Dorrell, Lady Elizabeth's mother, was visiting. That year the dovecote at

---

54 H23, fo. 202r.
55 H23, fos 124r, 173r, 174v.
56 H29, fo. 297.
57 H23, fo. 157v; H22, heading Beighton + date; CA, H29, fo. 297.
58 P. Edwards, *Horse and man in early modern England* (London, 2007), pp. 83–6.
59 H29, fo. 130; H22/Beighton + date; CA, H29/297. The eddish is the regrowth of grass after mowing.
60 H29, fos 136, 197.

Babworth produced 18 dozen pigeons.[61] Cavendish also benefited from the further seigneurial perk of keeping rabbits, a privilege that annoyed the tenants because the creatures ate the growing crops. He kept a warren in several of his manors, including one at Babworth, which William Ludlam rented for £12 a year. Then, in autumn 1610, Cavendish transferred the warren – along with 200 couples of rabbits – to Beighton. Ludlam remained as warrener, receiving a house and lands at Beighton and £4 a year in wages. Rabbits were a profitable option for marginal land: they bred prolifically, providing meat at six months and a saleable fur.[62]

Like his fellow grazier Lord Petre of Ingatestone Hall (Essex), Cavendish mainly produced hay and fodder crops on his demesnes: hay predominated, followed by oats and pulses.[63] Indeed, it seems as though his demesne produced so much hay that he could sell the tithe hay harvested on the estate: at Beighton and Birley in 1607–8 tithe hay brought in £12 1s 2d.[64] He did grow some bread corn, including small acreages in the Wortley manors. At Beighton in 1605 his officers sowed oats and rye in part of Blackcliffe and wheat and rye in the Halldelves, and on the arable land in High Field. At Babworth in 1610 they sowed the Hall Yard with seven and three-quarters quarters of oats and the Lay Close with ten quarters three strikes of rye. The latter field yielded 33 quarters five strikes of rye, a ratio of 1:4. The following year they sowed rye in the Old Warren.[65] Nonetheless, he obtained most of the corn he needed for the household by purchase in the markets in Chesterfield or Mansfield, in corn rents or as tithe.[66] In the rental of Beighton for 1607–8 the accountant noted: 'Tithe corn whereof most part sent to Hardwick and Owlcotes for my lords provision and some part sold and is to be accounted for'. That year it brought in 20 quarters, two strikes and two pecks of wheat; four quarters seven strikes of rye, nine quarters, one strike of barley; 38 quarters four strikes of oats; and 16 quarters two strikes of peas. At Bollom in 1605–6 Mrs Smith paid a corn rent of ten quarters of barley and at Hayton John Garlick supplied 26 quarters of barley. In 1610–11 the respective amounts were ten quarters and 32 quarters.[67] Much of the barley that Cavendish received as corn rent or as tithe was malted for the household. Although South Leverton was the main source of malted barley, Babworth and Retford supplied significant amounts. Between 19 August and 11 November 1608 Fretwell transported 40 quarters of malt from Babworth. Three months later James Ellis carried 15 quarters of malt from Babworth to Warsop – that is, half of the barley that had been growing at Retford.[68]

---

61   H22 Babworth, Beighton + dates.

62   *Ibid.*; Edwards, *Horses and the aristocratic lifestyle,* pp. 50–2.

63   *Ibid.,* p. 52.

64   *Ibid.,* pp. 52–4; H22 Beighton + date.

65   Edwards, *Horses and the aristocratic lifestyle,* p. 52; H22, Babworth + Beighton + dates.

66   Edwards, *Horses and the aristocratic lifestyle,* pp. 53–4.

67   H22, Babworth, Beighton + dates.

68   H29, fos 47, 123.

IV

Ironworking in South Yorkshire was being carried on in the Middle Ages, especially on the estates of religious houses, a number of which possessed bloomeries and forges. At Wortley the Poll Tax return for 1379 lists four smiths and a master.[69] In 1543, the year that he died, Thomas Wortley, the great-grandfather of our Francis, owned 'a furnace and lands in Thurgoland in the parish of Silkstone'.[70] A lease that Francis sealed on 2 April 1621, after coming into his inheritance, described his ironworks as 'divers iron smithies & premises for working & delfs & mines of ironstone in Thurgoland, Dodsworth & Silkstone, with leave to get 12 score dozens of charcoal out of the wood in the district of Wortley with services of colliers & gravers …'.[71] Roger Dodsworth, the antiquarian, noted when travelling through Yorkshire in the period 1619–30 that the River Don 'leaveth Wharncliffe Chase … on the North, belonging to Sir Francis Wortley, wher he haith great iron works'. He also passed Sir Francis's ironworks known as 'Midgeley Bank Smythies', which the latter had leased from Thomas Barnby in January 1620 for £40 per annum.[72] In addition, as Roebuck reveals, the Wortleys possessed 'enormous' reserves of timber on Wharncliffe Chase and around Pilley.[73] Indeed, the 12 score dozens of charcoal mentioned above would have contributed to the manufacture of 24 tons of wrought iron a year.[74]

When Cavendish took control of the Wortley estate his officers already had extensive experience in dealing with the business of metalworking.[75] So, when in February 1605 Parker and Edmunds rode from Haddlesey to Wortley to view the smithies and meet the smiths they knew what they were looking for and the questions they had to ask. Seven months later Parker and Edmunds, returned to Wortley in the company of Robert Stuart, another of Cavendish's officers, and the founder, to view the ironworks as part of an inspection of the estate. Stuart and the founder spent 7s 6d over the three days of the visit, after which Stuart returned home by himself.[76] On another tour of the Wortley estate in August 1609 Parker again visited the smithies, paying 6d for drink when he met the smiths.[77] The estate documents also confirm that the local cutlery industry, based on Sheffield but augmented with the output of forges operating in the surrounding villages, provided an accessible market for their product.[78] At Beighton the rental lists two cutlers: Godfrey Tryton, who paid £1 4s for

---

69 Andrews, *Wortley ironworks*, pp. 10–13, 87.

70 *Forging ahead: a conservation statement for Wortley Top Forge* (2009), p. 7; Mott, 'Wortley Forges', p. 63.

71 Mott, 'Wortley Forges', p. 64. In 1624 Sir Francis erected a wire mill upstream of Top Forge: *ibid.*, p. 63.

72 *Ibid.*, p. 64 (also cited in Cliffe, *Yorkshire Gentry*, pp. 64–5).

73 P. Roebuck, *Yorkshire Baronets 1640–1760* (Oxford, 1980), p. 38.

74 Mott, 'Wortley Forges', p. 64.

75 For a discussion of Cavendish's metal-working activities: Edwards, *Horses and the aristocratic lifestyle*, pp. 58–64.

76 H23, fos 143v, 156v.

77 H23, fo. 79.

78 D. Hey, *The fiery blades of Hallamshire: Sheffield and its neighbourhood, 1660–1740* (Leicester, 1991), pp. 3–8, 54–7; and see Hoyle's essay on the Sheffield cutlers in this volume.

his cutler's wheel, and Nicholas Skelton, who paid 10s for his. John Boswell paid 1s for his smithy.[79] In this respect Francis Wortley was fortunate that such an important component of the economic resources of his estate had been placed in the hands of a person who was not only involved in the business but who was mindful of the need to safeguard his ward's patrimony.

V

In 1604 Cavendish became the legal guardian not only of Francis Wortley but of his two brothers and five sisters too, aged from about ten or 11 down to less than a year. As the eight or nine years covered by this study were critical ones in the lives of the children, the experience of growing up in Cavendish's household would have shaped their character and future. Although the accounts record the allowance given to Cavendish's son and heir, William, and daughter, Frances, they do not note those given to his step-children, as their mother paid them. Even so, Cavendish did give the children money as New Year gifts and other sums during the course of the year. In January 1605, the first New Year with his step-family, his own children, William and Frances, received £1 and 12s respectively, while Francis Wortley was given £1, Ann and Elizabeth 10s each and Eleanor 5s, perhaps a reflection of their age as well as their gender. In January 1609 Eleanor and Elizabeth received £3 between them.[80] As casual sums, Edward received £1 in April 1609 and May 1610; Eleanor £1 in February 1611; Elizabeth 10s in September 1609; and Francis £1 as a token in March or April 1609.[81] On 22 June 1609, moreover, Henry Travice, Cavendish's London receiver, noted that Cavendish gave his wife £100 towards the purchase of an annuity for her youngest child, Thomas, then about six years old.[82]

Cavendish contributed to the cost of clothing his step-children as well as his own sons and daughter, even if Lady Elizabeth was buying items too. In April 1608 Cavendish spent 13s 6d on taffeta cloth for doublets for himself and Francis. That month he paid 14s to Mr Ruddock for making a cloak, gown and hood for Francis and a further 2s for a cloak for the boy's servant.[83] For the girls, the accounts record the acquisition of gowns, waistcoats, gloves, stockings and shoes.[84] In December 1604 Brooke and his son received 7s 6d for six days' work helping Clarke to sew gowns for Lady Elizabeth, her daughter Eleanor and her step-daughter Frances.[85] In the same month a Derby glover supplied two pairs of gloves for Lady Elizabeth, two pairs for Eleanor and three pairs for Frances, as well as three skins, all for 9s.[86] In March 1606 Roger Fretwell accounted for 5s spent on 'stuff' for Eleanor: an ell of sacking for a pair

---

79   H22, Heading Beighton, 1606–7, 1608–9.
80   H23, fo. 141r; H29, fo. 83.
81   Edward: H29, fos 66, 159; Eleanor: fo. 223; Elizabeth: fos 76, 221; Francis: fo. 90.
82   H29, fo. 54.
83   H29, fo. 242.
84   H23, fos 139v, 143v, 173r, 180r, 187v; H29, fos 55, 219, 222, 318.
85   H23, fo. 139v.
86   H23, fo. 139v.

of bodices (1s 3d); three yards of whalebone (3d); a yard of cobweb lawn (1s 2d); a yard of bone lace (6d); three pairs of gloves (10d); and a pair of white stockings (1s).[87] Of the two references to Sarah Wortley in the accounts, one refers to the purchase of a gown 'ready made' for her at London for £3 12s 4d.[88] The cost of clothing William's children William and Frances and their half-brother John are listed in greater detail, as is (to a lesser extent) expenditure on Edward Worsley (possibly a nephew of his first wife, Anne), who was brought up with Cavendish's children between August 1609 and April 1611. Even so, Cavendish spent a recorded sum of £12 1s to clothe Edward, comprising three suits (two made-to-measure); a hat; a cloak; two doublets; 36 buttons; ribbon; 12 points and four bands (and making more); four shirts (made-to-measure); a girdle; eight pairs of hose and stockings (and footing another pair of stockings); five pairs of shoes; and a pair of spurs.[89]

Between Michaelmas 1602 and Michaelmas 1605 Cavendish's chaplains (Mr Oats, then Mr Bruin) received £20 a year to lead household prayers and £10 a year to teach his son. Did they also teach Cavendish's step-children or did Lady Elizabeth pay for it? Moreover, one wonders whether Thomas Hobbes, who tutored Cavendish's son William and the latter's son William, the third earl, had any contact with the Wortley children.[90] Clearly, the boys had a formal education, as Francis matriculated at Magdalen College, Oxford, in 1609 and Thomas matriculated at Trinity College, Oxford, in 1621. Edward, the middle brother, entered the Inner Temple in London in 1612.[91] The children were also taught social skills befitting a gentleman or lady. A stray reference to payment to Thomas Banes, the singing master of his own children, for tutoring Eleanor Wortley suggests that they also tutored the young Wortleys. On 28 August 1606 Banes was paid 5s for teaching her to sing and in November 1610 one Maynard received £9 for teaching Eleanor Wortley and Ann Aston to play the lute and viol. In January 1610 Ann Aston's dancing master earned £2 for teaching her for two months.[92]

Cavendish introduced his step-sons to the masculine pastime of hunting. In August 1605 he spent £4 on Francis and his younger brother Edward when he took them hunting in Langwith Park. Perhaps it was a treat to celebrate Francis's fourteenth birthday on the fifteenth of the month. Indeed, Cavendish gave 7s 6d to the wife of Mellors, the keeper of the park, for the food she provided.[93] Cavendish had created Langwith Park at the turn of the sixteenth century, stocking it with deer donated by a number of his peers.[94] Nonetheless, during the wardship of Francis Wortley the

---

87 H23, fo. 173r.

88 H29, fo. 318.

89 H29, fos 72, 87, 90, 96, 97, 110, 115, 123, 127–8, 133, 135, 141, 180, 184, 221.

90 These were the two functions of Protestant chaplains in a household: Cliffe, *Country house*, p. 133; Edwards, *Horses and the aristocratic lifestyle*, pp. 216–22. For Mr Oats: H10A fo. 243v, H23 fos 106r, 120v, 124r, 134v; for Mr Bruin: H23, fos 139r, 144r, 148v, 159v; for Thomas Hobbes: G. Trease, *Portrait of a Cavalier: William Cavendish, first Duke of Newcastle* (London, 1979), pp. 25, 58.

91 Thrush (ed.), *History of Parliament. The Commons, 1604–29*, vol. vi, p. 844.

92 H23, fo. 177r; H29, fos 218, 150.

93 H29, fos 155v–156r.

94 Edwards, *Horses and the aristocratic lifestyle*, pp. 208–9. But none from Sir Richard Wortley.

keeper of Wharncliffe Park, close to Wortley Hall, regularly brought deer and venison to Hardwick.[95] In July 1610, for instance, one of Cavendish's servants received 10d for going to Wortley with a warrant for a stag. Thereupon, the keeper selected and killed a stag and brought it to Hardwick, earning 6s for his pains.[96] In November 1613 a reference to a horse purchased for 1s for its carcass – to be fed to Francis's hounds – indicates that he kept a pack of hounds at Wortley once he had entered into his estate.[97] For a gentleman such as Francis, hunting deer did not merely provide meat for the larder but also symbolised the élite way of life.[98] Hunting deer, especially *par force* hunting the hart with hounds, was considered to be good preparation for war, but Cavendish's accounts provide virtually no evidence that he gave his step-sons actual training in the use of arms.

By 1608 the 17-year-old Francis was becoming more independent. In April he and his manservant stayed in London, Cavendish paying 12s 6d to hire a chamber for two weeks, and for heating and beer.[99] By the end of 1610 it seems as though he had married Grace Brouncker.[100] It is not known whether Cavendish exercised his right to choose his ward's wife (and the initial wardship contract seemed to safeguard Francis's rights), but her father, Sir William Brouncker of Melksham (Wiltshire), was a courtier and an acquaintance of Cavendish's.[101] The king knighted Francis at Theobalds on 15 January 1611 and five months later the young man bought one of the first baronetcies. At the time he was serving in Prince Henry's household as gentleman of the privy chamber extraordinary, but Cavendish's money probably contributed to the purchase price of £1,095.[102] Three of Francis's sisters had married by 1612. Ann married Sir Rotherham Willoughby of Aston Rowant (Oxon) in the spring of 1608 and as part of her portion Cavendish gave her £100. She had had a child by January 1609.[103] Elizabeth received the same amount on her marriage to Sir Henry Crofts of Little Saxham (Suffolk) in December 1610. Cavendish spent £3 to hire musicians for the wedding.[104] Within a year Eleanor had become the wife of Sir Henry Lee of

---

95   References to deer and venison from Wortley or to the keeper of Wharncliffe: H23, fos 141r, 155v–156v; H29, fos 21, 68, 72–3, 76, 132, 138, 204, 334.

96   H29, fo. 132.

97   H29, fo. 340.

98   Edwards, *Horse and man*, pp. 120, 125–9.

99   H29, fo. 16.

100 Thrush (ed.), *History of Parliament. The Commons, 1604–29*, vol. vi, p. 845.

101 The Privy Council, anxious about the possible marriage of Cavendish's niece, Arbella Stuart, twice sent Brouncker to Hardwick Hall early in 1603: Edwards, *Horses and the aristocratic lifestyle*, p. 88. For Arbella Stuart (1575–1615), who had a marginal claim to the English throne see *ODNB*. Shortly afterwards, Brouncker presented Cavendish with a fine stallion he had bought him. He gave him another horse the following year: H23, fos 116r, 125r, 192r; H29, fo. 113.

102 Thrush (ed.), *History of Parliament. The Commons, 1604–29*, vol. vi, p. 845.

103 H29, fos 44, 83.

104 H29, fos 219, 221.

Quarrendon (Bucks.).[105] According to Mott, Mary married Henry, Baron of Hilton, and Sarah married Sir Sutton Coney.[106] Edward obtained a wife only in 1627, when on 2 July he married Elizabeth, the widow of Sir Samuel Tryon and the daughter of the wealthy London merchant John Eldred.[107]

VI

Cavendish and his wife and children lived at Hardwick but regularly stayed at Beighton and Wortley. Visits began a month after the couple were married: they travelled to and from the two places in August 1604, although on both occasions William returned home before his wife.[108] Similarly, when they travelled down to London for the burgeoning season there they did not always go together. Separation was typical of upper-class life at the time because, as I have argued elsewhere, wives might share various social activities with the husbands but were excluded from the masculine circles connected with their administrative, economic, legal and political business.[109] While apart William and Elizabeth corresponded with each other. Freake, a footman, regularly ran between them with letters, as in August 1604, when he received 1s for taking a letter to Lady Elizabeth at Beighton.[110] The children might accompany William and Elizabeth, but the accounts generally do not reveal the identity of family members in the party. We do know that Ann travelled with her mother and step-father when they drove to the capital in October 1605, and in August 1609 it cost Cavendish 15s 9d for a carrier to send Francis's trunk, weighing two and a quarter hundredweight, back to Hardwick.[111] The children also visited their maternal grandmother, Mrs Dorrell, who lived at Cawston (Warks.). In March 1606 Ann must have gone there because the accounts record the cost of taking her gown to Coventry, the nearest dropping-off point on the carrier network.[112]

Without his family Cavendish might ride on horseback with his retinue, but when travelling with them he went by coach, as did Lady Elizabeth when she made separate visits.[113] When Misses Eleanor and Ann Aston, accompanied by their attendants, travelled down to London in July 1610 they rode in the new litter. The trip cost £5 16s

---

105 For Sir Henry Lee: H29, fo. 262; for Lady Lee: H29, fo. 265; for the christening of their son: H29, fo. 266.

106 Mott, 'Wortley Forges', 68.

107 Thrush (ed.), *History of Parliament. The Commons, 1604–29*, vol. vi, p. 844.

108 H23, fos 126v, 134v, 137v, 139v, 143v, 144v, 146v; H29, fos 72, 113, 183. Other entries merely refer to letters coming from or going to Beighton or Wortley.

109 Edwards, *Horses and the aristocratic lifestyle*, p. 161.

110 References to letters between Cavendish and his wife or to and from Wortley or Beighton: H23, fos 126v–127r, 135r, 139v, 141r, 143v, 146v, 156v, 189r, 193r; H29, fos 72, 193; for the Freake example: H23, fo. 126v.

111 H23, fo. 161v, l H29, fo. 73.

112 H23, fo. 180r.

113 Edwards, *Horses and the aristocratic lifestyle*, pp. 161–7.

5d.[114] Unfortunately, on a visit to Wortley in October 1609 the coach broke down *en route* and the local smith had to carry out running repairs on the road. Subsequently, Bramley, the coachmaker, made a new axle for the vehicle.[115] When Mrs Dorrell visited her daughter and family at Hardwick she either rode in her own coach or in one sent to pick her up. In Michaelmas 1605 her coachman took her, but six years later Cavendish's coachman spent 17s to go to Cawston and back.[116] Naturally, when the children married they acquired coaches of their own. In October 1612 Francis, who by then must have been living in Wortley Hall, rode down to London in his coach to meet his mother and step-father.[117] A year earlier Elizabeth had ridden on a litter when she travelled to Hardwick, the horses being put out to graze on the Pentrich pastures.[118]

VII

By the turn of the sixteenth century wardship had become a source of profit for the crown rather than a means of raising an army for war. The purchase of a wardship might have been motivated by a desire to protect the family's interest against interlopers, but less scrupulous grantees of wardship also considered the fiscal element of the transaction when bidding for a ward, weighing up the cost of the fine and annual rent against the income to be derived from exploiting the ward's estate and the disposal of his or her hand in marriage. Even conscientious guardians benefited from the arrangement: Sir Thomas Temple claimed that he was entitled to some recompense for his expenditure of time and money on husbanding the Stantonbury (Buckinghamshire) inheritance of the co-heiresses Dorothy and Mary Lee. Wardship also had a social dimension. Apart from arranging a ward's marriage, the guardian was responsible for his or her education and providing him or her with the skills and social graces suitable for his or her station in life. In his handbook *The Book of the Courtier* (translated into English in 1561), Castiglione discussed the importance of horsemanship and military prowess, but also emphasised such social skills as singing, dancing and playing a musical instrument.[119]

From an economic perspective Cavendish was the ideal guardian. As his estate lay close to that of his ward, his officers could administer it effectively. Moreover, Cavendish was personally involved in the management of his estate, carefully overseeing the actions of his men and minutely scrutinising their accounts. Francis's inheritance was therefore in safe hands. Cavendish, as a grazier, benefited from the extra acreage at his disposal, giving him greater flexibility when moving livestock around the joint estate, and he quickly seized the opportunity. The hiring of George Brooke, an inhabitant of a Wortley manor and a large-scale drover and dealer,

---

114 H29, fo. 133. A litter comprised a furnished frame carried on the backs of two horses.
115 H29, fo. 113.
116 H29, fo. H23 fo. 159v; H29, 72, 240; Edwards, *Horses and the aristocratic lifestyle*, p. 126.
117 H29, fo. 302.
118 H29, fo. 242.
119 B. Castiglione, *The Book of the Courtier*, trans. G. Bull (1967, rev. edn London, 1976), pp. 94–6, 118; Edwards, *Horses and the aristocratic lifestyle*, p. 204.

significantly aided the expansion of his grazing business, especially the development of his links with the London market. He even loaned Brooks thousands of pounds and leased him his grazing ground in Westley Park at Sawtry in Huntingdonshire. Integration served Francis well too because, as his lands were being run alongside a larger estate, he benefited from the additional contacts and the expansion of his own economic interests. Harmonisation was facilitated by the compatibility of the two estates one with the other: agriculturally, grazing predominated while, industrially, metal-working was a significant feature. If the absence of income ledgers precludes an analysis of profit and loss, the fact that Cavendish's enterprises continued to grow through and beyond the period of wardship indicates that they flourished. So, too, must have the economy of the Wortley estate under his stewardship.

Cavendish's temperament and his careful management of his assets may have made him the perfect manager of his ward's estate, but was it suitable for the guardian of a 12-year-old boy and his two brothers and five sisters? If only the copious correspondence that passed between him and his family had survived we may have discerned a loving husband and father behind the rather aloof façade. Riden argues that he really did love his wife, pointing out that he showered her with gifts before and after the wedding and made a generous settlement in her favour. And he had to work at it. Lady Elizabeth continued to style herself Lady Wortley until Cavendish was ennobled a year later and in February 1610 he paid for a monument to her former husband in St George's Chapel at Windsor, where he was interred.[120] Even if the larger part of the charges of the children were met by their mother out of her income, Cavendish's spending on his step-children is indicative of his love for his wife and his affection and concern for her children.

Cavendish did not stint on his own children, providing them with the wherewithal of an aristocratic upbringing. Tutors gave them a classical education and taught them modes of behaviour and the social graces appropriate to their status. They learned to ride at an early age and did so on fine horses chosen for their size and temperament.[121] Moreover, numerous references in Cavendish's accounts indicate that he treated his step-children in the same way as he did his own. By 1612 most of them had left home: one son and three daughters had married and Francis and Edward had gone off to study, the one at Oxford and the other at the Inns of Court in London. While it is possible that Cavendish arranged Francis's marriage to Grace Brouncker, the wardship contract seemed to guarantee his step-son's rights and arguably he wanted to marry her. Unlike Cavendish, Francis sought a career at court, entering the household of Prince Henry at the time of his marriage. Significantly, Cavendish did not arrange a marriage between his son and heir William and one of his step-daughters, although he may have been aiming higher. In 1608 his son married Christiana, the daughter of Edward Bruce, Lord Kinloss, Master of the Rolls. To sum up, Francis Wortley was fortunate to have his step-father as his guardian. He husbanded Francis's estate and brought him up in a manner that fitted his status, providing him with the

---

120 Riden, *Household accounts*, vol. i, p. 13; H29/152 for the reference to Sir Richard Wortley's monument: H29, fo. 152.

121 Edwards, *Horses and the aristocratic lifestyle*, pp. 85, 92.

economic base and the social skills essential for a gentleman seeking to enhance his status and pursue an active public life. In this respect, this case study acts as an antidote to the numerous examples of unscrupulous guardians to be found in estate archives or the records of the law courts, as well as those that fill the pages of Bell and Hurstfield, the authors of books on the history of the Court of Wards and Liveries. It was a fortunate match for Lady Elizabeth too. She married a person who cared for her children and raised them in a manner suitable for their status, and who also loved her. Indeed, he indulged her, whether buying luxuries for her or accommodating her desire for a life at court and the associated social round.[122]

---

122 *Ibid.*, pp. 187–91, 196–7.

Chapter 4

The steel industry in England, 1614–1740

Dorian Gerhold

Steel was important in the Industrial Revolution, especially for making tools such as saws and files, weapons and industrial components such as springs, but until the eighteenth century most steel used in England was imported. What eventually made it possible to substitute English steel for imports and to develop a flourishing steel industry was a process called 'cementation', which produced 'blister steel'. Cementation began to be used in 1614, when it was introduced from abroad, and it dominated English steelmaking until the 1850s. Cementation furnaces were at first few, with the details of the process kept as secret as possible, and information about them is fragmentary. Much of the story was told by K.C. Barraclough in 1984, in what remains the standard work,[1] but important information has been added, especially by Paul Belford on Sir Basil Brooke and Coalbrookdale, by David Hey on Sheffield and Rotherham and by David Cranstone and John Bowman on north-east England.[2] This article aims to provide a more connected account of the development of steelmaking in seventeenth- and early eighteenth-century England, adding new information and placing the south Yorkshire steelmakers described by Hey in a national context.

First the cementation process and the steel it produced must be introduced. The cast or pig iron produced by a blast furnace can contain up to 5 per cent carbon, and is brittle but useful for making into cast shapes. Extracting all the carbon from it in a finery forge results in wrought or malleable iron, which can be hammered into different shapes. Steel in the seventeenth and eighteenth centuries had an intermediate carbon content, of 0.5 to 1.5 per cent. It was difficult and expensive to make, but was stronger and harder than wrought iron, and its hardness and strength could be increased by a separate heat treatment subsequent to manufacture.[3] It was different from modern mild steel, which largely replaced wrought iron in the 1850s, and would now be known as tool steel.

The several different ways of making steel were variations on two themes: either the process of refining was stopped at a point where just the right amount of carbon remained, or carbon was added subsequently to wrought iron.[4] Continental

---

1 K.C. Barraclough, *Steelmaking before Bessemer. Vol. 1, Blister steel: the birth of an industry* (London, 1984).

2 See works cited below. My debt to them, especially those by David Hey, is greater than appears in the footnotes, because I have often drawn directly on documents first identified by them.

3 Barraclough, *Blister steel*, p. 1; Paul Belford, 'Industrialisation and identity in Shropshire: the Brookes of Madeley, 1544–1646', PhD thesis (University of York, 2015), p. 231. I am grateful to Richard Williams for advice on metallurgy and comments on an earlier draft of the first part of this article.

4 For the full range, see Barraclough, *Blister steel*, pp. 11–12.

manufacturers almost exclusively used the first method, and there was some use of it in England in the sixteenth and seventeenth centuries, though without lasting success.[5] Cementation was an example of the second method, adding carbon, and became the usual method in England, partly reflecting the country's lack of iron ore suitable for making the best steel. The cementation process is first clearly recorded at Nuremberg in 1601, though there is a possible reference to it from Prague in 1574.[6]

Cementation created steel by heating wrought iron and charcoal together in an airtight container, thereby increasing the carbon content of the iron. The process required a reverberatory chamber with a fire below. Inside were one or more chests or pots made of fire-resistant sandstone. They contained wrought iron bars separated by charcoal, the whole being topped by sand and sealed from the air for firing. The temperature was raised to about 1100° centigrade, making the steel red-hot but not melting it. Firing might take six or seven days, and cooling about 12 days in winter and 18 in summer, so the whole process lasted three or four weeks.[7] Cementation allowed the production of steel on a much larger scale than the methods previously used for adding carbon. The businesses remained very small – one man might be needed for the furnace and several for the associated forge – though most owners had other interests in the iron industry and often in other industries too. The steel produced was known as blister steel because of the protrusions on its surface. It was not homogenous, because the carbon penetrated the outer edges of the bars more effectively than the inner parts. Therefore, until Benjamin Huntsman developed a way of melting steel in the 1740s, it had to be heated again and forged under a water-powered hammer, which is why cementation furnaces were often associated with a water mill.

The expertise involved included designing the furnace, selecting the iron, charcoal and coal, determining the composition and loading of the chests or pots, keeping an even heat, judging when to stop the process, selecting the steel for forging and not reheating the steel to too high a temperature or too many times. The three possible ways in which techniques could spread were agreement (with some sort of licensing system); workmen taking their knowledge and expertise to new owners on new sites; and owners of furnaces using their skilled workmen to establish new furnaces in additional locations.

This article considers the development of the industry in chronological – and so geographical – order. It begins with Sir Basil Brooke at Coalbrookdale (Shropshire) and his rival Dr Robert Flood at Limehouse to the east of London in the 1610s (sections I and II). Attention then shifts to Rotherham, Sheffield and south Yorkshire (section III), to Stourbridge (Worcestershire) and Kingswinford (Staffordshire) (section IV) and to the north-east of England (section V). Evidence of steelmaking in other locations is considered in section VI, and the findings are brought together in a conclusion.

---

5   Belford, 'Industrialisation', p. 234; Rhys Jenkins, 'Notes on the early history of steel making in England', *Transactions of the Newcomen Society*, 3 (1922–3), pp. 17–18.

6   Barraclough, *Blister steel*, pp. 48–9. For doubt about the 1574 reference, see Belford, 'Industrialisation', p. 235.

7   R.R. Angerstein (trans. T. Berg and P. Berg), *R.R. Angerstein's illustrated travel diary, 1753–1755* (London, 2001), pp. 252, 271–2.

I

In April 1614 a patent for making steel was granted to William Ellyott and Mathias Meysey, both described as gentlemen of London. The patent makes clear that the process intended was cementation: converting iron and steel was to be

> performed by meanes of a reverberatorie furnace with potts luted or closed to be putt therein containing in them certaine quantities of iron with other substances, mixtures and ingredients, which being in the said furnace brought to a certaine proportion of heate doth make or convert the same iron into steele, which steele with other heats temperatures and hammering to be afterwards given to the same doth make it good and fitt for the uses before mentioned.

The justification for the patent was the kingdom's reliance on imported steel and the patentees' 'painful labours' in finding a new way of making steel. They were to have the sole benefit of the new method for 21 years, paying £10 a year to the Exchequer.[8] Nothing is known about Ellyott, but Meysey belonged to a gentry family of Shakenhurst in Worcestershire.[9]

Until now, Ellyott and Meysey have always been taken at face value as the men who brought the new technique to England, and there has been much discussion about how they turned to Sir Basil Brooke for help. However, it is clear from the contemporary records that Meysey and Ellyot were merely the front men for Brooke, and it was Brooke who brought the technique to England and implemented it. A government source referred to 'the grant to Mesy & Eliot for the use of Sir Basill Brook kt for the making of steele', and objectors to the patent described it as 'granted to Ellyott & Meysey pattentees on the behalf of Sr. Bazill Brooke knight'. In addition, they contrasted the steel they preferred only to steel made by Brooke, indicating that the patentees' steel came entirely from Brooke.[10] The reason for the patent not being in Brooke's name was probably that such monopolies were intensely unpopular and a major political issue, and Brooke himself was a prominent Catholic, which would have made things worse. Once the attempt at a monopoly was abandoned in 1620, there was no need for Ellyott and Meysey. The link between Brooke and Meysey may have been the Middle Temple, of which both were members.[11] How Brooke acquired the technology is unknown, but the Nuremberg company was evidently interested in selling it for use elsewhere,[12] and Brooke had travelled widely on the European mainland.

Until recently it was uncertain where Brooke made his steel, but this was resolved in 2003–05 by the excavation of his two steel furnaces at Coalbrookdale, in the parish of Madeley, Shropshire. The excavation confirmed that the method used was cementation. Research by Paul Belford has clarified Brooke's strategy. Brooke

---

8   TNA, C 66/2017, no. 15. (The quotation is slightly repunctuated.)

9   C.T. Martin (ed.), *Minutes of Parliament of the Middle Temple*, 4 vols (London, 1904), vol. ii, p. 549; VCH, *Worcestershire*, vol. iv (1924), p. 238.

10   BL, Lansdowne Ms 160, fo. 185 (see also fo. 219); TNA, SP 14/105, nos 134, 136.

11   Martin (ed.), *Minutes of Parliament*, vol. i, p. 348, vol. ii, p. 549.

12   Barraclough, *Blister steel*, pp. 49–50.

owned the manor of Madeley, which was a major producer of coal. After the first two years, when wood was used, the furnaces were heated using coal. The rural location would have helped in keeping the technique secret. The iron ore from the Shropshire coalfield contained phosphorous and so was unsuitable for steelmaking, but Madeley was linked by the river Severn to the Forest of Dean, which provided iron virtually free of phosphorous. Indeed, Brooke took direct control of part of that iron production in 1615. At Coalbrookdale Brooke not only built steel furnaces but also apparently created the Upper or 'Great' Forge, where the blister steel could be forged. As there are later references to the 'old' and 'new' furnaces, there may have been just one furnace at first, to which a second was added subsequently. It was common for steelmaking sites to have two furnaces, so one could be fired while the other cooled.[13]

Brooke's choice of site highlights some of the factors affecting the location of furnaces. Converting iron to steel made little difference to its weight, so, other things being equal, the furnace could be anywhere on a reasonably direct route, or one with water transport, between the source of the iron and the final users. Three other factors then came into play. Coal had to be available cheaply, which meant location on a coalfield or close to water transport. As the iron accounted for 90 per cent or more of total costs, coal was a minor cost, often only around one per cent of the total, but that would quickly rise and eat into profit margins if it had to be conveyed any distance by land, which doubled the pithead price after about seven miles and so in proportion as distance increased.[14] The only furnaces in this period not on a coalfield were at Birmingham, Keynsham and London. The second was water power for hammering the blister steel, though this could be nearby rather than on exactly the same site as the furnace. The third was access to customers, as the steel varied greatly in quality and customers liked to inspect what they were buying. Customers were widely scattered, but with concentrations in the Black Country, Birmingham, the Sheffield area and London. However, it may have been almost as good to have a warehouse close to customers, as Brooke did at Southwark.[15] Its location suggests that Brooke's steel was conveyed to London by water, as steel conveyed by land would have arrived to the north or west of the city rather than across the river from it. Nevertheless, the high value and varying characteristics of steel sometimes made long-distance land transport worthwhile; for example, in the 1700s some of Ambrose Crowley's was sent by water from north-east England to London and thence by land to Birmingham.[16]

---

13 This paragraph is based on Belford, 'Industrialisation', pp. 215–16, 237–54. See also Paul Belford and Ronald A. Ross, 'English steelmaking in the seventeenth century: the excavation of two cementation furnaces at Coalbrookdale', *Historical Metallurgy*, 41 (2007), pp. 105–23; Malcolm Wanklyn, 'Iron and steelworks in Coalbrookdale in 1645', *Shropshire Newsletter*, 44 (June 1973), pp. 3–6. A shipment of two tons of steel down the Severn is recorded in 1619 (UK Data Service, GPB 1575–1765 database, 1247/08/02/20). The suggestion (Belford, 'Industrialisation', p. 243) that shipments of steel down the Severn increased in the 1630s seems unfounded; only two shipments are recorded in the GPB database.

14 Barraclough, *Blister steel*, pp. 225–8; John Hatcher, *The history of the British coal industry*, vol. i, *Before 1700: towards the age of coal* (London, 1993), p. 13.

15 TNA, STAC 8/25/17; SP 14/105, no. 136.

16 M.W. Flinn, *Men of iron: the Crowleys in the early iron industry* (Edinburgh, 1962), p. 141. In 1737 the conveyance of iron from London to Birmingham was said to cost from £3 10s to £4 by land

Brooke obtained a second patent, again in the name of Ellyott and Meysey, in 1616. There was one technical change: the fuel was now to be coal instead of wood. Much more significant was the prohibition of imported steel (except as manufactured items) from 25 March 1617. The patentees were required to have 60 tons of steel, as good as that made in Germany or elsewhere, in their warehouses in or around London by that date and to sell it for not more than 6d per lb (a high price equivalent to £56 per ton). They were also to pay £293 16s 8d a year to the king as compensation for loss of customs on imports, with 'a yearlie encrease of fiftie poundes by yeare'.[17] In 1619 they claimed to have 140 tons in their warehouses and to have provided 'many reverberatorie fornaces and hammers that goe with water', spending over £10,000.[18]

The prohibition on imports prompted determined opposition and plans to establish a rival steelmaking enterprise. An attempt by one Palmer, a Dutchman, to obtain a patent to make steel seems to have been beaten off easily in 1617.[19] In 1618 scythemakers in Worcestershire, Warwickshire, Staffordshire and Shropshire were said to be levying 6d per dozen scythes to fund petitions and other actions against the patent.[20] The patentees began suits in the courts of Exchequer and Star Chamber in 1618 and 1619 against importers of steel, who replied that the patent was invalidated by the poor quality and high price of the patentees' steel; they also stated that the patentees were selling Flemish steel and claiming they had made it themselves.[21] More determined opposition was provided by Dr Robert Fludd, who, as we shall see, was launching his own steelmaking project at this time. In May 1618 the patentees complained that Fludd had set up furnaces and was breaching their monopoly. Fludd responded in October with complaints from steel-users about Brooke's steel. The Privy Council dismissed the complaints, but in January or February 1619 Fludd submitted written complaints from large numbers of London tradesmen about the patentees' steel, which they claimed was inferior to Fludd's steel. Those complaining included the king's gunfounder for iron ordnance and shot, the prince of Wales's gunmaker and the locksmiths to the lord chancellor and the queen, as well as many gunmakers, cutlers, edge-tool makers, crossbow makers and others. Fludd claimed that the patentees' steel 'is noe steele but hardened iron: which by often putting into the fire returneth into mere iron againe'.[22] The situation changed following a treaty with the Dutch in 1619. The Dutch complained about the prohibition on imported steel and in November 1619 Brooke gave up the patent, requesting a new one that allowed him to make steel but omitted the prohibition on imports.[23]

All that can be said about the quality of Brooke's steel is that it was satisfactory for some purposes and not for others, as England's blister steel continued to be for

---

and £2 by water (*Journal of the House of Commons*, 23 (1737–41), p. 109b).

17   TNA, C 66/2102, no. 11.

18   TNA, E 112/101, no. 1226.

19   *APC, 1616–17*, pp. 394–5.

20   TNA, STAC 8/25/17.

21   Ibid; TNA, E 112/101, no. 1226.

22   *APC, 1618–19*, pp. 135, 279, 291; TNA, SP 14/105, nos 134–7.

23   *APC, 1618–19*, p. 462; *1619–21*, pp. 2–3, 77. No such patent seems to have come into force.

at least another century. According to Fuller in 1662, it could be used for items such as knives and scissors, but not for fine edges such as those of dissecting knives and razors.[24] The Nuremburg steelmakers had made the cementation process feasible, but there is no reason to think that they had perfected it. The Privy Council dismissed the complaints about quality, but once the political circumstances had changed it implicitly accepted them. In early 1619 Fludd claimed that the patentees were seeking to import 3,500 tons of steel, and that they were providing Flemish steel to customers so that they would not complain about the quality, and supporters of the patent in 1619 'did not insist upon the goodnes of the steele made for the present, but said they hoped it would still be made better and better, and withal confessed that they wraught Flanders steele in the mixture of the steele made by Sir Basill Brooke'.[25] Brooke cannot really have expected to supply the whole of England with steel as good as German steel from one or two furnaces at Coalbrookdale, or even just to supply London, and perhaps the objectors were right in thinking that one of the purposes of the second patent was to monopolise the importing of steel.

Brooke's property at Madeley, including his iron and steel works, was seized by parliament in 1642, and Brooke himself was imprisoned and died in the Tower in 1646, though his family later recovered Madeley. Steelmaking continued at Coalbrookdale until at least 1653, and its continuance until 1693–4 is suggested by numerous shipments of steel down the Severn. In 1682 there were 26 of these, totalling 24½ tons, equivalent to the capacity of perhaps one and a half furnaces. Although some of that steel may have been from furnaces at Stourbridge or Kingswinford, the cessation of shipments in 1693–4 could indicate the end of steelmaking at Coalbrookdale.[26] There was a 'steelhouse' there in 1696, but it was not necessarily in use, and the steel furnaces were demolished in 1726.[27]

II

Even before the second patent was granted a competing offer had been made by 'the French undertakers for the transmutinge of iron into steele'.[28] This was the venture headed by Dr Robert Fludd, philosopher, alchemist and physician, who had travelled widely on the continent.[29] The Privy Council later noted that Fludd had brought over experts in steelmaking, including John Rochier (also recorded as Rocher and Durocher), 'a Frenchman skilful and experte in making steele'.[30] The source of any French expertise is unexplained, though if the term 'Frenchman' was used loosely

---

24 T. Fuller, *The worthies of England* (London, 1662), pp. 347–8, quoted in Belford, 'Industrialisation', p. 256.

25 TNA, SP 14/105, nos 135–6; TNA, *APC, 1619–21*, pp. 2–3.

26 *Calendar of the proceedings of the Committee for Compounding* (London, 1892), part v, p. 3298; GPB database.

27 TNA, C 8/570/37; Belford and Ross, 'English steelmaking', pp. 108–9.

28 BL, Cotton Ms, Titus B V, fo. 255.

29 *ODNB*, 'Robert Fludd'; William H. Huffman, *Robert Fludd and the end of the Renaissance* (London, 1988), pp. 13, 28.

30 *APC, 1619–21*, pp. 284–5; BL, Add. Ms 64883, fo. 60; TNA, SP 14/105, nos 137.

it might have applied to someone from Piedmont, where steel was being made by the cementation process in 1627, not far from where Fludd spent much of his time in 1598–1604.[31] The proposers claimed to have spent £1,000 since their arrival in England and stated that they, 'as maisters of their craft, offer the present perfection thereof', whereas the patentees were 'yett to learne the arte'. They would pay £50 a year, compared with the patentees' £10. They would use only pit coal, whereas the patentees had used much wood from the Forest of Dean.[32] In 1618 they had a furnace producing enough steel for tradesmen to test its quality.[33]

In September 1620, with Brooke's patent out of the way, the Privy Council agreed that Fludd and Durocher could have a patent to make steel, with a monopoly of their process for 21 years. A third of the profits were to be paid to the king.[34] By February 1622 the patent had not yet passed the great seal, but the works were nearing completion. Sir John Suckling wrote that 'I have been twice at Lymehouse where the houses, furnaces, and watermill are buylt for the making and working of the sayd steele, it being a very faire busines and likely to proove very profitable, and against it no just exception can be taken.' He added that he had not previously pressed for the patent to be passed 'in regard the housing and other necessaries were but lately finished, and not ready to make any steele till this present moneth'.[35] There is a possible site close to Limehouse, though strictly in Ratcliff Hamlet, where a Steel House Lane appears on a later map on the north side of Commercial Road.[36] The watermill used was presumably one of those on the Lea. In 1621 John Durocher and his wife were living in Portsoken Ward, just outside London's city wall on the east side.[37]

The patent apparently never passed the Great Seal, perhaps because Fludd and Durocher decided they could make steel without it and keep the promised third of profits. The last reference to this enterprise records the appearance at Whitehall in May 1625 of

> [the] widow of John Rocher the inventor of transmuting iron into steel who being defrauded of his third part of the benefit of his patent by Dr Flood & Caleb Rawlins died for greif. [She] prayeth for a reference to Mr Attorney or anie other to examin & take order or certifie.[38]

Although Durocher had died and the profits were contested, the complaint indicates that there were profits worth complaining about. The assumption that the enterprise soon

---

31 Barraclough, *Blister steel*, p. 162; ODNB, 'Robert Fludd'.

32 BL, Cotton Ms, Titus B V, fo. 255.

33 *APC, 1618–19*, p. 135; TNA, SP 14/105, nos 135, 137.

34 *APC, 1619–21*, pp. 284–5, 319.

35 S.R. Gardiner (ed.), *The Fortescue papers*, Camden Society new series 1 (London, 1871), pp. 177–8.

36 The lane is not recorded until Horwood's map of 1813; probably there was a building known as the Steel House, and the name only later became attached to a newly created lane.

37 R.E.G. Kirk and Ernest F. Kirk (eds), *Returns of aliens dwelling in the City and suburbs of London*, Publication of the Huguenot Society, 10, pt 3 (Aberdeen, 1907), p. 250.

38 BL, Add. Ms 64,883, fo. 60 (the quotation is slightly repunctuated).

foundered is based only on the silence of the records and, even if it did, it seems that the Durocher family's steelmaking expertise was applied elsewhere, as discussed below.

Another patent for steelmaking was granted in 1626 to Thomas Letsome, a citizen and merchant taylor of London, Nicholas Page and Lord Dacre for sole use of a 'true and perfect way of making steel' devised by Letsome and Page. It resulted in a steelworks at Ballintree, County Cork, in 1629, which continued until at least 1634. The process is unknown, but the use of coal suggests a reverberatory furnace and cementation.[39]

III

Steelmaking in south Yorkshire probably started in 1628, though there is no definite evidence until 1643. The first steelmaker there was Charles Tooker, described in 1628 as a gentleman of Rotherham.[40] Where he was from and how he acquired knowledge of steelmaking is unknown,[41] but the fact that he was described as a gentleman makes it unlikely that he discovered the secrets of steelmaking by working in a steel furnace himself. In 1628 he purchased from Thomas Cock a piece of former arable land 49 yards long in a place called Canklowe Moorgate, just south of Rotherham town, on which Cock had recently built a house.[42] This was almost certainly the house later known as Moorgate Hall, where Tooker's descendants would live until at least 1806. It had nine hearths in 1665.[43] A small piece of moorland adjoining was enclosed at the same time, and was described as 'for his smythye gardyn there', or 'for his smythy garden & croft'.[44] These descriptions indicate that iron was being worked in some way. Although we cannot be sure that steel was being made, there is no evidence of Tooker or the Moorgate site being involved in any other branch of the iron industry, and no reason to think that someone described as a gentleman would have bothered to operate a small-scale smithy. What seems at first sight to be a third piece of land, adjoining the small piece of moorland and leased in 1692 for 900 years by the churchwardens of Rotherham to John Tooker, grandson of the first Charles Tooker, was almost certainly the property purchased in 1628, subsequently mortgaged and

---

39 TNA, C 66/2392, no. 2; H.R. Schubert, *History of the British iron and steel industry from c.450 B.C. to A.D. 1775* (London, 1957), p. 325.

40 RA, 363-G/2/10/14/3.

41 There were a number of Tooker families in various places, some including a Charles. According to Hunter, the family was from Wiltshire and Somerset, but the basis for this statement is unknown (Joseph Hunter, *South Yorkshire*, 2 vols (Wakefield, 1828–31), vol. ii, p. 25). Note that the first proposal for making steel in America came from John Tucker or Tooker of Southold (Barraclough, *Blister steel*, p. 142; <https://www.geni.com/people/Capt-John-Tooker/6000000022514044420>, accessed 30 August 2019).

42 RA, 363-G/2/10/14/2 and 3. In March 1628 Tooker was listed at Moorgate in a church rate, though the location of the rate itself is unknown. <https://www.genuki.org.uk/big/eng/YKS/WRY/Rotherham/RotherhamChurchRateRoll1627>, accessed 1 August 2019. Children of Charles Tooker were baptised at Rotherham from 1629 onwards (SA, transcript TI 45).

43 Hunter, *South Yorkshire*, vol. ii, p. 25; TNA, E 179/210/393.

44 RA, 363-G/5/1, pp. 517, 520.

lost by the Tookers.[45] In 1692 it was described as having been leased to the second Charles Tooker (who died in 1680) and to have contained not just a house but 'two furnaces & a smithy & severall other buildings'. By 1692 most of these buildings had been demolished,[46] but, as we shall see, the furnaces were replaced elsewhere in Rotherham. As well as the furnaces, both the first and second Charles Tookers leased from Sir John Reresby at Thrybergh, several miles to the north-east, a watercourse 'which was used … for a steele millne or forge & comonly called Thriburgh steel forge'. When water was scarce, Reresby's corn mill was to have priority.[47]

There was good reason for starting steelmaking in south Yorkshire in the late 1620s. By the seventeenth century there was a well-established cutlery industry in Sheffield, which used imported steel.[48] The Swedish iron industry was transformed by Dutch migrants in the 1620s, and Swedish iron proved to be exceptionally suitable for the cementation process. Almost immediately it began to be exported, at first via Amsterdam but from the 1660s directly to London; such imports expanded rapidly from about the 1640s. English steelmakers everywhere eventually came to use Swedish iron almost exclusively, and usually the highest-quality iron, known as Orground iron.[49] London aldermen were examining the use of Swedish iron for steelmaking in 1631, 40 tons of Swedish iron was conveyed up the Severn in 1647 for Richard Foley (who had taken the Coalbrookdale works the previous year), the steelmaker at Kingswinford in Staffordshire was using only Swedish and Spanish iron in 1686 and Ambrose Crowley was using some Swedish iron at Stourbridge in 1692.[50] It was undoubtedly cheaper to bring Swedish iron to the Rotherham area for conversion to steel close to its final users than for the iron to be taken to the west Midlands, converted to steel there and

---

45   It was mortgaged in 1629 to William Dickenson (RA, 363-G/2/10/14/5), was transferred to Thomas Dickenson in 1640 while occupied by Tooker (RA, 363-G/2/10/14/6), and was almost certainly among the properties 'late Shaw and Dickinsons, and by them given to the poore' in 1672, which included one occupied by Mr Tooker (SA, PR87/120, list of rents), that one subsequently being leased by the churchwardens to John Tooker in 1692. The deeds of this property from 1613 to 1692 are filed together.

46   RA, 363-G/2/10/14/7. Another copy is at RA, 425–2.

47   RA, 425–2. The works at Thrybergh was a forge and not, as Hey indicates, a furnace (David Hey, 'The South Yorkshire steel industry and the Industrial Revolution', *Northern History*, 42 (2005), p. 93).

48   Hey, 'South Yorkshire steel industry', p. 91.

49   Chris Evans and Göran Rydén, *Baltic iron in the Atlantic world in the eighteenth century* (Boston, 2007), pp. 31, 35, 53, 66, 105, 294, 298; Peter King, 'The iron trade on the River Severn in the seventeenth and eighteenth centuries', text of lecture delivered on 5 January 2016 <academia.edu/20308210>, accessed 9 August 2019, p. 4.

50   W.H. Overall and H.C. Overall (eds), *Analytical index to the series of records known as the Remembrancia, 1579–1664* (London, 1878), p. 528; GPB database, 1248/14/03/06 (see also other shipments from 1680 onwards; for Foley, see Belford, 'Industrialisation', p. 239); Barraclough, *Blister steel*, p. 154; M.W. Flinn and Alan Birch, 'The English steel industry before 1856, with special reference to the development of the Yorkshire steel industry', *Yorkshire Bulletin of Economic and Social Research*, 6 (1954), p. 166. Belford, 'Industrialisation', p. 242, suggests that Brooke was using Swedish iron in 1634, citing TNA, E 112/181, no. 155, but the case referred to seems to be TNA, E 112/235, no. 86, and the reference is to 'osmond iron' (which was not necessarily Swedish) being used at the Tintern wireworks.

conveyed to south Yorkshire. This must quickly have become apparent to Sir Basil Brooke, and perhaps he licensed his technology to Tooker in response. In 1717–18 Swedish iron for use at the Ballifield furnace near Rotherham, worth about £16 per ton, cost 22s to convey from London, of which 15s was the land carriage from Bawtry to Ballifield.[51] The Swedes themselves made little steel, as they lacked coal. Spanish iron made serviceable steel, but not steel of the highest quality.[52]

On 9 May 1643 Tooker petitioned Sir John Reresby, reporting that he had fallen into distress because:

> on the Sonday before Michaelmas last past or thereabouts, yt happened & fell uppon my work howse a suddayne fyer, which was uppon that Sonday which was the first insurrection of Sheaffeild & Rotherham to my losse then of fower score pounds at the least by reason whereof I was hindred of my woorke of makeing steele untyll this day: & nowe this last weeke all my goods that I have was taken from mee by the common soldiers beinge supposed to be of the factious company commonly called Roundheads: but for satisfacon I doe take yt uppon my salvation I never did, either in thought word or deede, indirectly or directly doe by any ways or meanes any active matter agaynst the kings majestie or to any of his subjects.

He asked for some paid service 'fytting for a poore gentleman' or some role in garrisoning Rotherham for the king.[53] His son, who became a marshall in the parliamentary army, later had some accounts disallowed because he was said to have been absent from duty at his father's house, and responded that 'truely S[i]r I was bound to doe what I could for him, being very old: and all that hee had was taken from them when the Lord of Newcastles earmye did take the towne of Rotherham where he lived.'[54] That too was in May 1643, and blaming the Royalist commander for Tooker's losses was by then more politic than blaming Roundhead soldiers.

Steelmaking evidently continued at Rotherham under the second Charles Tooker. In the 1650s he began a campaign to acquire a monopoly of steelmaking, claiming that he and one Morossey had discovered a new process of making steel. It was agreed under Cromwell that he should have a patent. In 1662 petitioners against the patent argued that 40 years previously Sir Basil Brooke, Sir William Bowes and others had made as good if not better steel and that, since the Restoration, George Harrison and John Ardron had done the same and at cheaper rates.[55] The proposed patent was disallowed in 1662, but

---

51 Barraclough, *Blister steel*, p. 76; *Journal of the House of Commons*, 22 (1732–7), p. 851b. An 'Act for making the Don navigable from Doncaster to Tinsley near Sheffield' was obtained in 1726, but the work was not completed until 1751 (G.G. Hopkinson, 'The development of inland navigation in south Yorkshire and north Derbyshire, 1697–1850', *Transactions of the Hunter Archaeological Society*, 7 (1956), pp. 231–3).

52 Evans and Rydén, *Baltic iron*, p. 132.

53 WYL, 156/R/1/7.

54 BL, Add. Ms 21,418, fo. 370.

55 TNA, PC 2/55, p. 614. Unlike the 1667 patent, the one granted by Cromwell apparently never passed the great seal. The Ardron referred to was John Ardron, not George Ardron. There seems

in 1666 Tooker tried again, and a patent was obtained in the names of Sir John Reresby and Sir Thomas Strickland, who claimed that they themselves had invented a new way of making steel. This time the patent passed the Great Seal, but petitioners made similar arguments against it, noting that Tooker had agreed to pay Reresby £100 a year and that he had been 'an active officer in the late wars against his Majestie'. This patent too was disallowed. Reresby later observed that 'by denying another part of the profit, who knew the secret as well as hee [Tooker], the patent was reversed, and we lost all'.[56]

The reason for Tooker's attempts to obtain a patent may have been the competition or the threat of it from new furnaces nearby. The petitioners had indicated that this competition began after the Restoration, and the start of it may therefore be marked by the articles of agreement of 1 August 1661 between Peter Ardron (*d.* 1670), his son John Ardron (1627–85), both of Treeton, and Peter's son-in-law George Harrison, of Richmond in Handsworth parish.[57] Harrison had a half-share in the venture and the Ardrons a quarter-share each, and the stock was valued in 1669 at £562 15s 8½d.[58] The steelmaking took place at Treeton, three miles south of Rotherham. Peter Ardron had '2 steele howses' adjoining his house there in 1668. He was a long-established farmer, having leased 84 acres there in 1650.[59]

The failure of the patent seems to have persuaded Tooker to co-operate with his rivals. In September 1667 he transferred a quarter-share of the steel mill at Thrybergh to Robert Harrison senior of Richmond and Robert Harrison junior of Handsworth Woodhouse, both described as yeomen.[60] No later than June 1668, Charles Tooker, Nicholas and John Ardron, Robert Harrison senior and junior, Thomas Stacey and Francis Barlow 'did agree amongst themselves about the well ordering & manageing the mistery of makeinge of steele in theire owne trade and of sellinge & disposinge thereof to theire respective best advantages'.[61] Barlow was innkeeper at one of Sheffield's major inns, the Cock, and Thomas Stacey lived at Ballifield Hall, Handsworth.[62] The participants had four steel furnaces in 1668, which must have been the two at Rotherham and the two at Treeton. When they agreed to raise a sum of £30, or £7 10s on each furnace, Tooker was to pay only £7 10s, which suggests that he was in partnership with someone else at the Rotherham furnaces.[63]

---

to be no surviving evidence of the role Sir William Bowes played in steelmaking.

56 TNA, C 66/3087, no. 1; TNA, PC 2/59, p. 310; Andrew Browning (ed.), *Memoirs of Sir John Reresby* (Glasgow, 1936), p. 63.

57 TNA, C 8/222/38.

58 TNA, C 22/18/22. Nicholas Ardron's share was then £135 4s ½d. In 1670 the stock was valued at £303 8s 4d, of which £22 was desperate debts, but this was probably a half-share (TNA, C 8/222/38).

59 SA, ACM S79. See also Peter Ardron's probate inventory at TNA, C 6/229/45 and the Ardron family tree at BL, Add. Ms 24474, fo. 169.

60 RA, 425–2. There seems to have been some sort of agreement to share the services of Roger Hellifield as early as September 1663 (TNA, C 22/795/17, George Harrison).

61 TNA, C 6/278/29.

62 David Hey, *The fiery blades of Hallamshire: Sheffield and its neighbourhood, 1660–1740* (Leicester, 1991), pp. 152–3, 172, 186.

63 TNA, C 6/278/29.

Tooker's steelmaker in the 1660s was Roger Hellifield of Rotherham, who described himself as a blacksmith. Hellifield later claimed that Tooker had agreed in 1665 to pay him £15 a year for life and a further £20 a year if he employed him to make steel, and that he had then served Tooker for four years. Tooker replied that the £20 and £15 were only to ensure that Hellifield faithfully concealed the mystery of steelmaking, and that the £20 had been paid for three years, but that otherwise he had agreed the following:

> the summe of two shillings for himselfe & seaventeene pence for his servant or striker for every hundred of steele that the said complainant [Hellifield] should cut into gadds by the direccon of this defendant dureing the said terme & also the summe of five shillings for every time that the complainant should lay in iron into this defendants furnice to make steele & two shillings & two pence for his labour in takeing the same forth againe also the summe of sixteen pence to the complainant for himselfe & ten pence for his servant for every day that he or they should worke for & serve this defendant or his heires.[64]

According to John Ardron, Nicholas Ardron had agreed to pay Hellifield £20 a year plus £5 for each heat of steel, but Tooker's agreement had been made instead, and the Ardrons and George Harrison had then paid half of the £20.[65] Hellifield had worked for Tooker since 1660, and in a hearth-tax list of 1665 the name 'Charles Tuke' is followed by Henry Ludlam, William Hellifield (Roger's father, also a blacksmith) and Roger Hellifield.[66] Hellifield and Tooker fell out several times over people taken on by the former for 'gadding' (cutting the steel into smaller strips), with Hellifield describing Tooker on one occasion as a 'blockhead', and particularly over the employment in 1666 of Richard Shercliffe, who Tooker considered a 'cunning fellow' who might learn the secret of steelmaking, even though gadding itself was not part of the secret. Some time after that Tooker stopped paying the £20 on the grounds that Hellifield had caused the secret of steelmaking to be revealed to others, though William and Roger Hellifield were still living near the Rotherham furnaces in 1672[67] and lawsuits between Tooker and Hellifield did not begin until 1673.

According to Tooker, the employment of Shercliffe had resulted in the secret of steelmaking being discovered by other people a few miles away, who had built furnaces and made steel; as a result Tooker's business, in which he and his father had invested £1500, had declined in value from £200 a year to £20 a year. John Ardron confirmed that since 1665 'there have severall steele furnices beene built whereof the trade of the said defendant [Tooker] is very much decayed'.[68] The one new furnace recorded was at Kimberworth, about a mile west of Rotherham, belonging to Lionel

---

64 TNA, C 6/228/33.

65 TNA, C 22/795/17, John Ardron.

66 TNA, C 22/795/17, William Hellifeild and George Harrison; TNA, E 179/210/393. Roger, son of William Hellyfield, was baptised at Rotherham in 1638 (SA, transcript TI 45).

67 TNA, C 22/795/17; C 6/228/33; E 179/262/13 and 15.

68 TNA, C 6/228/33; C 22/795/17.

Copley. A hearth tax list of 1672 records that 'Will[ia]m Hellefeild or Mr Copley' were assessed for four hearths 'per steele furnish' there.[69] William Hellifield was probably Roger's son.[70] Whatever Shercliffe's role, the Hellifields appear to have made their steelmaking expertise available to Copley, a long-established Rotherham ironmaster, and enabled him to enter the steel trade, the clearest example of steelmaking spreading to a new location in this way. Roger Hellifield later worked for Copley, stating that he had been employed by him 'for carrying on certain ironworkes & other affaires', and accounts of the Copley business record him purchasing wood to make charcoal and collecting debts.[71] The Kimberworth steel furnace may have been short-lived. It is recorded in the inventory made after Copley's death in 1675,[72] but not subsequently.

There was a major shift in the location of south Yorkshire steelmaking around 1710, away from Rotherham and Treeton and towards Sheffield and its immediate surroundings. Nicholas Ardron died in 1670 and by 1676 John Ardron and James Bate, his brother-in-law, each had a half-share of the Treeton furnaces.[73] They were still operating in 1685, when John Ardron's half-share of the 'stock belonging [to] the steale house' was valued at £250,[74] but there are no further references to them.

Tooker died in 1680. A part-share in the Thrybergh mill then passed to William Staniforth,[75] and probably Tooker's share in the Rotherham furnaces too. Staniforth died not later than 1708, and in 1709 Dysney Staniforth sold to Field Sylvester of Sheffield a steel furnace with smithy and 'tenting house' 'in or near the beast markett' in Rotherham (i.e. near the Crofts, some distance from Moorgate Hall).[76] This suggests that the Moorgate furnaces had been replaced by a single one nearer the town at some stage. Field Sylvester had from 1689 or earlier organised the steel business of John Fell and Denis Hayford's iron partnership, delivering iron to local steelmakers and then selling the steel to the partnership (the steelmakers presumably acting on commission). As well as satisfying local demand, there was a 'north steele trade'; there are many references to steel sent to Lancashire and in the 1690s Sylvester was

---

69 Wakefield Library, West Riding Hearth Tax return 1672, quoted in David Hey *et al.* (eds), *Yorkshire West Riding Hearth Tax assessment Lady Day 1672*, British Record Society, Hearth Tax Series V (London, 2007), p. 54.

70 William Hellifield of Kimberworth, blacksmith, aged 28, gave evidence in a Chancery suit in 1675 (TNA, C 22/795/17).

71 TNA, C 6/246/48; C 5/287/17. Subsequently he was associated with Copley's successor, William Simpson (C 6/241/87).

72 TNA, C 5/287/17. It contained little of value in 1675, but unless a heat was in progress that might be expected. There was only seven hundredweight of rough steel and three hundredweight of 'bad gad steele' at Kimberworth, but there was six tons of 'raw steele' at Rotherham Forge.

73 TNA, C 8/222/38; C 6/71/25. See also C 22/84/3.

74 TNA, C 6/269/7; C 6/71/25.

75 Memorial flagstone in Rotherham church; WYL, 156/R/19/21 and 156/R/15/58.

76 TNA, C 6/346/58; SA, Wheat 1966. For the beast market see Anthony P. Munford, *A history of Rotherham* (Stroud, 2000), pp. 16–17, 92.

also supplying steel to Birmingham on his own account and had a partner in London.[77] In 1710 the partnership paid Sylvester £10 11s 3d 'for one quarter of Mr Stanyford's furnace at Rotherham and ye tools', valuing the furnace and tools at only £42 5s. From about that time the partnership provided the iron and paid Sylvester only for converting it to steel. Sylvester died in 1717 or 1718, and by January 1718 the furnace had been demolished.[78]

Three new furnaces were established within a few miles of each other just east of Sheffield, and two of these can be seen as a continuation of the Rotherham and Treeton enterprises. George Harrison of Handsworth had a steelmaking business in Handsworth parish by 1707, recorded slightly later as being at Richmond in that parish and having one furnace. After his death in 1707 it passed to the related Roper family by 1710, to George Steer by 1735 and (still with one furnace) to Samuel Shore junior, John Fell and Elizabeth Parkin in 1736.[79] Ballifield furnace, also in Handsworth parish, existed by 1710 and possibly by 1696 (when John Twigg of Ballifield, steelman, is mentioned) and had a continuous history to at least 1765. The furnace was rented from the Stacey family of Ballifield Hall, who had been allied to Tooker and others and were related by marriage to the Harrisons.[80] A document now lost recorded that in May 1719 'George Steer first began to lay iron in furnace to make steel at Darnall', and this may have been what was later recorded as Attercliffe furnace, as the parish was Attercliffe-cum-Darnall.[81]

Within Sheffield Samuel Shore leased land near Castle Hill, Sheffield, in 1709 and had the lease extended in 1714 'in regard he hath lately erected a new steele house and severall other buildings upon the premises'.[82] Shore and Henry Ball, steelmaker, agreed in April 1709 that, for a seven-year term, Shore would employ only Ball to 'make, slitt and gadd' steel, paying him 10s for every making of steel or 'heat' and 2s to his aged mother, and that Ball would not assist in making steel for anyone else; this was then changed to 6s per week plus 6d to widow Ball.[83] Shore still had just one furnace in Sheffield in 1716, but by 1737 had two furnaces on the north-west edge of the town, in what became known as Steelhouse Lane.[84] His forge capacity seems to have been at Woodhouse Mill, east

---

77 Barraclough, *Blister steel*, pp. 69–74; SA, SIR 1/1/1, first pagination, pp. 68, 86, 87, 92, 93, 97, second pagination, pp. 131–2, third pagination, p. 119; SIR 12, pp. 7, 88, 198; SIR 13, p. 334; TNA, C 5/118/40.

78 Barraclough, *Blister steel*, pp. 74, 76; SA, MD401.

79 Hey, *Fiery blades*, pp. 186–7; SA, Tibbitts 699.

80 Hey, *Fiery blades*, p. 188.

81 Alexander B. Bell (ed.), *Peeps into the past, being passages from the diary of Thomas Asline Ward* (London, 1909), p. 237; Barraclough, *Blister steel*, p. 75. The other claimed references to Darnall are mistaken: Samuel Shore's furnace in 1709 was at Castle Hill, Sheffield, rather than Darnall (SA, ACM5376, first pagination, p. 75; cf. Hey, *Fiery blades*, p. 190), and George Steer's furnace in 1735–6 was at Richmond rather than Darnall (SA, Tibbitts 699; cf. Barraclough, *Blister steel*, pp. 75, 77n).

82 SA, ACM5376, first pagination, p. 75.

83 Barraclough, *Blister steel*, p. 77; Robert Eadon Leader, *Sheffield in the eighteenth century* (Sheffield, 1901), p. 71. George Ball of Norton, steelmaker, is recorded in 1695, and George Ball and John Ball, both of Sheffield, steelmakers, died in 1700 and 1701 respectively (Hey, *Fiery blades*, p. 190).

84 Hey, *Fiery blades*, pp. 191, 192.

of the city, as in 1723 he agreed to take part of the water from the mill dam there 'for the management of his steele forges'.[85] Shore (1676–1751), the son of a mason, had been a chapman (or hardwareman) in 1700, but eventually became an ironmaster, steelmaker and merchant. In the 1730s he was in partnership with Griffin Prankerd of Bristol in an ambitious scheme to engross the supply of the best Swedish iron to Britain and channel it through Bristol and Hull instead of London.[86] The other Sheffield furnace was in Balm Green, next to the present City Hall, first recorded in 1716 under Thomas Parkin, who was making steel by 1714. Parkin was an established and successful ironmonger. When he died in 1729 the steel business passed to his granddaughter Elizabeth Parkin.[87]

IV

An early steelworks at Stourbridge, which has escaped notice hitherto, was probably in existence by 1641. James Durocher of Stourbridge, described as a 'steelmaker', died in April 1669 and the parish registers for Old Swinford, in which Stourbridge lies, record him getting married there in August 1641 and having children baptised there from 1642 to 1656.[88] The surname is too rare for the name to be a coincidence, so it is likely that one or more members of the Durocher family transferred the expertise deployed in Fludd's venture to Stourbridge, and therefore that English steelmaking was not entirely a development from Sir Basil Brooke's enterprise. Durocher appears in a hearth tax list for Stourbridge in 1666 as 'James Darasia', with two hearths, the low number possibly indicating that he was a workman rather than the owner.[89]

After 1669 there is a gap in the record at Stourbridge, but by 1682 Ambrose Crowley, father of his more famous namesake, was making steel there and, again, there is a possibility of continuity, but not a proven link.[90] Crowley had been living in Stourbridge by 1657, initially as a nailer.[91] By 1682 he had two steel furnaces on the north side of Mill Lane, adjoining the town mill and in the angle between Mill Lane and a channel of the river Stour.[92] He also held the Royal Forge and Clatterbach Forge nearby and other property.[93] The furnaces passed in about 1710 to the management

85 SA, ACM5376, third pagination, p. 24.

86 Hey, *Fiery blades*, pp. 189–92; Evans and Rydén, *Baltic iron*, pp. 107–9.

87 Hey, *Fiery blades*, pp. 193–4; Barraclough, *Blister steel*, p. 77n; David Hey, *A history of Sheffield* (Lancaster, 2005), p. 88.

88 TNA, PROB 11/330/304; Worcestershire Archive and Archaeology Service, Old Swinford parish register.

89 TNA, E 179/260/6. His will indicates that he had purchased property and built new houses.

90 Flinn, *Men of iron*, p. 12. No reference is given for the 1682 date, but p. 10 refers to a survey of rents in Stourbridge in 1682 (among the Palfrey papers at Worcestershire Archive and Archaeology Service), which is probably the source. However, no such survey is listed in the sketchy online catalogue of the Palfrey collection.

91 Flinn, *Men of iron*, p. 10.

92 The site is shown on a plan of 1868 at DA, DPIT/8/3.

93 Flinn, *Men of iron*, pp. 12, 13. For an inventory of Crowley's goods in 1721, see TNA, PROB 3/20/150. See also Barraclough, *Blister steel*, pp. 215, 216.

of his son James Crowley; after Ambrose Crowley's death in 1720 to Thomas Harvey, ironmaster of Evesham, and then to Benjamin Harvey, ironmonger of Stourbridge; in 1733 to Francis Homfray, ironmonger of Stourbridge and formerly Ambrose Crowley's nail warehouseman; after the death of Francis in 1737 to his widow Mary Homfray; in 1749 to his son John Homfray, ironmaster of Stourbridge; and later to John's son John Addenbrooke Homfray, ironmaster of Old Swinford. When the latter sold the site in 1780 the purchaser had already replaced the steel furnaces with other buildings.[94]

The steel furnace at Kingswinford, four miles north-west of Stourbridge, is one of the best known of the early steel furnaces because of the description given in Robert Plot's *The natural history of Staffordshire* (1686), but it seems to have been short-lived. Plot wrote that 'At the tile house at Bromley in the parish of Kingswinford one John Heydon hardens whole barrs of iron quite through, i.e. he makes them into steel.' Only Spanish and Swedish bar iron was used; this was called 'bullet iron', probably referring to the 'double bullet' brand of iron from Osterby forge, one of the highest-quality Swedish irons. The furnace was small by later standards, with three coffins or chests each containing half a ton of iron.[95] 'John Heydon' was John Haden, variously described as an ironmonger and a steelmaker. He was probably the John Haden baptised in the parish in 1639, the son of a nailer, and married there in 1662.[96] Haden also acted as factor for a Bristol ironmonger, buying rod iron for him and having it made into nails and other items in return for a salary and costs.[97] In a dispute over a contested right of way he stated in July 1687 that about 12 years previously he had rented a house and land called 'the Tyledhouse'. That dates his lease to about 1675, which was probably when the steelmaking began.[98] While Plot referred to 'the tile house', suggesting a furnace converted from another use, all the other contemporary references are to 'the tiled house', which presumably meant a house roofed with tiles. The last known reference to steelmaking at Kingswinford is from 1692.[99] John Haden died in December 1692, apparently in debt, and in 1695 the tiled house was sold to Edward Cooke with the buildings belonging but no mention of a furnace.[100]

V

Steelmaking in north-east England was distinctive in that it took place in a region with only a limited tradition of ironworking, the workers were at first brought in from elsewhere and much of what was produced was sent out of the region.[101] Its advantages were

---

94 Flinn, *Men of iron*, pp. 27–8; DA, D6/1/D3/1 and 3; DPIT/7/4; Evans and Rydén, *Baltic iron*, p. 307.

95 Barraclough, *Blister steel*, pp. 57, 154.

96 DA, transcript of the parish register of Kingswinford; TNA, C 7/153/21.

97 TNA, C 7/153/21.

98 TNA, C 8/390/32.

99 Barraclough, *Blister steel*, p. 199.

100 TNA, C 7/153/21; TNA, E 112/739, No. 57, list of surrenders and Edward Cooke's answer; TNA, E 134/10Wm3/East20, Edmund Haden.

101 David Cranstone, 'From slitting mill to alloy steel: the development of Swalwell ironworks', *Industrial Archaeology Review*, 33 (2011), p. 41; John Bowman, 'The iron and steel industries of the Derwent valley: a historical archaeology', DPhil thesis (University of Newcastle, 2018), pp. 93, 95, 259.

presumably its transport links by sea and river and the ready availability of coal. It is much clearer in this region than elsewhere how the expertise was acquired. Steelmaking was brought to the region in about 1687 by Denis Hayford (*c*.1635–1733). After Lionel Copley's death in 1675 his business in south Yorkshire, including Kimberworth, had been taken over by a partnership consisting of Hayford, William Simpson and Francis Barlow, so Hayford had access to steelmaking expertise.[102] With William Cotton, William Simpson and John Fell, Hayford formed 'the Company in the North', apparently for operations in the Derwent valley,[103] and Hayford on his own purchased a 'steele mill or mill for ye making or drawing of steel' at Blackhall Mill, nine miles south-west of Newcastle, in about 1687. Hayford claimed to have purchased an existing steel mill, which had been operating since 1680 or 1681, but nothing is known about this earlier venture. No furnace is mentioned there and, although this is not conclusive, it is possible that the steel was at first made at the Newcastle furnace recorded in the 1690s, as Hayford's steelmaker worked at Newcastle before moving to Blackhall Mill and the Newcastle furnace was later recorded as being owned by Hayford.[104] There was a furnace at Blackhall Mill by 1719.[105] It is possible that at first Hayford used iron made from a suitable local ore smelted at the blast furnace at nearby Allensford, which he and partners leased from 1692 to 1713.[106]

It was also in or about 1687 that German workers from Solingen settled at Shotley Bridge, a few miles upstream from Blackhall Mill, to make swords. Hayford supplied the steel for the sword makers, and the coincidence of dates, as well as the fact that his steelmaker, William Bertram, was originally from Remscheid near Solingen, suggests that Hayford's venture at Blackhall Mill was established mainly for the sword makers' benefit.[107]

Hayford, who lived near Staveley in Derbyshire, said in 1717 that he went to Blackhall Mill 'usually but once or twice in a year and some years not so often to take ye accounts of his servants or for some such purpose'.[108] It was apparently Bertram who provided the expertise to make shear steel and double shear steel, which were used for the best cutlery and edged tools.[109] Instead of simply forging the blister steel under a water-powered hammer, the bars of blister seal were broken into short lengths, bound together, heated to about 1400° centigrade and then hammered

---

102 TNA, C 5/287/17, Simpson's answer.

103 *ODNB*, 'Denis Hayford'.

104 TNA, C 11/1399/2; C 121/1744/7; Barraclough, *Blister steel*, p. 65. However, in a Chancery suit relating to access and encroachment there was no need to mention a nearby furnace unless it was directly relevant. Barraclough gives no reference for the Newcastle furnace in the 1690s.

105 Barraclough, *Blister steel*, p. 209.

106 Bowman, 'Iron and steel industries', pp. 90–1; Barraclough, *Blister steel*, p. 64.

107 Bowman, 'Iron and steel industries', pp. 85, 90; Cranstone, 'From slitting mill', p. 41; Angerstein, *Travel diary*, pp. 267–8.

108 K.C. Barraclough and B.G. Awty, 'Denis Hayford: an early steel master', *Historical Metallurgy*, 21 (1987), p. 16; TNA, C 11/1399/2.

109 Cranstone, 'From slitting mill', p. 41; Barraclough, *Blister steel*, pp. 64–6. Bertram came to England after working in Sweden, but Swedish expertise was in iron rather than steel.

to produce a square bar with a high degree of consistency. The process could be repeated with a second or even third cementation to create double shear steel.[110] In 1753–4 blister steel was sold for about £26 per ton, faggot steel (drawn out into slimmer bars) for about £31 per ton and shear steel for about £53 per ton (or £93 if it had undergone cementation a third time).[111] The technique was at first confined to Blackhall Mill, and to only part of its output, but spread to nearby Derwentcote in the 1730s (through one of Bertram's apprentices), to the Crowleys' works nearby in the 1750s and to Sheffield in 1767.[112] Hayford died in 1733 and Bertram in about 1740, but steelmaking continued at Blackhall Mill under Bertram's son. The Newcastle furnace was still operating in the 1750s, together with a second furnace there.[113]

The second steelmaking enterprise in the north-east was established by Ambrose Crowley, son of Ambrose Crowley of Stourbridge. The heart of the younger Crowley's business was in London, where he was a major wholesaler of iron and steel products, and he continued to live there. He had access to steelmaking expertise from his father and they exchanged technical and experimental information. His first steel furnace in the north-east was built by Walter Parker, who had previously built or repaired Crowley's father's 'great furnace' at Stourbridge.[114] Crowley's first ironmaking venture in the north-east was at Sunderland in 1682, and was not very successful, but in 1691 and 1699 he acquired sites at Winlaton, five miles north-east of Blackhall Mill, and by 1696 he was a major supplier to the navy. His first steel furnace at Winlaton Mill began operating in 1701 and two new furnaces had replaced it by the end of 1711. In 1707–10 he acquired control of a recently established ironmaking site at nearby Swalwell, and two steel furnaces were begun there in 1711. The two Winlaton furnaces were still operating in 1728 but had closed by 1754, perhaps when the Crowleys purchased the Teams furnace in 1735 (discussed below).[115] In the 1730s the Crowleys were consuming 300 tons of Orground iron per year, between a fifth and a third of the total imported to England.[116]

Two other steel furnaces were established on the Derwent or the Tyne in or about the 1730s. One, at the High and Low Teams works, two miles east of Swalwell, was built by William and Richard Thomlinson. From 1720 to 1733 they also ran the forge at Derwentcote, about a mile east of Blackhall Mill. In 1733 Richard Thomlinson, who was an ironmonger with a warehouse at Wapping in east London, offered for sale his iron manufactory 'at and near Newcastle upon Tyne', containing a slitting mill, a steel furnace, a forge, two blade mills and workshops. This seems to have referred to both the Teams and Derwentcote sites, which were sold separately. The new lease of Derwentcote in 1733 mentions a forge but no steel furnace, whereas at Teams in 1735

110 Schubert, *History*, p. 329; Angerstein, *Travel diary*, pp. 259, 269.
111 *Ibid.*, pp. 21, 252, 259, 271.
112 *ODNB*, 'Denis Hayford'; Bowman, 'Iron and steel industries', pp. 92, 216, 234; Angerstein, *Travel diary*, pp. 269, 272.
113 Barraclough, *Blister steel*, pp. 65, 67.
114 Bowman, 'Iron and steel industries', p. 93; Flinn, *Men of iron*, p. 13; Cranstone, 'From slitting mill', pp. 41, 54.
115 *Ibid.*, pp. 41–2, 44; Bowman, 'Iron and steel industries', pp. 93–6.
116 Evans and Rydén, *Baltic iron*, p. 111; *Journal of the House of Commons*, 22 (1732–7), pp. 851b, 853b.

the Crowleys took over, among other things, a slitting mill, a steel furnace, a forge and workshops. The Teams furnace was thereafter worked by the Swalwell steelmaster in close association with Swalwell. At Derwentcote a steel furnace was added not later than 1742, and is now the earliest surviving cementation steel furnace.[117] In summary, the number of steel furnaces in the north-east rose between 1686 and 1719 from nil to six, and then stayed at about this number to 1740.

VI

At Birmingham, the first steel furnaces seem to have been established early in the eighteenth century, probably in or about 1714. In that year William Kettle, a Birmingham ironmonger, purchased a plot 6 yards by 40 yards on the north side of Whitealls Lane (later Steelhouse Lane) and adjoining another plot previously conveyed to Kettle.[118] 'Kettle's Steel Houses' are shown on the north side of Steelhouse Lane on Westley's map of Birmingham in 1731. Westley's map also shows 'Carlesse's Steel House' in Coleshill Street, but the date of its construction is unknown. In 1720 Alstromer reported three or four steel furnaces in Birmingham using 200 tons of Swedish iron a year, 150 tons of this going to Kettle, and in 1737 Birmingham was using 220 tons of the 900 to 1500 tons of Swedish iron imported for steelmaking each year.[119] In the 1730s John Kettle at Birmingham and Francis Homfray at Stourbridge consumed almost all the Orground iron imported by Griffin Prankerd through Bristol.[120] Kettle's business continued until about 1797, when steelmaking in Birmingham ceased.[121]

There may also have been a steel furnace at Rowley Regis, about seven miles west of Birmingham, by 1711. The will of William Barnesley, steelmaker of Rowley Regis, was proved in 1711, and in 1743 a steel furnace at Corngreave, Rowley Regis, owned by William Machin of Birmingham, was offered for sale.[122] By 1713 there was a steel furnace at Tern Hall in Shropshire (now the site of Attingham Park). In 1710 the mills there were let to Thomas Harvey, ironmonger of Stourbridge, Griffin Prankerd, merchant of Bristol, and others. According to a letter of April 1713 they had erected a mill for rolling brass plates and iron hoops and slitting bar iron into rods for nails, 'since which we have erected a wire mill, a forge and a furnace for converting of iron into steel and shops for about 40 men'. The works continued until 1755, but there

---

117 Cranstone, 'From slitting mill', p. 44; D. Cranstone, *Derwentcote steel furnace: an industrial monument in County Durham* (Lancaster, 1997), p. 19; *Daily Journal*, 24 September 1733.

118 Birmingham Archives, MS 3726/5 (581529); MS 3033/3/375 (252577). Kettle was not already in possession. Samuel Timmins, *The resources, products, and industrial history of Birmingham and the Midland hardware district* (London, 1866), p. 212, dated Kettle's steel business to the end of the seventeenth century. John Russell, a Birmingham ironmonger, supplied a parcel of steel to the elder Ambrose Crowley in 1676, but this is not evidence that Russell himself was a steelmaker (TNA, C 5/468/42; C 5/549/41; C 5/628/99).

119 Barraclough, *Blister steel*, p. 94; *Journal of the House of Commons*, 22 (1732–7), pp. 851b, 853b, 854b.

120 Evans and Rydén, *Baltic iron*, p. 66.

121 Timmins, *Resources*, p. 212.

122 TNA, PROB 11/520/373; Marie B. Rowlands, *Masters and men in the West Midland metalware trades before the Industrial Revolution* (Manchester, 1975), p. 141.

is no further evidence of steelmaking and Harvey, evidently the leading partner until his death in 1731, may have lost interest in steelmaking there once he acquired the furnaces at Stourbridge in 1720.[123]

The first definite evidence of steelmaking in the Bristol area is from a Swedish visitor, Kalmeter, in 1725. He wrote that:

> At the end of Keynsham, right next to the brassworks, lies a steelworks with furnaces and one hammer for forging. The steel here is made from Oregrund iron or other Swedish iron, although Spanish, Russian and even English iron has been used from time to time. The proprietor also converts iron for the merchants of Bristol on a hire basis. For the conversion of iron into steel he charges £2 per ton; forging costs a further £1 per ton.[124]

It was run by the Shallard family, at first John Shallard (*d.* 1735) in partnership with his son William (*d.* 1736), and then by Christopher Shallard (1718–1754).[125] Apart from one reference to a baptism in 1703, the Shallards are recorded in the Keynsham parish register only from 1718 onwards, and that may mark the beginning of steelmaking there.[126] One other furnace falls just within our period: in 1739 Sampson Lloyd, a steel importer, and John Willetts erected a steel furnace at Tetbury in Gloucestershire.[127]

Several other places are said to have had steel furnaces, but direct evidence is lacking. According to Joseph Moxon, writing in 1677, 'The English steel is made in several places in England, as in Yorkshire, Gloucestershire, Sussex, the Wilde of Kent, &c. But the best is made about the Forrest of Dean.'[128] No evidence has been found for cementation furnaces in the Weald, Gloucestershire or the Forest of Dean at that date, and these places, if making steel at all, seem more likely to have been using other steelmaking techniques.[129] Least is known about steel furnaces in London. The younger Ambrose Crowley, writing about steelmaking, referred in 1700 to 'the furnaces about London' and their characteristics, and Angerstein indicated in 1754 that there were furnaces in London.[130] The only one so far identified was at Dartford, where 'a parcel of right Dartford steel, converted by the late famous Mr. Kemp' was offered for sale in 1721. This was said to be the last such steel available, as Kemp had died two years before.[131] Nothing is known about Kemp.

---

123 B. Coulton, 'Tern Hall and the Hill family, 1700–75', *Transactions of the Shropshire Archaeological and Historical Society*, 66 (1989), pp. 97–102. See also TNA, C 11/324/12. Only tiny quantities of 'gad steel', 'blistered steel' and 'old steel for files', totalling just over two hundredweight, are listed at the Tern works in Thomas Harvey's inventory of 1732 (TNA, PROB 3/31/86).

124 Barraclough, *Blister steel*, p. 97.

125 Evans and Rydén, *Baltic iron*, p. 311.

126 Keynsham parish registers, <https://keysalthist.org.uk/online.htm>, accessed 21 August 2019.

127 Rowlands, *Masters and men*, p. 141.

128 Joseph Moxon, *Mechanick exercises, or, the doctrine of handy-works* (1677), p. 55.

129 Schubert, *History*, pp. 325–6.

130 Barraclough, *Blister steel*, pp. 96–7; Angerstein, *Travel diary*, p. 175.

131 *Applebee's Original Weekly Journal*, 27 May 1721.

VII

This article makes possible a better appreciation of how the technology of cementation steelmaking spread and at what speed. The technology arrived in England through two separate enterprises, those of Sir Basil Brooke and of Dr Fludd and John Durocher. At least one major improvement was brought from abroad later, namely the manufacture of shear steel. The technology probably spread in three ways, though only two can be documented. The undocumented one is by agreement or sale of technology, of which Brooke and Charles Tooker are possible examples. Another is by workmen or members of their families moving to a new employer, as in the case of the Hellifields in about 1670. The third is by owners of steel furnaces moving skilled workers to new areas, as in north-east England.

Caution is necessary regarding the number of furnaces, not only because the dates of the known furnaces are sometimes uncertain but also because some are known from only a single chance reference. There may have been a few that are not recorded (or are yet to be discovered), especially in London. Nevertheless, the number of known furnaces is unlikely to be far from the actual number at any date. There were no more than six up to 1661, for most of that period at three sites (Coalbrookdale, Stourbridge and Rotherham). The number fluctuated from six to eight up to 1710, and then rose rapidly, to 17 in 1714–17. There were 18 or 19 in 1718–25 and usually 20 or 21 in 1726–40 (Table 4.1). From about 1711 there were similar numbers in each of the three main areas – the west Midlands, south Yorkshire and north-east England – but those in north-east England seem to have had double the capacity of the ones elsewhere, making north-east England about as important in steelmaking as the rest of the country.

At least as important as the number of furnaces was the growth in their capacity. In 1686–92 the furnaces in Yorkshire and at Kingswinford were described as having a capacity of only one to one and a half tons, whereas in 1720–5 the furnaces near Sheffield had a capacity of six tons and those at Stourbridge three and four tons. At the same time one at Swalwell had a capacity of ten tons, and all the furnaces in the north-east seem to have remained larger than those elsewhere: in 1754 those at Blackhall, Newcastle and Derwentcote had capacities of ten to 11 tons, double that of the Birmingham furnaces, and one at Swalwell could then convert 14 tons.[132] In 1680, assuming seven furnaces, ten heats a year each and capacity of one and a half tons per furnace, overall capacity would have been about 105 tons per year, probably only a small increase since the 1620s. In 1720, with about 18 furnaces, the same ten heats per year and a capacity of about five tons each but ten tons in the north-east, overall capacity would have been about 1200 tons, an 11-fold increase in 40 years. The figure for 1737 would have been slightly higher (1300 tons), which is consistent with estimated annual imports of 900 to 1500 tons of Swedish iron for steelmaking.[133]

Given that the iron bars used accounted for 90 per cent or more of the cost of steel there was limited scope for economies of scale, so the increased size of furnaces may have been as much a consequence as a cause of growing use of English-made steel. There is neither likelihood nor evidence of significantly lower costs overall, and it is also unlikely

---

132 Barraclough, *Blister steel*, pp. 58–9, 77, 80, 95, 154, 209, 216, 218; Angerstein, *Travel diary*, pp. 252, 261, 271–2.

133 *Journal of the House of Commons*, 22 (1732–7), pp. 851b, 853b, 854b.

Table 4.1
Numbers of furnaces, 1650–1740.

Date	West Midlands	South Yorkshire	North-east	Other	Total
1650	4	2	–	–	6
1660	4	2	–	–	6
1670	4	4	–	–	8
1680	3	4	–	–	7
1690	3	3	1	–	7
1700	2	3	1	–	6
1710	2	4	2	–	8
1720	5	5	6	2	18
1730	6	6	7	2	21
1740	6	6	6	3	21

Sources: See text.
Note: The table incorporates many assumptions, and the figures are therefore approximate.

that steel-users would have abandoned high-quality imported steel purely on grounds of price, so the increased use of English-made iron is likely to have resulted from higher quality rather than lower price. Most improvements in the technology probably occurred incrementally through trial and error, but evidently something significant changed at the start of the eighteenth century. A worker who left one of the Swedish ironworks was credited with a great improvement in the quality of English steel around 1700,[134] but what expertise he might have brought is unknown, especially as Sweden's expertise was in ironworking rather than steelmaking. One important change was the use of a better quality of iron, and especially the switch from English iron to Swedish iron, but this happened much earlier. Another aspect was improvement in the forging of blister steel, and especially the making of shear steel, but at first the latter was produced only in small quantities at one site. The crucial change around 1700 remains to be identified. It coincided approximately with a shift in the location of steel furnaces, usually moving closer to their customers.

Despite the improvement in English-made steel, foreign steel continued to be imported for some purposes, and the imported steel was more valuable: in the 1700s Crowley's selling prices were 4d per pound for English steel and 6d per pound for imported German steel.[135] Nevertheless, whereas in the seventeenth century England had been marginal to European steelmaking, and most steel had been imported from Germany, from about 1700 great progress was made in supplying England's steel demand from its own furnaces, albeit using imported iron.[136] The foundations had been laid from 1614 onwards, but it seems to have been in the decades around 1710 that English steelmaking became a substantial industry, providing the basis for major growth during the rest of the eighteenth century and beyond.

---

134 Cranstone, 'From slitting mill', p. 41.

135 Evans and Rydén, *Baltic iron*, p. 139; Chris Evans and Alun Withey, 'An enlightenment in steel? Innovation in the steel trades of eighteenth-century Britain', *Technology and Culture*, 53 (2012), p. 537; Flinn and Birch, 'English steel industry', p. 166.

136 Evans and Withey, 'Enlightenment in steel?', pp. 534–7.

Chapter 5

Out of the shadows:
searching for lost Domesday landscapes

Ian D. Rotherham

Over the last 20 years, European ecological history and the nature of the so-called primeval landscape have been hotly debated.[1] These discussions have informed policy debates about the 'rewilding' of landscapes, but most advocates of rewilding have failed to understand the historical drivers that helped create modern countryside.[2] It in this context that cross-disciplinary research by historians, archaeologists and ecologists across the UK and Europe has taken place, with intensive studies in the South Pennines and Peak District, which we discuss here. This has been driven by the need to understand the past, to inform the present and to guide future countryside management. One outcome has been the recent discovery of 'shadow woods' and the recognition of the lineage of modern-day heaths and moors from medieval wood-pastures and wooded commons.[3] At the time of Domesday (1086) the core study area (situated just west of Sheffield) had many thousands of acres of wood-pasture but few 'woods', and this provides a glimpse into landscape origins. The study region was one about which David Hey wrote extensively.[4] Today the ecological 'shadows' of the wood-pastures remain in moors, heaths and bogs, but are largely unrecognised. This has major significance for any future 'wilding'.

In order to fully understand the complexities of modern treescapes descended and evolved from historic landscapes, it is necessary to take a multi-disciplinary approach. Experience suggests that in practice this is rarely achieved and consequently many studies lack the joined-up research by historians, ecologists, archaeologists, mycologists and soil scientists which would be the ideal. However, in the present study emerging paradigms in British historic landscape development have been tested and refined through a case-study approach

---

1   F.H.W. Vera, *Grazing ecology and forest history* (Wallingford, 2000); O. Rackham, *Woodlands* (London, 2006).

2   I.D. Rotherham, 'The call of the wild. Perceptions, history, people and ecology in the emerging paradigms of wilding', *ECOS*, 35 (2014), pp. 35–43.

3   I.D. Rotherham, *Shadow woods: a search for lost landscapes* (Sheffield, 2017).

4   D. Hey, *Derbyshire, a history* (Lancaster, 2008); D. Hey, 'The grouse moors of the Peak District', in P.S. Barnwell and Marilyn Palmer (eds), *Landscape history after Hoskins*, 3, *Post-medieval landscapes* (Macclesfield, 2007), pp. 68–79; D. Hey, *A history of the Peak District Moors* (Barnsley, 2014); D. Hey, 'A manorial history at Holmsfield', in *Essays in Derbyshire history presented to Gladwyn Turbutt*, Derbyshire Record Series (Chesterfield, 2015), pp. 1–20.

applying multi-disciplinary research across a number of regions. This chapter reports the wider findings in the context of the core study area of the Peak District and south Pennine moorlands. The studies have involved extensive field survey of ecological, soil and archaeological features, map-based interpretation, archival study and inspection of aerial photography and LiDAR imagery. In particular, teams of trained community 'citizen scientists' have helped survey and map indicator species, mainly plants, which help identify anciently wooded sites.[5] This information can be used to create computer-based maps that can be interrogated to reconstruct images of past landscapes.

I

Before considering the regional heritage of moorland and woodland in the south Pennines and Peak it is necessary to be more precise about the nature of a 'wood', as opposed to merely woodland.[6] Moorlands, heaths and commons also require definition, as it was generally from these landscapes that woods were enclosed.[7]

Woods

These are treed sites enclosed from the wider countryside, named and managed over subsequent centuries. Trees were protected from large grazing herbivores at least during the early years of the coppice cycle or after major tree-felling to allow regeneration of the wood.

Wood-pastures

These are treed landscapes that mix tree cover with open ground for large grazing herbivores, both wild and domesticated. The most widely recognised forms of wood-pastures are parks, chases, forests and wooded commons.

Lost woods

Enclosed woods often suffered damage, loss or destruction over the centuries following their establishment. So lost woods are sites that were enclosed and named but where the tree cover was subsequently removed, whether by conversion to farmland or as a result of urban development or the building of infrastructure such

---

5   I.D. Rotherham, 'A landscape history approach to the assessment of ancient woodlands', in E.B. Wallace (ed.), *Woodlands. Ecology, management and conservation* (New York, 2011), pp. 161–84; P. Glaves, I.D. Rotherham, B. Wight, C. Handley and J. Birbeck, *A report to the Woodland Trust. A survey of the coverage, use and application of ancient woodland indicator lists in the UK* (2009).

6   Rotherham, *Shadow woods*.

7   *Ibid.*; Glaves *et al., Report to the Woodland Trust*.

as roads, or simply by being opened up and reverting to a grazed landscape.[8] Some ancient woods, such as Gardom's Coppice in the Peak District, still exist but have been 'lost' from memory and even from maps. This ancient wood, now shrouded by secondary birch growth, has over 1,000 veteran coppice trees that were overlooked by contemporary ecological surveyors mapping ancient trees and woods.[9]

Ghost woods

When a wood is lost its destruction may be total, with the tree cover completely removed. However, in many cases the ghost of a lost wood can be seen in the landscape, where physical features such as woodbanks, walls, charcoal hearths, lanes and so on survive. In many cases, veteran trees and ancient woodland botanical indicators mark the area of a past wood now etched into the modern landscape. Even in intensively farmed or highly urbanised areas, these indicators survive alongside field names and place-names associated with woodland use.

Shadow woods

The concept of 'shadow woods' as lost Domesday landscapes is one of the most exciting outcomes from the on-going research.[10] These are remnants of once extensive Domesday wood-pastures that survived unenclosed into the medieval period as wooded commons. In other words, it was from landscapes such as these that our woods originated. Remarkably, having survived episodes of medieval and then parliamentary enclosure, some areas of wood-pasture remain. Some Peak District moors were described on nineteenth-century maps as 'wood-pastures'. In the current research they were initially identified by detailed field surveys of indicators, soils and other evidence. Not being 'woods', these sites often have limited documentary evidence associated with them.

Lost woods and shadows

Perhaps the biggest issue in terms of shadows and ghosts is that of being able to see them, to recognise them and then to understand them. First of all, we need to see them in the landscape. It has been an interesting experience to go in search of lost landscapes, of hidden ecologies and forgotten histories. Yet once you begin to see the evidence and to read the signs, a whole new landscape comes to life. It has been there all the time, but we have simply failed to see it.[11]

---

8   H. Lewis, 'Interactions between human industry and woodland ecology in the South Pennines', unpublished PhD (Universities of Bradford, Hull and Sheffield Hallam, 2019).

9   Rotherham, *Shadow woods*.

10   *Ibid.*, Rotherham, 'A landscape history approach'.

11   Lewis, 'Interactions'.

The key questions to be considered in this chapter relate to the origins of enclosed 'ancient woods', the development of unenclosed wood-pastures and the nature of the countryside within which enclosure took place. The practice of managing woods by formal coppice was known to the Romans. Coppice woods mostly originated, however, after Domesday, though some may go back to the preceding Saxon countryside.[12] Once enclosed, the 'woods' were managed over centuries as simple coppice or coppice-with-standards; those which survive today are our 'ancient woodlands'. Botanical indicators of ancient woodlands are plants that provide robust evidence of antiquity and continuity often back to these medieval landscapes, but not, as is often assumed, to some semi-mythical 'wildwood'. Domesday provides evidence that these woods were enclosed from the extensive wood-pasture of the time. The areas remaining unenclosed were then mostly a mix of royal forest and wooded commons.

II

England is unique in possessing the Domesday Book, compiled in and around 1086 as a record of taxable land use by the conquering Normans.[13] Domesday is of particular interest because it tells us, manor by manor, the extent of the lands in various uses. Especially interesting are the descriptions of wooded landscapes or woodlands. While Domesday does not always give details of woodland, where it does it tells of a countryside dominated by open wood-pastures but with little enclosed coppice wood.

While we know that in Roman times there was extensive clearance of woods and forests from lower-lying areas in particular, in the post-Roman period the woodlands probably spread back across abandoned farmland and other cleared areas. It is not unusual for today's ancient woodlands to have Romano-British remains such as villas and farmsteads within them. Furthermore, if we go back beyond the Romans, the earlier settlers undoubtedly cleared wooded landscapes in both upland Britain (such as the Peak District and Pennines, for example) and lowland areas such as Dorset, Wiltshire and East Anglia. Evidence of forest or woodland clearance comes from sediments washed down into low-lying areas such as the Cambridgeshire Fenlands and the Wash, the Nottinghamshire Trent Valley, the Thames Valley and elsewhere. Pollen and insect records, cultivation evidence and other sources tell of clearance from an early date and of grazing landscapes maintained with much-reduced tree cover from the Neolithic, the Bronze Age and the Iron Age. Open brecklands, sheep-walk downs and similar areas were cleared and used from ancient times. However, even in these cleared landscapes the character of open, grazed lands with occasional trees or thickets is that of wood-pasture. Furthermore, as land that was poor but easy to cultivate was cleared of trees, ploughed, burnt and grazed, its soils were leached of those minerals originally present. These areas included rolling chalk and limestone downs and wolds and nutrient-poor acidic sandstones, granites and gritstones.

---

12   Rotherham, *Shadow woods.*
13   *Ibid.*, O. Rackham, *The history of the countryside* (London, 1986).

Once these soils are disturbed their future land use is limited by lack of nutrients; extensive grazing is often all they can sustain. (Once petro-chemicals and technology became available, many such areas quickly succumbed to ploughing and intensive farming.)[14]

From this cursory discussion it is clear that tree cover has retreated over time from many areas. Its removal began with the first major periods of human settlement. In fact, much early occupation by people specifically targeted areas that were easy to clear, such as open forest and woodland on higher ground or poorer soils. Intensive land use was unsustainable and many areas never recovered from consequent nutrient depletion. Post-clearance vegetation recovery was influenced and affected by large grazing herbivores, either domesticated or wild, or both. It is also clear that woodland and tree cover ebbed and flowed over centuries with changing human cultures and as populations rose and fell. Woodlands retreated through the Bronze Age and Iron Age, and especially with the Romans. However, they expanded again through the Saxon and Viking colonisations, only to retreat again as human populations rose. with warm weather and farming advances in the medieval feudal period. Then, as the Black Death ravaged Europe's population, the human pressure on countryside resources reduced swiftly and dramatically, and woodland and wood-pastures expanded again.

During the earlier post-Conquest period England's population grew and parishes and manors expanded. Land clearance began on better areas around settlements, progressing outwards to boundaries with adjacent settlements and onto poorer soils. Wooded areas were inexorably squeezed by the need for resources, especially for arable land for tillage. Woods and trees survived on poor soils and inaccessible terrain and in more remote parts of parishes. However, in a medieval landscape it was vital to balance resource usage and availability and both trees and woodland were essential to survival. While, in the pre-Domesday countryside of few people and plentiful resources, conservation and management were not essential, by the thirteenth and fourteenth centuries each community would be painfully aware of vulnerability to shortage. With growing human populations across Europe, peripheral lands came under increasing pressure,[15] and the key assets of the manor needed to be carefully managed if they were to be sustained. This realisation was probably at the core of the 'Charter of the Commons' of 1217, that 'Magna Carta of the rural landscape'.[16] The manor was parcelled up into areas, each of which had rights and uses assigned them. For the production of sustainable wood and timber, enclosed 'woods', with protection from grazing animals, were necessary. The exclusion of stock (and if necessary local peasants) was enforced by an employed woodward. In many lowland areas timber and wood were sourced from sometimes-extensive hedgerows.

---

14   I.D. Rotherham, 'Cultural severance and the end of tradition', in Rotherham (ed.), *Cultural severance and the environment. The ending of traditional and customary practice on commons and landscapes managed in common* (Dordrecht, 2013), pp. 11–30.

15   Rackham, *Woodlands*, pp. 117–25.

16   Rotherham, *Shadow woods*; Rackham, *History of the countryside*.

Gradually, too, and usually (but not always) with royal permission in the form of a grant of free warren and a licence to impark, manorial lords enclosed further areas as hunting parks.[17] These varied from the very small – perhaps a few fields in size – to the very large. Such land grabs were often hugely unpopular with commoners, as they involved countryside over which they had formerly exercised customary rights. With their day-to-day and year-to-year survival depending on access to vital resources, peasants and other commoners were naturally protective of their rights.[18]

III

In the Domesday countryside, individual manors were carved out of the landscape often by the partition of larger landholding units. In the lowlands the fluid, dynamic, pre-enclosure countryside was morphing into the fixed medieval pattern.[19] Most manors had fields in common use for arable; temporary, uncultivated fallow (land left uncultivated to replace depleted nutrients); and temporary or seasonal pasture. This system included grazing animals: cattle for dairy products and hides, sheep for wool, pigs for meat, and beasts of burden. It needed hay meadows, often along watercourses, where winter flooding provided free fertiliser. Land beyond the arable fields and meadows pastured livestock and often included extensive heaths and commons managed as wood-pasture and wooded common. Depending on location and topography, a manor might also include bogs, moors, fens and coastal flats or dunes. With little fresh forage available, keeping and maintaining stock through the long winters of the 'Little Ice Age' was a challenge.[20]

Medieval enclosure fixed lands such as parks, woods and fields inside clear boundaries. Areas such as heaths, commons, moors, bogs and fens were still open and less rigorously or less intensively managed. The boundaries of fields, lanes and other areas might include banks and hedges, which over time became important sources of fuelwood, wood for charcoal manufacture and building timber. This pattern continued until the parliamentary enclosures of the late eighteenth century. Commoners might retain certain rights within the pale (the fixed boundary ditch, bank, wall, hedge or fence) or wood-bank of the park or wood. However, these were severely curtailed and mostly overseen and administered on behalf of the lord. In some cases, local peasant pig-herders might pay for autumn access to the park or wood for pannage, when the pigs were fed on the autumn crop of acorns, sweet chestnuts or beech mast to fatten up prior to winter slaughter.[21]

In this largely unenclosed landscape, fen, bog, moor, heath and commons remained open and still covered extensive areas. In dry inland areas and along

---

17 I.D. Rotherham, 'The historical ecology of medieval deer parks and the implications for conservation', in R. Liddiard (ed.), *The medieval park: new perspectives* (Macclesfield, 2007), pp. 79–96.

18 Rackham, *History of the countryside*.

19 Rotherham, *Shadow woods*.

20 Rackham, *History of the countryside*.

21 M. Jones, *Sheffield's woodland heritage*, 4th edn (Sheffield, 2009).

sandy, wind-swept coasts, commonlands were joined by sand dunes and associated habitats to form interconnected networks and mosaics of unimproved areas.[22] However, many rural commonlands were characterised by trees, both managed and unmanaged, and by wildflowers today typical of woodlands. In some countryside areas these trees were undoubtedly managed by coppicing, pollarding and stubbing (cutting at a height between low coppice and high pollard so as to leave 'stubs'). This was probably piecemeal and informal, in marked contrast to management within the wood-bank or park pale. Importantly, over time the woodland element, particularly trees, was reduced on areas of common wood-pasture; wood-pasture became less wooded and morphed into modern heath or moorland. Large trees succumbed to the lack of protection. The older surviving trees were coppices of hazel, holly and oak and veterans of smaller species such as hawthorn, rowan and similar. Wet areas had both alder and willow as self-coppicing trees.

The forms that the manorial landscape took varied with place and topography. A Midland parish might have a typical three-field system of two fields in arable and one rested as fallow, where an upland parish might have variants on infield–outfield cultivation. However, there are also upland examples of strip-field systems and lynchets (linear strips). The intensity of use varied with the demands of population growth and the lack of available labour in times of population decrease. Furthermore, the key to long-term success was the careful management of nutrients and fertility through balancing grazing, dunging and harvesting. Get this wrong and the chances of survival and good health diminished. This landscape also had to supply fuels for cooking and keeping warm and materials with which to build shelters and to manufacture tools and other necessities. Alongside arable and hay-meadow, commonlands supplied fuelwood, building stone, fuels (such as turf, gorse and fern), herbs, small game, fowl, wood for small construction and grazing for livestock, including, in lowland wet areas, geese.[23] These were all essential to life in the medieval English countryside.

Clearly, in unravelling the fates and timelines of these resources, ownership, rights and control are important. Enclosed medieval woods were valuable assets that generated both resources, such as fuel and building timber, and income. These were carefully and rigorously protected and managed. Wooded commons were important in the rural economy for the upkeep of the peasantry and the poor. A potential conflict could and did arise when competing common rights led to problems such as over-grazing, preventing tree regeneration. Important in these nutrient-poor, acidic upland wood-pastures were woody species such as holly and gorse, both widely harvested as herbage for grazing livestock. In the lord's woods or park a degree of control might be imposed by the landowner, whereas on the commons management was more easily compromised and restrictions flouted.

---

22 Rotherham, *Shadow woods*.

23 Donald Woodward, 'Straw, bracken and the Wicklow whale', *Past and Present* 159 (1998), pp. 43–76.

IV

Despite popular myth, today's ancient woods are not 'wildwood'. After many centuries of often intensive management, they are only tenuously linked to such landscapes.[24] Within their boundary banks, ditches, walls, fences and hedges, medieval woodlands under newly imposed, closeted management regimes grew tall trees for timber and dense underwood or coppice for fuelwood and charcoal. Through longer timber cycles and shorter coppice cycles, grazing animals were strictly controlled to prevent damage to regrowth.[25] 'Woods' were increasingly valued for their economic rather than subsistence benefits, producing income from timber, tanyard bark, wood-fuel and charcoal-making for their owners. Specialist workers oversaw, cared for and managed woodland operations. Within the wood both timber cycle and coppice cycle involved periodic oscillations of environmental conditions, especially light, moisture and humidity. In managed coppice, wood was periodically cut back almost to the ground, allowing full penetration of sunlight to the woodland floor. Springwood regrowth then came back and gradually darkness fell once again on the ground flora. With the taller timber trees a similar cycle occurred over decades rather than years. These cycles generated pulses of light and warmth, of drought and desiccation, and then darkness, humidity, shade and moisture.

The regular cycles of managed woods were imposed on top of annual seasonal cycles (winter–spring–summer–autumn). The spring flora or vernal flowering exploits early-season light in the wood while soils are still moist. In the dappled shelter of the wood, early insect pollinators actively undertake fertilisation, seeds are set and ripening occurs by the time the canopy closes and shuts out summer sun. By mid- to late summer, the ground is desiccated and hardened by the water demands of tall 'forest' trees in mature woodland. Spring flowers wither and dry, retreating back into over-wintering bulbs or rhizomes or simply entering a dormant phase of inactivity. In many cases, woodland flowers do not *need* prolonged shade; in fact, the very opposite. They thrive in sunlight as long as there is also moisture and an absence of more competitive species. The early phase of the coppice cycle, for example, is characterised by a dramatic blooming of primroses, early purple orchids, bluebells, cowslips, wood stitchwort, wild garlic, lesser celandine and more.[26] However, shade is essential to maintain woodland ground flora in competition with the taller, more competitive herbs and shrubs that characterise open habitats. Shade and drought eliminate competitors, allowing woodland species to thrive. This 'boom and bust' process of 'hide and seek' with sunlight and moisture is played out seasonally as tree canopies dictate, and over cycles of years and decades as coppice is cut and trees harvested. Woodland spring flowers are well adapted to their particular ecological niche. Philip Grime showed how species

---

24 Rotherham, *Shadow woods*; O. Rackham, *Trees and woodlands in the British landscape* (London, 1976); O. Rackham, *Ancient woodland: its history, vegetation and uses in England* (London, 1980).

25 I.D. Rotherham, *Ancient woodland: History, industry and crafts* (Oxford, 2013).

26 Rackham, *History of the countryside*.

such as bluebell are supercharged with cellular nucleic acids so that they explode into early spring growth by 'inflating' huge numbers of pre-formed cells, the building blocks of growth,[27] enabling the flowers to complete cycles of flowering, pollinating and seed-setting before the summertime closure of the woodland canopy shuts out the light.[28]

V

The publication of Oliver Rackham's seminal early books in the late 1970s and early 1980s prompted a reassessment of the nature of the English countryside and especially of its woods and trees.[29] For the first time there were coherent explanations of the remarkable histories and longevity of woods. The 'ancient wood' concept, relating to sites dated to pre-1600 (Rackham) or pre-1700 (Peterken), gained wider recognition – a watershed moment in the general appreciation of the importance of countryside history and environmental history.[30] However, with this awareness developed a popular misconception that these 'ancient woods' were relicts of primeval 'wildwood': ancient, untouched European landscape. This misunderstanding sat comfortably alongside ideas of both British and Western European landscapes originally being clothed by extensive forest from coast to coast.[31] Both these ideas are fundamentally flawed and misleading, but even today they remain widely prevalent in the media and accepted by the general public. One basic problem with the wildwood idea is that the landscape was much wetter, with fens, marshes and bogs covering perhaps half the land area, much of which had relatively few trees.[32]

There remains the question of whether ancient woods are the *descendants* of wildwood. Research into indicator plants and historic sources shows sites recognised as 'ancient woods' today often have remarkable timelines evidenced back to the Middle Ages.[33] However, they are not 'wildwood', and nor are they descended from wildwood as envisioned by the public. Ancient woodland is strongly eco-cultural, its ecology driven by human management over the centuries. What is more, many ancient woods have had long periods as open countryside with few trees or, at least, little close-canopy 'woodland'.

Most ancient woods in the English lowlands show evidence of Romano-British villas and field systems, Iron Age hilltop enclosures, plough-marked stones from prehistoric

---

27   J.P. Grime, J.G. Hodgson and R. Hunt, *Comparative plant ecology. A functional approach to common British species* (Dordrecht, 2007).

28   Rotherham, *Shadow woods*.

29   Rackham, *History of the countryside*; Rackham, *Trees and woodlands*; Rackham, *Ancient woodland*.

30   Rackham, *History of the countryside*; G.F. Peterken, 'A method for assessing woodland flora for conservation using indicator species', *Biological Conservation*, 6 (1974), pp. 239–45; G.F. Peterken, *Woodland conservation and management* (London, 1981).

31   Rackham, *History of the countryside*.

32   I.D. Rotherham, *The lost Fens: England's greatest ecological disaster* (Stroud, 2013).

33   Lewis, 'Interactions'; Rackham, *History of the countryside*; S.P. Day, 'Origins of ancient woodlands', *Landscape archaeology and ecology*, 1 (1993), pp. 12–25.

cultivation and more.[34] Many woods also have evidence of long-term Saxon and Viking occupation or cultivation, which raises questions about where the woods were at that time. As already noted, woods were essential for survival and for producing fuelwood and charcoal (for metal-smelting). In which case, if ancient human settlements were within what today are woods, then the woodland in those earlier times was somewhere else, but where? Furthermore, modern-day 'ancient woods' were mostly enclosed and managed during the medieval period and through intensive interventions of regular cutting and harvesting, their character was transformed.

Therefore, in order to find links to former 'wildwood', it is necessary to look elsewhere. Domesday resonates with the visions of both Vera and Rackham, implying a savanna-like ancient landscape with areas of dense woodland or forest.[35] This more open, fluid wood-pasture connects wilder, freer countryside and this is where we should look for 'wildwood': not inside the ancient woods, but in the wider unenclosed areas that survive.[36]

Over centuries, people transformed the land to create eco-cultural landscapes.[37] While much traditional management slowly modified the environment and created 'countryside', its effects were sometimes dramatic and deeply damaging to ecology. Being reliant on local resources, communities worked to utilise countryside sustainably, but environmental, social and economic factors sometimes forced detrimental impacts. Land use ebbed and flowed as human populations and their demands varied through time and space. However, if over relatively long timescales the management of local resources was not sustainable, then a community's existence was at risk. Such deterioration has fuelled ideas such as Hardin's exposition on the 'tragedy of the commons'.[38] A challenge for modern perceptions is to imagine a countryside on which you depend directly for survival and daily subsistence. To do so is to get inside the lives and countryside of long-lost forbears and to understand the implications of local subsistence.

From perhaps the mid-eighteenth century, a reliance on local countryside resources for subsistence became less important as the twin revolutions in industry and agriculture gathered pace.[39] In particular, petrochemical energy (from first coal and then oil) allowed communities to break out of locally based cycles of energy and

---

34   C.D. Pigott, 'The history and ecology of ancient woodlands', *Landscape History and Archaeology*, 1 (1993), pp. 1–11; Day, 'Origins of ancient woodlands'.

35   Vera, *Grazing ecology and forest history*; Rackham, *Woodlands*.

36   Rotherham, *Shadow woods*; Rotherham, 'A landscape history approach'.

37   An eco-cultural landscape is the result of human–nature interactions over long periods and has significant bio-cultural heritage. See I.D. Rotherham, *Eco-history. An introduction to biodiversity and conservation* (Knapwell, 2014); I.D. Rotherham, 'Bio-cultural heritage and diversity: emerging paradigms in conservation and planning', *Biodiversity and conservation*, 24 (2015), pp. 3405–29 and M. Agnoletti and I.D. Rotherham, 'Landscape and biocultural diversity', *Biodiversity and Conservation*, 24 (2015), pp. 3155–65.

38   G. Hardin, 'The tragedy of the Commons', *Science*, new series 162 (1968), pp. 1243–48. Hardin later modified his position to maintain that it was the tragedy of the *unregulated* commons.

39   Rotherham, *Eco-history*; Rackham, *History of the countryside*.

nutrients. Especially across Western Europe and North America, these processes triggered a dramatic breakdown in relationships between humanity and nature, a process that can be called 'cultural severance'. This seismic transformation reflected the ending of traditional or customary management (and control of resources) by local communities.[40] Today, cultural severance proceeds in less-developed countries within the space of a few decades, whereas in now economically advanced places such as Great Britain it took centuries.

By the end of the eighteenth century wide areas of Britain's countryside had experienced cultural severance as traditional and customary forms of management ceased. Until coal became available to burn for heating and homes acquired the necessary technology to burn it safely, wood and turf from the common remained important fuels, but with improved transportation even remote areas switched from traditional fuels to mineral coal. Common woodland ceased to be important. In a few isolated areas vestiges of community-based subsistence rights lingered to the early twentieth century, but most were lost.[41] A tipping point was the extinguishment of common rights by parliamentary enclosure. Most English commons were enclosed and 'improved', establishing the large, isolated farms characteristic of the early nineteenth century. Nevertheless, these modern farms still relied on people-power and animals to function: former peasant commoners became farm labourers hired by the season and often dependent on poor relief when work was short.[42]

The Peak District moors about which David Hey wrote were enclosed as sheep moor and grouse moor and policed by gamekeepers and bailiffs.[43] The *nouveau* urban poor attempting to escape the dire environmental conditions of industrial towns and access one-time commons for recreation were now 'trespassers'. This was on what had been 'their' (or their parents') common land over which they exercised specific rights but in practice had largely unhindered access for daily activities. Essentially, rural land was largely depopulated, with traditional occupations and utilisation displaced by modern capitalism, labour by machinery. The landscape of extensive heath, moor, common, bog, fen, wood and forest, with areas of relatively intensive farming in champion countryside, was transformed.[44]

Parliamentary enclosures were key triggers in transforming the countryside by removing the extensive commons to leave only tiny lowland fragments with tenuous

---

40   I.D. Rotherham, 'The importance of cultural severance in landscape ecology research', in A. Dupont and H. Jacobs (eds), *Landscape ecology research trends* (New York, 2008), pp. 71–87; Rotherham, 'Cultural severance and the end of tradition', pp. 11–30.

41   Rotherham, *Eco-history*; Rotherham, 'Importance of cultural severance'; Rotherham, 'Cultural severance'.

42   The most recent account stressing the loss of rights and pauperisation of former commoners is J.M. Neeson, *Commoners: common right, enclosure and social change in England, 1700–1820* (Cambridge, 1994).

43   Hey, 'Grouse moors'; Hey, *History of the Peak District Moors*.

44   Rotherham, *Eco-history*.

inter-connections.[45] Wetlands were drained incrementally, a process taking around two centuries to complete. The changes were almost total in the lowlands and transformational but less immediately obvious in the uplands, which is where shadows of past landscapes are mostly found today.[46]

V

Rewilding and wilderness are current topics in conservation debates.[47] Within the broad spectrum of individuals and organisations seeking to create wilder future landscapes there are those seeing heaths and moors as models of rich and sustainable biodiversity. Others feel that heaths are anachronistic landscapes, impoverished and degraded from 'woodland' by human-imposed grazing animals. Yet other rewilders consider large grazing herbivores as key to wilder places (for example, as at Knepp Castle or Wild Ennerdale).[48]

There is a further twist. By supporting plants associated with woodland – bluebell, honeysuckle, greater or wood stitchwort, bilberry, wood sage, creeping soft-grass and more – many heaths are difficult to place within contemporary ideas of landscape ecology. When examined closely, the ecologies of these areas – woods, moors, heaths, fens, parks, forests, and bogs – all have much in common. Moreover, most heaths are clearly human-modified, with intensive past utilisation in subsistence countryside. Evidence of human use and occupation is recorded in field boundaries, prehistoric settlements, ceremonial stones and rock carvings, flint scatters and features dating up to the nineteenth century.[49] Some rewilders view these as cultivated lands, degraded and over-exploited by human occupation and utilisation. Humans arrived, cleared natural 'wildwood', cultivated land – which, given the nature of the poor soils, was unsustainable – and sites descended into low-grade heathland. They argue that releasing sites from human intervention would allow nature to become more 'natural' and 'free-willed'.[50] In practice this

45 I.D. Rotherham, 'Habitat fragmentation and isolation in relict urban heaths: the ecological consequences and future potential', in I.D. Rotherham and J. Bradley (eds), *Lowland heaths: ecology, history, restoration and management* (Sheffield, 2009), pp. 106–15.

46 Rotherham, *Shadow woods*.

47 Rotherham, 'The call of the wild'; Rotherham, 'Cultural severance in landscapes and the causes and consequences for lowland heaths', in Rotherham and Bradley, *Lowland heaths*, pp. 130–43; J. Denton, 'Comment: conservation grazing of heathland: where is the logic?', *British Wildlife*, 24 (2013), pp. 339–47.

48 C. Burrell and T. Greenaway, 'Observations on the Knepp Cattle Wildlife Project', in *The interactions between grazing animals, people and wooded landscapes,* (*Landscape archaeology and ecology*, 9 (2011)), pp. 160–8; J. Gorst and G. Browning, 'Wild cattle and the "wilder valley" experiences. The introduction of extensive grazing with Galloway cattle in the Ennerdale Valley, England', in I.D. Rotherham (ed.), *Trees, forested landscapes and grazing animals: a European perspective on woodlands and grazed treescapes* (Abingdon, 2013), pp. 269–81.

49 Hey, *History of the Peak District Moors*.

50 Mark Fisher, 'Wild nature reclaiming man-made landscapes', *ECOS*, 34/2 (2013), pp. 50–58.

often means allowing secondary ecological successions (the long-term changes in ecological communities of plants and animals) that end in species-poor dense birch wood, bracken beds or gorse. As a consequence, even today these lands are disputed.

There is undoubtedly some truth in this overall broad assessment, but the problem is in the interpretation. In the Peak District and Pennine uplands, for example, we know that early settlers colonised the region from the Mesolithic and Neolithic Ages onward.[51] By Bronze Age and Iron Age times the uplands held significant human populations who left legacies of stone circles, burial mounds or barrows, marked or carved boulders and massive hilltop enclosures. Records of fossil pollen from modern peat bogs show shifts from treescapes to the grasslands, heaths and weeds associated with arable cultivation.[52] The opening up and burning of vegetation and the ploughing of acidic, skeletal soils caused massive leaching of nutrients and downwash of soils through erosion. This process created the modern landscape of upland moor, heath, bog and scattered woodland. The leaching of organic acids and minerals such as iron down the soil profile triggered the deposition of 'iron pans', which impaired drainage and led, via subsequent waterlogging, to the formation of peat bogs.

Evidence for these changes is seen in the upland soils washed downhill to form floodplains along east England's lowland rivers. Similar patterns occurred across the uplands of Dartmoor, Exmoor, Bodmin Moor and elsewhere. Environmental factors influenced human activity, with early communities colonising when the climate was warmer and less wet. More open upland landscapes with fewer and smaller trees than in the lowlands were amenable to clearance and settlement; thin turf was cut and burnt to release nutrients for arable land managed in a manner akin to an infield–outfield system, which helps manage and recycle nutrients effectively. In at least some cases transhumance prevailed, whereby pastoralists took animals to upland grazings and shelters during the summer months, moving back downslope in the winter. This was the case with Dartmoor into the twentieth century and in north-west Scotland until at least the eighteenth century. Though they are declining, similar systems occur around the world today.[53]

VI

Individual case studies are enormously helpful and informative in the search for lost landscapes. Here we consider the evidence for 'shadow wood' sites on the National Trust's Longshaw Estate and the adjacent Eastern Moors Estate in the Derbyshire Peak District. These display evidence of continuous pastoral management up to the

---

51   Hey, *History of the Peak District Moors*.

52   V.M. Conway, 'Ringinglow Bog near Sheffield, pt 1, Historical', *Journal of Ecology*, 34 (1949), pp. 149–81; 'pt 2, The present surface', *Journal of Ecology*, 37 (1949), pp. 148–70.

53   T.C. Smout, *Nature contested. Environmental history in Scotland and northern England since 1600* (Edinburgh, 2000).

Figures 5.1 and 5.2. Longshaw wood-pasture in the eastern Peak District at around 1,000 feet altitude. Photo: Ian Rotherham.

Figure 5.3. Upland willow carr and open heather moorland on the flanks of the Peak District's Eastern Moors at around 1,100 feet altitude. Photo: Chris Percy.

present day.[54] Longshaw is on the west-facing flank of the Eastern Moors and the study area extends up and over the moorland and down to the east-facing slopes around three miles away. Evidence in the landscape indicates that people and their animals were present from pre-Roman times to the modern period. The results of this human impact include a remarkable heritage of biodiversity comprising in some cases almost uniquely rich grassland ecology and small but ancient culturally modified trees.

Burdett's maps of Derbyshire (1767, 1791) are notoriously unreliable in their depiction of both woodland and unenclosed land such as commons, and here he showed no woodland at all. However, on lower ground ancient woods surround Longshaw, including the evocatively named Yarncliff Wood, the 'Eagle Cliff Wood' (woodland enclosed when eagles bred on nearby crags). These are all ancient woods that Burdett omitted to map. Increasingly, too, spreading across heather moorland, are new secondary, semi-natural, birch woods. The open wood-pastures at Longshaw, although heavily grazed even today, have extensive patches of woodland flowers, though these are reduced in stature (Figures 5.1, 5.2). This is one of the UK's best sites for the large red 'hairy wood ants' with huge, domed nests: again, markers of ancient landscapes. Longshaw's claim to ecological fame is in its richly diverse fungi,

---

54   Rotherham, *Shadow woods*; Rotherham, 'A landscape history approach'.

particularly the waxcaps (*Hygrocybe*), and these again are indicators of unimproved grasslands and wood-pastures.[55] Longshaw is one of the most biodiverse sites in Western Europe for these species.[56] Despite recent human impacts on the English uplands, the wider moors and bogs remain hugely important for wildlife. Birds such as golden plover, red grouse and hen harrier thrive on heather moors. Furthermore, areas that either escaped the most intensive usage or are now recovering under conservation management are habitat for rare wildlife and a diverse ecology rarely found elsewhere. However, the over-grazing of uplands by sheep, combined with burning, extensive drainage and removal of peat cover, has decimated many wildlife species. In particular, during the 1970s and 1980s publicly funded upland farming involved so-called 'sheep headage payments' that encouraged damaging, unsustainable grazing.[57]

Around the core study site today the dominant landscape is heather moorland with peat bog and bracken (Figure 5.3). Viewed by many as the 'natural' landscape, it is the result of eighteenth- and nineteenth-century enclosure and management by gamekeepers and tenant sheep-farmers in 'improved' farmsteads. In the early nineteenth century this remote and rather wild landscape attracted the duke of Rutland to Longshaw for its potential for shooting upland game birds on a grand scale. He acquired vast areas of moorland as the manorial lord of several manors, displacing the pastoralist commoners. The imposing ducal shooting lodge, built about 1830 and complete with family chapel and two moorland keepers' lodges, facilitated the shooting of red grouse and black grouse on an almost industrial scale.[58] There followed nearly two centuries of intensive upland management of burning, grazing and draining for maximisation of grouse and sheep, impacts that were compounded by gross air pollution associated with the burgeoning Industrial Revolution.[59] When leisure visitors pour to the Peak District National Park today they perceive this landscape of intensive farming of sheep and grouse, imposed onto an ancient eco-cultural landscape, as 'wild'.[60]

It is important to set this case study into a historic context. As noted earlier, the Domesday account provides insight into a lost countryside. According to Melvyn Jones, Domesday for Derbyshire shows widespread wood-pasture; of 252 manors listed 118 had wood-pasture but only 35 had *silva minuta* (coppice woods). The wood-pasture was very extensive around the Eastern Moors and Longshaw. Edale, with outliers at Aston, Shatton and Tideswell, had over 13,000 acres of wooded commons. Closer to the core site, Hathersage (with outliers at Bamford, Hurst, Offerton and Stony Middleton) had 4,032 acres of wood-pasture. Yet, fast-forward 700 years, and Burdett's 1791

55 Rotherham, *Shadow woods*.

56 S. Evans, *Wax-cap grasslands: an assessment of English sites*, English Nature Research Reports, 555 (2003).

57 Rotherham, *Eco-history*.

58 Hey, 'Grouse moors', pp. 70–1: for enclosure and Rutland's purchases, Hey, *History of the Peak District Moors*, pp. 125–9.

59 Rotherham, *Eco-History*.

60 Rotherham, *Shadow woods*.

map of Derbyshire has only one wood in north-east Derbyshire west of Sheffield (at Padley, which is part of the study area). There was nothing whatsoever at Hathersage or in Edale. The modern 'Ancient Woodland Inventory' shows a good number of ancient woodland sites around the lower parts of the study area (*c*.100 metres above sea level) but none on the higher ground (*c*.300 to 400 metres above sea level).[61] Again, Burdett's maps of 1767 and 1791 omit any reference to woods here, but their presence is confirmed by soils, place-names, botanical indicator species, platforms for charcoal burning and surviving ancient coppice trees dated at well over 500 years old. Nearby plantations from the early 1800s are very clearly different in character and origin from the ancient woods. The main produce from these upland coppice woods was underwood for charcoal manufacture, whereas the later plantations provided owners such as the dukes of Rutland or of Devonshire with both aesthetic pleasure and a timber crop. The latter remained very important until timber imports from the Baltic states became more widely available in the eighteenth century and later.

Much of the landscape here (evidenced by fire-sites and flint scatters) was part-cleared during the Mesolithic (perhaps 5,000 years BC) and in part farmed during the Bronze Age (*c*.1,500 BC), and Iron Age (*c*.800 BC).[62] Later settlers undertook some farming, but many hunted wild grazing animals, particularly red and roe deer, mountain hare and wild boar. Romano-British settlement in the region extended some cultivation onto relatively high ground. These activities removed much of the thin tree cover and caused mass wastage or downwash of soils from the higher ground and from slopes. These changes are evidenced by pollen and sediment profiles in local peat bogs. Soils became impoverished of nutrients, generally acidic and often waterlogged owing to the formation of impermeable 'iron pans' in the soils, following the sequence of developments outlined above.

With deteriorating climate and poorer soils, settlement and cultivation moved downslope and the higher ground was mostly used for grazing livestock and for small cottager farmsteads with some meadow and ploughland. In the twelfth century much of the area was incorporated into the Peak Forest, a royal hunting forest throughout which the forests laws applied. The main beast of the chase here was the red deer. It is likely that many of the enclosed 'woods' were established to protect the trees and coppice wood from grazing deer and domestic livestock. The forest jurisdiction survived until around 1674. The character of the grazing appears to have encouraged the remarkable biodiversity of the short-grazed grasslands here, which also contain evidence of shadow woods in the form of extensive patches of woodland indicator plants.

Continuity of grazing in this area after enclosure was through small farms and cottages located much higher on the hill than present-day settlement and some upland grazings associated with lower-lying settlements. These people probably

---

61 J.M.S. Bevan, D.P. Robinson, J.W. Spencer and A. Whitbread, *Derbyshire inventory of ancient woodland (provisional)*, Nature Conservancy Council (1992). The current version is online at <https://data.gov.uk/dataset/9461f463-c363–4309-ae77-fdcd7e9df7d3/ancient-woodland-england>.

62 D. Garton, 'The North Peak environmentally sensitive area: the impact of erosion on archaeology', *Landscape Archaeology and Ecology*, 4 (1999), pp. 55–8.

grazed the smaller breeds of cattle, plus sheep and pigs. Oak trees were probably managed to produce rich crops of acorns to fatten pigs in the autumn. Some areas under monastic control were dedicated to relatively intensive sheep grazing for wool. These upland farmers harvested small wood and timber too from the upland wood-pastures and wooded commons. While tree cover reduced further, some 'woods' or wooded commons with trees were maintained as important resources.

The abolition of common rights by parliamentary enclosure allowed upland commons to be used exclusively for sheep grazing and grouse shooting. At Longshaw, the estate of the duke of Rutland was developed for shooting. Yet the scale of grazing by sheep and sometimes cattle now exceeded previous levels. Tree cover declined and intensive grazing restricted or prevented regeneration. Some prickly species, such as ancient hawthorns and holly, persisted alongside oaks on remote, rough boulder slopes, crags and wet areas. Large areas of the moors described by David Hey, which were former wooded commons and wood-pastures, were burned on rotation under private ownership to support sheep and grouse, and drained. Once botanically diverse heathy wood-pastures were dramatically reduced in species richness; often to a mix of poor grasses, heather, and bracken.[63]

In the 1930s campaigns to protect the landscape as a national park and to acquire the countryside for conservation and public access commenced. The Longshaw Estate was bought by the National Trust in 1931 after a public appeal and the wider Eastern Moors Estate was acquired by the Peak District National Park in the 1980s. Significantly for landscape and biodiversity, there was continuity of grazing, though periods of tree planting converted some remaining shadow woods into plantations. Grazing levels peaked in the 1970s and 1980s, driven by grant aid, but have since reduced under the influence of conservation-orientated management regimes. Sheep have in part been replaced by cattle and some sites are being rewetted by the blocking of drains. In some cases, these changes have triggered significant ecological recovery.

The slopes of both sides of the higher ground of the Eastern Moors, east-facing and west-facing, have remarkable areas of bluebell-rich vegetation marking former wooded commons, today's shadow woods. These areas combine with ancient wet willow carrs of multi-stemmed veteran trees, scatterings of old hawthorns and rowans, ancient 'medusoid' oaks on higher crags and waxcap-rich acid grasslands to form a complex time-capsule of biodiversity. Roadside grasslands that escaped heavy grazing have rich patches of woodland flowers (bluebell, dog's mercury and wild garlic), which are unexpected at this altitude. These too mark the locations of shadow woods. The wet areas across the moors are characterised by species-rich willow carrs with very old willow trees. The ground flora here is rich in bryophytes such as sphagnum mosses, but also flowering plants such as lesser skullcap and a range of orchids, with bluebells, wild garlic, dog's mercury and greater stitchwort. These areas appear relatively undisturbed and are probably some of the most 'natural' communities in the Peak District National Park. Furthermore, observations nationally have identified similar communities. This

---

63   Rotherham, *Shadow woods*; P. Anderson and D. Shimwell, *Wild flowers and other plants of the Peak District* (Ashbourne, 1981).

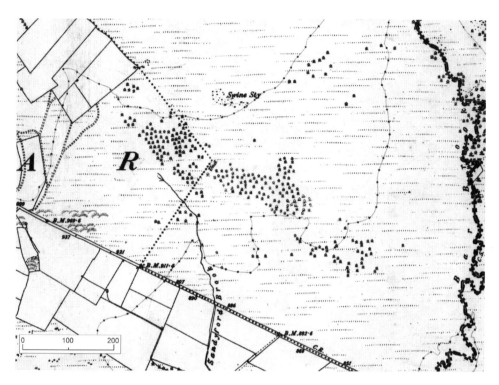

Figure 5.4. Big Moor shadow wood on the 1882 Ordnance Survey map, located on the south-west-facing slopes of the Peak District above Chatsworth Park.

may indicate that these willow communities were formerly more widespread in earlier, undrained countryside – an exciting variant of the shadow woods.

VII

The writings of David Hey brought the history and heritage of these south Pennine moorlands to the attention of a wide audience. Furthermore, new multi-disciplinary research has provided fresh insights and interpretation with applications nationally.[64] However, the future conservation of these historic landscapes remains a major challenge, in part because their ecological timelines and the implications of their evolution are unrecognised by key actors. The origins of moors, heaths, and bogs – which now form landscapes of leisure and recreation – as wood-pasture and wooded common have been misunderstood by most site managers. A danger of this omission is that some conservation priorities may be misaligned and accidental damage to the

---

64 Rotherham, *Shadow woods*; I.D. Rotherham, 'The magic and mysteries of Ecclesall woods', in M. Atherden, C. Handley and I.D. Rotherham (eds), *Back from the edge. The rise and fall of Yorkshire's wildlife*, 2nd edn (Sheffield, 2018), pp. 85–106.

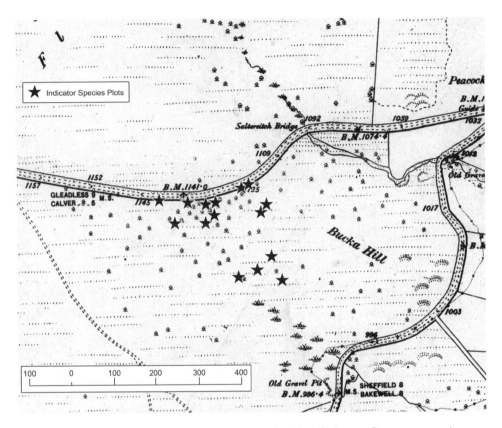

Figure 5.5. Big Moor shadow wood at Bucka Hill on the 1882 Ordnance Survey map and located on the east-facing slopes of the Peak District.

ecology and the heritage continues. In the ancient willow carrs, for example, estate managers have sought to cut the veteran trees to 'open them up' and to 'regenerate them'.[65] In terms of conservation of these long-term unmanaged communities, this is a mistaken approach, unjustified by historical practice.

A priority for management is the recognition of the remarkable eco-cultural nature of this landscape.[66] Problems arose, for example, when the rich bluebell habitats and communities on the east-facing flanks of the area were recognised. The response has been to plant trees. This is inappropriate, as it turns some-time eco-cultural wood-pasture and wooded common into plantation 'woods'. In order to address such issues it is important to understand more about the dynamics of this vegetation, how it survived to the present day and what the future management options might be. Clearly, until the enclosures these communities extended downslope into nearby lower-lying

---

65   Personal observation.
66   Rotherham, *Shadow woods*.

Figure 5.6. Ancient multi-stemmed willow at Houndkirk Moor at around 1,100 feet altitude, on the south-east-facing slope situated just west of Sheffeld. Photo: Chris Percy.

farmland and upslope onto what is now heather moor.[67] This interpretation implies that heather moor resulting from two centuries of draining, burning and intensive sheep-grazing is degenerate wooded common with the trees largely removed. This assertion is confirmed by the Ordnance Survey six-inch maps of the area surveyed in the 1850s and 1880s, which mark scattered trees on today's moorland, showing that it was then 'wood-pasture' (Figures 5.4, 5.5).

These biodiversity-rich communities are in effect time-capsules descended from Domesday landscapes to the present day. If the necessary ecological processes can be unlocked, then these areas might in future serve to re-diversify the now species-poor moorlands. It is likely that the countryside here was more 'woody' downslope and more 'heathy' upslope. Perhaps planting scattered trees in the upper area would speed the process, but natural succession and regeneration are generally preferred. However, the conundrum is that the species-rich ecological

---

67 G. Scurfield, 'The Peak District in the early seventeenth century: pt 1, Hope, woodlands and lands adjacent', *The Peak District Journal of Natural History and Archaeology*, 1 (1999), pp. 1–12; G. Scurfield, pt 2, 'Hartington in 1614', *The Peak District Journal of Natural History and Archaeology*, 1 (1999), pp. 13–26.

communities depend on grazing but how much, by what and when are still unknown; there is much to discover.

In major debates on countryside origins from pre-medieval landscapes and ecologies it is often the case that history has been overlooked. Yet the work of historians such as David Hey and Melvyn Jones has changed our awareness of key processes in the landscape. The broad-brush account contained in Domesday Book provides a glimpse into the nature of anciently treed landscapes. Combining this approach with botanical indicators and issues of comparative plant ecologies and of fluctuating herbivore impacts allows a new vision of upland treescapes to emerge.[68] This has evolved in detail from studies in the countryside about which David Hey wrote so prolifically.

Work in progress shows that some of the coppice oak trees in this landscape, often dismissed by conservation agency colleagues as of little interest, may in fact be from 600 to 1,000 years old. Similarly, the massive, multi-stemmed willows have been tentatively aged by archaeologists as many centuries old (Figure 5.6). Taken together with the map-based and archival studies, the ecological indicators and the field archaeology, this all lends credence to claims of antiquity and continuity.

---

68   Grime, Hodgson and Hunt, *Comparative plant ecology*; Rotherham, *Shadow woods*; Rotherham, 'A landscape history approach'.

Chapter 6

Opposition to parliamentary enclosure in Nottinghamshire

John Beckett

The traditional view of enclosure was that it was a Good Thing. Sociologists and historians alike have argued that the transition to capitalist agriculture that underpinned European industrialisation could be explained only in terms of changes in the agrarian structure that facilitated a steep rise in the output and productivity of farms. Enclosure, it was argued, hastened this process by sweeping away the last vestiges of inefficient, common-field farming. In place of the troublesome open-field farmers – who laboriously toiled their strips with no interest in trying to bring about improvement – came entrepreneurial farmers occupying large, ring-fenced and highly productive holdings. Greater farming efficiency led to the release of labour from the land and the migration of surplus labour from the countryside to urban employments. This view was shared by many contemporaries. As Robert Lowe, who wrote the county report on Nottinghamshire for the Board of Agriculture in 1798, put it, 'the value of land has everywhere been raised by inclosure in greater or lesser degree, in some very greatly.'[1] This positive view of enclosure, shared by both contemporaries and modern commentators, was designed to give the impression that the process was a universal good in the context of English agriculture.[2]

To many contemporary witnesses of parliamentary enclosure its benefits far outweighed any drawbacks that they may, or equally may not, have noticed. Landlords saw the opportunity to raise rents, to do away with unmanageable common rights and to bring unruly open-field farmers to heel via a fixed-term lease or even a tenancy at will. For their part, farmers might object to the higher rents, but they could see the advantage of a ring-fenced farm on which the agricultural practice conformed with their own desires, rather than the common purpose supervised by the manor court. As for the potential human cost, some contemporaries saw it as minimal. R.W. Corringham, discussing the state of agriculture in Nottinghamshire in 1845, said little directly about enclosure (except for wanting the remaining unenclosed areas of the county to be enclosed). He acknowledged the underemployment of the agricultural labourer, and favoured the provision of allotments not only because they improved the condition of the poor but also because they reduced the burden the poor placed on ratepayers.[3] This lack of interest in the social consequences of enclosure seems

---

1 Robert Lowe, *General view of the county of Nottinghamshire* (London, 1798), p. 19.

2 David Hey, *The grass roots of English history: local societies in England before the Industrial Revolution* (London, 2016), pp. 83–5.

3 R.W. Corringham, 'Agriculture of Nottinghamshire', *Journal of the Royal Agricultural Society*, 6 (1845), p. 38.

complacent, but it is widely found. In sum then, enclosure seemed to be a Good Thing because it was believed to have increased the output and productivity of the land and enabled a growing urban–industrial population to be fed.

Other commentators argued that this all came at a cost, a cost that was shouldered by cottagers and others on the land who lost traditional rights to cut furze and turf from the common and to keep a cow. The major proponents of this approach were J.L. and Barbara Hammond, writing before the First World War, who argued that, although the small farmers might receive a share of land at enclosure, most of them were 'overwhelmed' by the legal costs and expenses of fencing and by the loss of fallow and stubble grazing. They had little option but to sell up and leave the land. '[T]he small farmer either emigrated to America or to an industrial town, or became a day labourer.' Furthermore, they added, the impact was felt not only by the first but also by subsequent generations:

> All these classes and interests were scattered by enclosure, but it was not one generation alone that was struck down by the blow. For the commons were the patrimony of the poor. The commoner's child, however needy, was born with a spoon in his mouth. He came into a world in which he had a share and a place. The civilization which was now submerged had spelt a sort of independence for the obscure lineage of the village.[4]

W.E. Tate had little time for what he saw as the negativity of the Hammonds, who, he argued, had grossly exaggerated the extent of opposition to enclosure. Writing in 1944 of parliamentary enclosure in general, he suggested that:

> Of the dozen odd enclosures dealt with in the [Hammonds'] book, every one has at least a counter-petition. Stray instances prove very little, however, and an unkind critic might suggest that these dozen instances are amongst the twelve most scandalous that could be found among some 6000.[5]

Tate's viewpoint was that a systematic analysis of opposition to parliamentary enclosure needed a firm evidential base, and this was not provided by cherry-picking juicy individual cases. He argued that the Hammonds had sought out rare and necessarily atypical cases of opposition to enclosure to create a politically inspired but historically inaccurate view of what had happened.[6]

Subsequent historians have enlarged upon the work of the Hammonds with the result that their view of the relationship between enclosure and agricultural

---

4   J.L. and Barbara Hammond, *The village labourer, 1760–1832: a study of the government of England before the Reform Bill* (London, 1911), pp. 97–103.

5   W.E. Tate, 'Parliamentary counter-petitions during the enclosures of the eighteenth and nineteenth centuries', *English Historical Review*, 59 (1944), p. 398.

6   J.V. Beckett, 'The disappearance of the cottager and the squatter from the English countryside: the Hammonds revisited', in B.A. Holderness and Michael Turner (eds), *Land, labour and agriculture, 1700–1920* (London, 1991), pp. 49–67.

improvement is now held to be seriously flawed. Research begun by Tate and subsequently continued by Michael Turner, has transformed our view of enclosure. Tate and Turner showed how enclosure carried out by parliamentary act affected one in every four acres (one in three in Nottinghamshire), but that, far from denuding the countryside of population, it left numbers in the majority of villages much as before.[7]

This finding does not, of course, imply either that opposition to enclosure was rife in the countryside or that it did not occur at all. One way of testing the issue is to look at a more limited study area than the country as a whole, and for this reason I have chosen to study what happened in one county. It seems appropriate to revisit this debate given that the historiography of enclosure is now very different to that with which Tate was familiar, and the range of archival materials available to historians is much greater than that to which he had access. There is also a much greater sensitivity among historians to regional economies and distinctions and these prove to be of significance in the new account of Nottinghamshire offered here.

Nottinghamshire has been well served for studies of parliamentary enclosure ever since Professor J.D. (David) Chambers and W.E. Tate were working on the subject in the 1920s. Tate compiled a list of all the county's parliamentary enclosures, which was initially published as an appendix to Chambers' book *Nottinghamshire in the eighteenth century* (1932).[8] The list itself, augmented with additional material, was published in 1935.[9] Chambers specifically acknowledged Tate's help but he used the survey findings primarily to discuss the course of parliamentary enclosure in relation to the different parts of the county.[10] His main interest in the effects of enclosure lay with the decline of the yeoman, and he paid little or no attention to any resistance locally to parliamentary enclosure.

Tate's research covered not just Nottinghamshire but parliamentary enclosure more generally. He continued to argue that opposition to it was minimal, a claim he based on information collected from the *Journals of the House of Commons*, in particular counter-petitions presented to enclosure bills. These counter-petitions were, he argued, the only real evidence of opposition to enclosure bills, and there were not many of them. Over the period 1745–1845 he counted 133 parliamentary enclosure acts for Nottinghamshire. In only 11 cases was a counter-petition presented (about 8 per cent) and, in most of these cases, he suggested, the petition came from larger landowners wanting to protect their own interests rather than from the poor and

---

7   W.E. Tate, 'The [eighteenth-century] enclosures of the townships of [Sutton] Bonington St Michael's, Sutton St Ann's, in the county of Nottingham', *TTS*, 34 (1930), pp. 133–50; W.E. Tate, 'A Nottinghamshire Enclosure Commissioner's Minute Book', *TTS*, 41 (1937), pp. 76–86; W.E. Tate, *A Domesday of English enclosure acts and awards*, ed. Michael Turner (1978); M.E. Turner, *English parliamentary enclosure* (Reading, 1980), pp. 135–51.

8   J.D. Chambers, *Nottinghamshire in the eighteenth century* (London, 1932), pp. 333–53.

9   W.E. Tate, 'Parliamentary land enclosures in the county of Nottingham during the 18th and 19th centuries (1743–1868)', *Thoroton Society Record Series*, V (1935).

10   Chambers, *Nottinghamshire*, p. 143; J.L. Purdum, 'Profitability and timing of parliamentary land enclosures', *Explorations in Economic History*, 15 (1978), pp. 313–26 [a study of five Nottinghamshire parishes].

the potentially dispossessed resisting enclosure.

Nor could this easily be disputed. At East Leake bills of 1781 and 1786 were dropped, but the driving force behind the 1781 counter-petition – Sir Thomas Parkyns – was determined to get the terms he wanted. The gentlemen who objected to the Lenton and Radford bill of 1799 were primarily concerned with the fate of horse racing on the Forest recreation ground in Nottingham, while the earl of Chesterfield's opposition to the Calverton bill arose from his belief that the proposed allowance of land in lieu of his rights as hereditary ranger of Thorneywood Chase was inadequate.[11] The primary objection at Kirkby-in-Ashfield in 1795 was from Thomas Webb Edge Esq., and at Spalford and Wigsley in 1813 from Samuel Russell Collet, Esq.[12] This was not the opposition of dispossessed small farmers and cottagers, but of landowners protecting their interests.

Tate also argued that in only five instances in Nottinghamshire were counter-petitions presented by small owners: in Everton (1759), Mattersey (1770), Misterton and Stockwith (1771), Calverton (1779)[13] and Morton and Fiskerton (1803). Of these five, the first four petitions failed to halt the enclosure and the fifth succeeded only in delaying it, albeit for 36 years. This collective evidence led Tate to the conclusion that opposition to enclosure in Nottinghamshire was limited:

> In Nottinghamshire at any rate, it appears that the picture of enclosure as forced from above by squire and parson upon a bitterly hostile countryside has little truth in it. Unless the parliamentary committees were in general composed of the most shameless and brazen liars, so that all entries in the *Journals* are a mere tissue of falsehoods, the movement was accepted by majorities of anywhere from 8:1 to 23:1.[14]

Tate's conclusion was that the evidence of the Nottinghamshire counter-petitions suggested that the whole process was largely uncontested. Nor, probably, would anyone disagree with this analysis. After all, Lord Lincoln, son of the duke of Newcastle and therefore well acquainted with Nottinghamshire, told the House of Commons in 1845 that

> in nineteen cases out of twenty, committees sitting in this House on private bills, neglected the rights of the poor. I do not say that they wilfully neglected those rights – far from it; but this I affirm, that they were neglected in consequence of the committees being permitted to remain in ignorance of the rights of the poor man, because by reason of his very poverty he is unable to come up to London to fee counsel, to procure witnesses, and to urge his claims before a committee of this house.[15]

---

11   M.E. Brown, 'Aspects of parliamentary enclosure in Nottinghamshire', PhD thesis (University of Leicester, 1995), pp. 219–22.

12   NA, DD 4P 62/37; Tate, 'Parliamentary land enclosures', p. 183.

13   There were two counter-petitions at Calverton, one from the earl of Chesterfield and one from William Huthwaite and others.

14   W.E. Tate, 'Opposition to parliamentary enclosure in eighteenth-century England', *Agricultural History*, 19 (1948), p. 142.

15   *Parliamentary Debates (Commons)*, 1 May 1845.

Parliamentary counter-petitions were, in Lincoln's view, the preserve of the rich man protecting his rights, rather than the potentially dispossessed cottager, the small farmer and the squatter who were the most likely to suffer from loss of privileges. Nor has this judgement been seriously challenged. Dr Margery Brown's reassessment of Tate's work unearthed material that he did not find but, like Tate, she concluded that, when measured from the official records, parliamentary enclosure in Nottinghamshire was 'seemingly relatively peaceful'.[16]

I

Do these official records tell the whole story? Even Tate accepted that relying purely on counter-petitions to estimate opposition to enclosure was likely to produce a limited picture. He noted of Nottinghamshire that many enclosure bills were not carried when they were first introduced and that there were plenty of examples where the proprietors were far from unanimous in promoting enclosure. This might not be *positive* evidence of opposition, but it implied that there was doubt. Tate accepted that opposition might be construed from the evidence of bills being dropped before completing their passage through parliament, something that happened in one-fifth of all cases (38 out of 133, i.e. 29 per cent).

A further issue was the quality of the archival material. A case in point was Norwell, in central Nottinghamshire. It was one of a group of late enclosed parishes in the county where an earlier bill had been introduced and then dropped, indicating that there was some opposition, although the bill that went through in 1826 did so unopposed.[17] Fortuitously a substantial cache of papers relating to the Norwell enclosure has survived, including two commissioners' minute books (1826–9 and 1829–34).[18] It is in these books that we can find evidence indicating that the process of enclosure authorised by the 1826 act did not go particularly smoothly. The Norwell commissioners were experienced in this sort of work and swiftly got down to what turned out to be a protracted business. Through 1828, for example, they had to deal with problems over the depasturing of sheep and cattle on open meadow land, as well as fencing, ploughing and a range of other pressing agricultural issues.[19] Norwell was a contentious enclosure, with disputes over roads, over the farming cycle, over who was entitled to which crop and much more. The case may not have been highlighted in parliament, but the long-drawn out process was itself a sign of opposition, certainly to the outcome if not also to the structure of the enclosure.[20]

Completing the enclosure could take considerable time if there was contention. At Norwell it was seven years (1826–33) and yet there was no sign on the ground of opposition: no riots, fights, brawls, rick burning, machine smashing, just a small

---

16   Brown, 'Aspects of parliamentary enclosure', pp. 194, 225.

17   Wallace Smith, *The enclosure of Norwell* (Retford, 1968).

18   NA, DD.M 55/21, 90. The catalogue entry at Nottinghamshire Archives for the enclosure of Norwell includes no fewer than 112 separate items.

19   NA, DD.M. 55/90, 7 December 1830.

20   Smith, *Norwell.*

amount of reorganisation, a few 'poorer cottages' being displaced from their strips and relegated to allotments, and the whole business completed on 10 October 1832. However, as the commissioners did not complete their work formally until August 1833 there is a hint here of internal controversy over the way in which the enclosure was handled.[21]

For more than half of the Nottinghamshire parliamentary enclosure cases there is the *possibility* of opposition measured in terms of counter-petitions, bills being withdrawn and proprietors failing to reach a unanimous viewpoint. Splicing the evidence from various sources together, I have identified 69 instances where parliamentary enclosure seems to have been entirely unopposed. By contrast, there are 84 cases in which it is possible to suggest that there may have been some sort of dissent, even if it took the form only of the successful enclosure bill being preceded by an earlier bill that was dropped. (The enclosures judged to be opposed or unopposed are listed in the Appendix.) Such evidence is, we may argue, insubstantial, but it suggests some degree of dissatisfaction with the process of parliamentary enclosure.

Yet even this conclusion may not get us anywhere near the true extent of opposition to enclosure. The question still arises of whether the small farmer, the cottager and the squatter really were the silent victims of enclosure, or whether they put up a fight: in other words, out of the various interest groups who might have opposed enclosure did any of them do so and, if so, how? In 1984 Dr Jeannette Neeson published a path-breaking study of enclosure in Northamptonshire. In her article, and a subsequent book, she rejected Tate's method of working and suggested that his emphasis on counter-petitions to parliament merely provided an index of *parliamentary* activity, and that this was 'no guide to protest at all'.[22] Neeson stressed the point originally made by Lord Lincoln: that the cottagers, squatters and small farmers identified as the chief victims of enclosure were in no position to submit counter-petitions to parliament, and that any opposition that they might mount was likely to take place locally, perhaps with a greater emphasis on direct action. Consequently, so her argument ran, Tate looked in the wrong place, and the real evidence of opposition was to be found in a much broader range of documentary sources, notably newspaper reports and judicial proceedings. Her views chimed with the findings from studies of Buckinghamshire and Warwickshire.[23]

Neeson also noted that opposition took different forms in different parishes and under different farming and tenurial conditions. Counter-petitioning was most likely in parishes with divided landownership and in which one or another owner believed their interests were not being properly protected. By contrast, popular opposition was most likely to occur in those parishes that still had extensive common land at the time of

---

21   Michael Jones, *Norwell Farms*, Norwell Heritage Booklet 5 (Nottingham, 2009), pp. 20–22.

22   J. Neeson, 'The opponents of enclosure in eighteenth-century Northamptonshire', *Past and Present*, 105 (1984), pp. 114–39; J. Neeson, *Commoners: Common right, enclosure and social change in England, 1700–1820* (Cambridge, 1993).

23   Michael Turner, 'Opposition to parliamentary enclosure in Buckinghamshire', *Southern History*, 10 (1988), pp. 94–128; J.M. Martin, 'The parliamentary enclosure movement and rural society in Warwickshire', *Agricultural History Review*, 15 (1967), pp. 32–9.

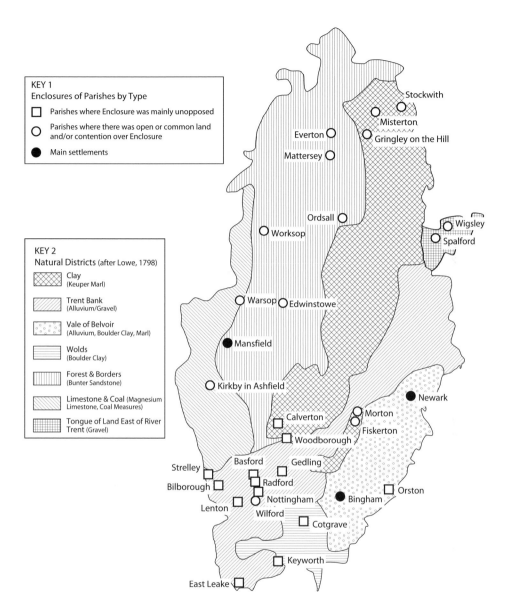

KEY 1
Enclosures of Parishes by Type

□ Parishes where Enclosure was mainly unopposed

○ Parishes where there was open or common land and/or contention over Enclosure

● Main settlements

KEY 2
Natural Districts (after Lowe, 1798)

Clay (Keuper Marl)

Trent Bank (Alluvium/Gravel)

Vale of Belvoir (Alluvium, Boulder Clay, Marl)

Wolds (Boulder Clay)

Forest & Borders (Bunter Sandstone)

Limestone & Coal (Magnesium Limestone, Coal Measures)

Tongue of Land East of River Trent (Gravel)

Figure 6.1. The enclosure of open fields and waste lands in the county of Nottingham (after Tate, 1935).

enclosure, particularly forest parishes where squatters and commoners were able to eke out a living without having been able to gain any sort of legal claim to ownership.

II

What happens when we apply Neeson's revisionist thinking to parliamentary enclosure in Nottinghamshire? Broadly speaking, if the Neeson model is correct, we would expect to find at least two different patterns within the county, the first on the claylands of the Trent Valley. Here some of the land was still in open fields, but a considerable acreage had been the subject of ancient enclosure. In these areas as well much of the common had been encroached upon. Popular opposition to enclosure was usually minimal. Figure 6.1 demonstrates this, particularly the cluster of parishes in the south of the county where enclosure was not opposed. The second pattern we might anticipate finding would be in the forest parishes with extensive common grazing and open heathland. If the Neeson model had any predictive power, then here we might expect to discover much greater levels of opposition to the enclosure process, when former waste and common land was parcelled up into private property. Here, customary rights and values had persisted long into the eighteenth century, not infrequently with rival interpretations as to what was meant by customary and common rights. Residents of Worksop claimed rights in 1749 over 141 acres of common bordering Welbeck Park, and the resultant enquiry highlighted a customary forest economy working at the margins of the Dukeries parks. John Strutt of Elkesley, aged 61, a wheelwright, claimed that 'the poorer sort of people of the parish of Worksop … burnt the bracken growing upon the said piece of ground without interruption from anybody', and that 'he used to fetch sticks to burn out of Welbeck Park'. Several villagers testified to taking in the common during the annual parish perambulation. The conviction among people that they had rights such as these could not be easily overturned. Even Tate, although he seems scarcely to have recognised the fact, found an imbalance between the Trent Valley and the Forest, because four of the five parishes in which he detected opposition from small owners were forest parishes.[24] We need to look at these two different patterns separately.

III

First, enclosure in the Trent Valley, on the open-field mixed farming areas of the county, was relatively painless. With little common surviving and few if any common rights to be exercised, most of the problems that occurred in this area were of the sort Tate was looking for, where landowners and tithe owners fell out over the way enclosure should take place and the subsequent distribution of land. This did not make them reckless; indeed, landowners were usually on the lookout for ways of avoiding disputes, as these could all too easily involve lawyers and become expensive. In several cases the enclosure *preceded* the legislation. At Cotgrave the bill was petitioned on 2 February

---

24   D.V. Fowkes, 'The Breck System of Sherwood Forest', *TTS*, 81 (1977), pp. 55–61.

1790 and passed the House of Lords on 6 May.[25] No one was waiting for the act, let alone the award. On 18 February William Sanday, acting for Charles Pierrepont, Earl Manvers, told William Pickin, the chief steward on Manvers' estate at Thoresby, that he was having difficulty setting out the farms and would value a visit to help agree the boundaries.[26] In other words the enclosure was sorted out before the act passed, hence its title: 'An Act to *confirm and establish* the division, apportionment, and inclosure of the open fields, meadows, pastures, commons, and waste grounds lying within the parish of Cotgrave ... and several exchanges of land within the said parish' (author's italics). Part of Sanday's problem was the preferential treatment of his son. There were clearly rumblings that Sanday junior had received special treatment with an unexpectedly large farm, but this was grumbling rather than opposition.[27]

Once the bill became law in May 1790 common rights were extinguished and the boundaries staked out so that the farmers could begin to cultivate the land in severalty.[28] The task of fencing, meanwhile, took several years to complete. Manvers spent large sums of money on boundaries, an expenditure that continued for about four years after the act passed.[29] In February 1793, for instance, he paid £2 2s 2d to Thomas Scrimshaw for 'setting down double posts and rails, making two dykes, and setting quick 9a 3r 0p at 4s. 4d. per acre in Cotgrave inclosure'. This may have delayed the final award but it was never going to alter the outcome.

Sanday rather liked this method of allotting the land in advance of the act, and he was keen to try it at Gedling until the lawyers intervened:

> With respect to Mr Sanday's recommendation to have the parish first surveyed, divided and allotted and then to subscribe to Parliament to confirm etc, it is a measure we never can subscribe to for a thousand reasons, and if insisted upon this inclosure must be dropped.[30]

For the enclosure to proceed an agreement was needed on the manorial rights and tithe allotments. By February 1792 it was agreed that the earl of Chesterfield and Earl Manvers would share the manorial rights between them.[31] In other words, potential disputes among the greater landowners (let alone between them and other interested parties) were resolved before the enclosure came anywhere near parliament, although, simply because there is some evidence of dissension, Gedling appears in the list of disputed enclosures.[32]

It was not quite as straightforward as this in Keyworth, but it was not very different. The act was passed early in 1798 without noticeable opposition. Within days the

---

25 NUMASC, Ma 2P/16/1.
26 NUMASC, Ma B 244/15.
27 *Ibid.*
28 NUMASC, Ma 2P/17.
29 NUMASC, Ma B 16/111 .
30 NUMASC, Ma B 99/3.
31 NUMASC, Ma B 99/9. The tithe lands had yet to be decided at this point.
32 NA, Ma B 99/20, 45.

commissioners were hard at work, and the award was completed in 1799. The lack of direct evidence, particularly the absence of commissioners' minute books or of related estate papers from the lord of the manor, makes definitive judgement problematic, but we can be sure that parliamentary enclosure was implemented with little or no serious trouble.[33] Enclosure in Keyworth seems to have had only a minimal impact on village life: 'the social pattern of the village had been relatively little affected by the change.'[34] There are plenty of similar examples. At Woodborough the enclosure bill was petitioned on 22 January 1795. The extent of support for the bill was then investigated by a committee, which reported on 5 May. The bill passed through its various stages, clearing the House of Lords on 27 May. No opposition seems to have been offered at any stage.[35]

IV

These relatively straightforward enclosures on the clay can be contrasted with enclosure in the forest areas, where the process involved considerable acreages of common land and, potentially, significant numbers of squatters and commoners. Many of the forest parishes were enclosed by legislation between 1750 and 1850, among them Edwinstowe – at the heart of the forest – in 1818. Here, common rights relating to the use of wood and scrubland waste for timber, food and fuel were still claimed in the eighteenth century. As late as the mid-1790s residents of Edwinstowe 'could supply themselves plentifully with firewood, during the whole year' from the royal woodlands at Birkland and Bilhagh, suggesting this was a customary claim if not a legally prescribed common right. Forest dwellers also had customary rights to grazing and the produce of the forest undergrowth. Some gathered bilberries 'which every summer were wont to be an extraordinary great profit and pleasure to poor people who gathered them and carried them all about the country to sell'. In 1793 at Edwinstowe the villagers exercised a variety of claims:

> they claim a right to acorns, when they fall, and take swine to feed on them, at certain rates per head, according to the plenty or scarcity of food. They also depasture their sheep in the woods, but not horses or horned cattle, for which the pastureage is not sufficient, and do not take in any sheep belonging to others to feed there. No other persons enjoy rights of common in those woods.[36]

---

33 Enclosure commissioners were expected to maintain minute books for each enclosure they handled. Unfortunately there were no instructions as to what the commissioners and their clerk were to do with the books when the award was completed, and the majority have disappeared: M.E. Turner and T. Wray, 'A survey of sources for parliamentary enclosure: the House of Commons' Journal and Commissioners' working papers', *Archives*, 19 (1991), pp. 257–88. Turner and Wray's survey was not comprehensive: ex inf. Dr Ben Cowell.

34 John Atkins, Bob Hammond and Peter Roper, *A village transformed: Keyworth, 1750–1850* (Keyworth, 1999), p. 139.

35 NA, DD.RC 14/27; DD.T/123/71.

36 Ben Cowell, 'Patrician landscapes, plebeian cultures: parks and society in two English counties, *c*. 1750–1850', PhD thesis (University of Nottingham, 1998), pp. 124–5.

It is ironic in these circumstances that a parish with so many cottagers and squatters passed through enclosure between 1818 and 1821 without overt opposition, although the late date might imply some earlier disagreement.

The same could not be said in the case of Sutton in Ashfield, a neighbouring forest parish. According to Tate the enclosure was unopposed, but it took seven years to move from the act of 1794 to the award of 1801, and during that process the large body of commoners committed various depredations. These took the form of trespassing on newly staked allotments on the common, and they occurred because former common-right holders took advantage of the fact that the enclosure commissioners neglected to publish the usual notice of a date for the extinction of common rights. The commissioners were forced to remedy this deficiency through a warning published in the *Nottingham Journal*.[37] At neighbouring Kirkby in Ashfield, where the act was passed in 1795, and which Tate records as opposed because the proprietors were not unanimous, enclosure took 19 years to complete (1795–1814). Here, there were fewer claimants to the substantial commons, but it was the land allotted in lieu of tithes that was the target of fence breakers.[38]

Warsop, in the same part of the forest, was one of the 38 Nottinghamshire parishes where Tate recorded enclosure as having been opposed because an earlier bill had been dropped. A new bill passed in 1818. Resistance to enclosure was not unexpected. John Cruso, a local land agent, writing in September 1811 to John Wylde, agent to the Galley Knight estate, noted that

> An enclosure act is perhaps more calculated to lay the present spirit than any other step, as it would set at rest what may have been in times past and put out of the way that which perhaps has always been the ground for contention by a division of the commons.[39]

Subsequent letters also speculated on the attitude of the commoners. Wylde told Cruso in December 1811 that

> the poorer claimants have been and still are alarmed for their common rights and believe they have no chance if an enclosure bill is previously consented to … I beg leave in confidence to say that should the inclosure be put off this time, I shall take the very first opportunity of canvassing myself … If Mr [Galley] Knight's tenants would only stock the forest (such as have a right to do) all would then be aware of the advantage of the Inclosure; but a few having the forest entirely to themselves it makes it so much their interest to oppose an Inclosure and whose real rights are very inferior.[40]

The first attempt to enclose by legislation failed in 1813 and no further progress was made until 1818. In the meantime Henry Galley Knight, the lord of the manor, was

---

37 NA, DD M 25/49; DD 4P/62/37.
38 NA, DD 4P/62/37; Brown, 'Aspects of parliamentary enclosure', pp. 228–9.
39 NA, DD 2106/5/1/12, 29/9/1811.
40 NA, DD 2106/5/1/15.

anxious to establish his rights of ownership of the commons.[41] John Horncastle told Cruso on 24 January 1818:

> although many of the proprietors will object to sign the Bill, I am of the opinion that they will not carry their opposition to parliament ... I had some applications for a promise of letting them rent some of Mr [Galley] Knights land if they signed the Bill. This I think was intended as a trap. I told them I should make no such promise. It would appear that I wished to buy their interest.[42]

Legislation passed in 1818, but the parish proved to be far from united. Eventually, the ratio of five landowners in favour to each one against was reached, after a long dispute between the larger landowners, notably Galley Knight, and the rector (Rev. Samuel Martin) over tithes.

The passing of the act was not the end of the troubles at Warsop. Once the commissioners started work, several claims were submitted respecting common rights on an area called the Sheepwalk. In December 1818 Cruso was presented by Horncastle with a list of ten local inhabitants who disputed Galley Knight's claims on the Sheepwalk. Galley Knight had claimed the whole area but the ten smallholders objected that they had rights of common because the land he claimed had been taken from the commons. The commissioners had to adjudicate: Galley Knight commented privately to Cruso that he would hope to keep all the lands but if some were to be lost he would still be 'perfectly satisfied'. He can hardly have been dissatisfied, as he was subsequently awarded most of the land he claimed. His opponents fared less well. John Smith, George Mitchell, John Norman and Thomas Moody, four of the ten men listed in the original letter, applied for poor relief and were noted as first-time applicants in the overseers' accounts for the parish by 1820.[43] The strategy of the smallholders appeared merely to be to hinder and delay the process as long as possible. In this they had some success, as the award was completed only in 1825.

In some instances the strategy was less peaceful, notably at Gringley on the Hill, another forest parish. The fifth Lord Byron of Newstead had opposed enclosure here in the late 1760s, but he sold his property to the duke of Devonshire in the 1770s and by 1796 agreement had been reached to sponsor an enclosure bill in parliament. According to Tate's criteria, Gringley was straightforward. There was no counter-petition, the bill passed on the first occasion that it was applied for and there were no delays. It appears in Tate's list as 'opposed' because the proprietors were not unanimous in their desire for enclosure, although the four-fifths majority of landowners to pass the bill (actually about 7 to 1) was easily gained. However, Gringley is surrounded by three of the five parishes where Tate noted the presentation of early counter-petitions from rural labourers, and the enclosure certainly did not go through without opposition.

---

41   NA, DD 2106/5/1–4.

42   NA, DD 2106/5/4/22.

43   NA, DD 2106/5/5/24; QDE 1–4, PR 2604.

This was a parish with a long history of resistance to any attempt to interfere with common rights and a significant acreage of common in the form of 'carr' land.[44] Clearly there was a major disturbance in the 1790s. Three men were subsequently charged with 'feloniously, wilfully, maliciously, demolishing, pulling down and destroying certain fences at Gringley-on-the-Hill'.[45] They were sent for trial at the county assizes in July 1798, when the *Nottingham Journal* reported on the case at some length:

> Bench bills of indictment were found by the Grand Jury against John Throop, John Barthroop and Thomas Cook, all of Gringley on the Hill, for felony in resisting the Act of Parliament for the Inclosure of the parish, by cutting down and destroying fences directed to be made by the commissioners for the said inclosure, and by that means preventing the other proprietors from cultivating the allotments assigned to them.[46]

Throop and Barthroop appear in the Land Tax Assessments as occupiers of some of the land allotted to the lord of the manor. As their lands were valued at under £1, they were probably smallholders. Their opposition was clearly violent.

What is much more difficult to establish is whether or not Gringley was in any sense typical. In other parts of the country enclosures such as this were fiercely resisted. At West Haddon in Northamptonshire, which had 800 acres of common, 'a tumultuous mob ... pulled up and burnt the fences designed for the inclosure ...', and did other considerable damage in 1765. Riots also occurred at Iver in Buckinghamshire in 1802, where there was 1,100 acres of common. Perhaps the most famous of all such instances was Otmoor, Oxfordshire, where there were disturbances in 1830–1 in conjunction with enclosure of the commons.[47]

If Nottinghamshire had a case similar to these examples it was perhaps at Selston. The open fields had already been enclosed by the 1790s, when the historian John Throsby described it as an 'enclosed lordship of cold clay land', with a village consisting of 'several detached houses and some cottages on the common'.[48] Bills for enclosing the common were introduced in 1799, 1819 and 1826, and an act was finally passed in 1865. It was 1877 before attempts were made to enforce its terms and 1879 before the award was completed. Fences started to appear in 1877 and it was not long before overt resistance appeared. Several fences were uprooted and burnt in September that year. Twenty-six men were arrested and committed for trial at the assizes. In the event 17 of the men were found guilty and the others acquitted. Even those found guilty were eventually released, but the enclosure went ahead although with a small amount of land set aside 'for the purposes of exercise and recreation for the inhabitants of the

---

44 NA, DD 2P 25/2–14; Brown, 'Aspects of parliamentary enclosure', p. 230.

45 *Nottingham Journal*, 28 April 1798.

46 *Nottingham Journal*, 4 August 1798; trial at County Assize Court beginning 25 July 1798.

47 David Eastwood, 'Communities, protest and police in early nineteenth-century Oxfordshire: the enclosure of Otmoor reconsidered', *Agricultural History Review*, 44 (1996), pp. 35–46.

48 John Throsby, *Thoroton's History of Nottinghamshire, republished with large additions*, 2nd edn, 3 vols (1796, fasc. repr. Wakefield, 1972), vol. ii, p. 266. Cold clay was a local term for heavy clayland.

neighbourhood'.[49] Selston, however, was both a late example and in some respects an unusual one, given that many of those claiming common rights were industrial workers, being employed either in the hosiery industry or by the Butterley Company's iron works at neighbouring Ripley. In the longer term the commoners lacked the numbers to challenge the great landowners and could muster neither the legal means nor the physical force to resist the ongoing process of change.[50]

V

Forest villagers may have seen their common rights extinguished in acts passed between about 1770 and 1820, but they did not necessarily accept that they had gone forever. Commoners began to exercise a variety of common rights and privileges such as grazing in the royal woodlands and rights of gathering the native ling or furze for the manufacture of soap.[51] John Throsby, passing by Clumber in the early 1790s, noted that 'Ling and broom are natives of this part of the forest. Before it was so much enclosed the people used to burn acres together, and plant fresh to be eaten young as food for sheep; but now most of that ground is occupied by corn.' Christopher Thomson, the self-styled 'artisan' author of Edwinstowe, claimed in 1847 that 34 parishes in the forest had been enclosed in the previous half century, and that there had been much suffering as a direct result:

> Time was, when the humblest peasant enjoyed his right of 'folcland' – the land of the folks; but dare the peasantry of Bassetlaw set a foot upon one acre within those thirty-four parishes? Truly, some persons have been enriched by the mapping-out, and ring-fencing of these commons; but are they the 'common people'? How many of the poor peasants are bettered by it? Doubtless, the peasantry are existing by thousands within these parishes; have the thousands been allowed to take the 'lion's share'?[52]

Unless forest rights could be proved in law, however, the Forest landlords were in a strong position to deny all forms of customary access to the forest resources. At enclosure only those who held 'ancient copyhold messuages' or cottages were taken into consideration, despite the fact that many others made claims to common rights based on possession of freehold land.[53]

Covert, if not overt, resistance continued through and beyond enclosure. Among some of the more substantial Nottinghamshire landowners with extensive acreages on

49   Edgar Eagle and John Heath, 'Selston and the enclosure of its common lands, 1877–1879', *TTS*, 90 (1986), pp. 64–8; also the comments in Report from the Select Committee on [the] Enclosure Act, BPP 1868–9, 304, pp. 73–4.
50   Cowell, 'Patrician landscapes', p. 120; Brown, 'Aspects of parliamentary enclosure', p. 43.
51   Cowell, 'Patrician landscapes', p. 119.
52   Christopher Thomson, *The autobiography of an artisan* (London, 1847), pp. 315–16; Cowell, 'Patrician landscapes', p. 127.
53   Cowell, 'Patrician landscapes', p. 137.

the sandy soils of Sherwood Forest, enclosure and the removal of common rights was central to the creation or – in most cases – extension of landscape parks. Parks were neither aesthetically nor agriculturally successful if outsiders retained the right to enter them to graze their animals or to crop trees. Thus, if a landowner wanted to enclose and empale a park he first had to abolish customary or common-right claims. If he did permit the use of sections of the park for grazing or fuel-gathering, he was most likely to do so on the basis of strictly controlled private leasing agreements or charitable bequests rather than as a customary or legal right.[54]

Enclosing land for emparkment was not necessarily straightforward. At Bestwood Park in the mid-1770s Mr Barton (tenant of the duke of St Albans) ran into trouble when he attempted to repair the pales of the ancient park so that he could turn it over to agricultural uses. The wooden pales had been in a state of disrepair for years, having been largely removed by 'poor people in the neighbourhood' for fuel. When Barton rebuilt the pale, the local residents who had previously used the park as open forest pulled it down at night to let their cows and sheep back in. Barton took several residents to court to contest their claim that 'time had established a right' for them to use the park as if it were a legal forest common right. By 1775 Barton had apparently won the case, but he still suffered 'extremely by his neighbours, pulling the hedges &c in various parts of the estate for firing but he has conquered them respecting their pretended right of commonage'.[55]

Once we begin to move beyond Tate's insistence on parliamentary evidence, a very different picture starts to emerge of opposition to parliamentary and indeed other forms of enclosure in Nottinghamshire. Fence-breaking occurred in boundary disputes between Nottingham and its neighbouring parish of Basford in the 1790s, and in the Lenton and Radford enclosure of 1799. John Musters of Colwick supported the Sneinton enclosure in 1796 because this meant that the open fields adjoining Colwick would fall into the exclusive possession of Earl Manvers. Musters asked Manvers to use this plot of land as a woodland plantation, thus helping to shield Colwick from the rougher inhabitants of Sneinton. However, as William Sanday pointed out, this was easier asked than answered because of customary rights in the areas. He could not recommend an oak plantation as proposed by Musters, owing to the fondness of 'Nottingham people' to 'crop the tops' of oak trees previous to every 29 May, Oak Apple Day, which was a celebration of the restoration of Charles II. Many local poor folk took this as a customary right to gather timber from all the woodlands on that day, whether commonable or private, and Manvers was hardly likely to plant trees which would almost immediately be robbed in the name of custom. Already by 18 February 1790, and well before the final version of the bill was drawn up (let alone passed), Manvers' land *in toto* appears to have been established, and the acreages of individual farms decided.[56]

Sneinton was not entirely free of contention, which was hardly surprising given that the parish adjoined Nottingham at its eastern boundary. Enclosure here was

---

54   *Ibid.*, pp. 113–14.

55   *Ibid.*, p. 134.

56   NA, M 3321/1–46, M 3323/3–37; Ma B 248/108.

first discussed in the 1780s but nothing was done until the mid-1790s, and the act passed on 23 March 1796. The Pierrepont family, the Earls Manvers, were the major beneficiary, and the process of dividing and allotting the individual portions began almost immediately. It took a number of months to complete. On 21 December 1796 William Sanday, agent for Manvers in Sneinton, wrote to William Pickin, his counterpart at Thoresby, asking him to get on with laying out the new farms and setting up the fences,

> for I dare say it will be difficult to please many of the [people of Nottingham], and living so near them, I should have no end of their trouble. When the allotments are staked out, the sooner he begins upon that business the better, if he is to do it, that I may begin to put down the fencing.'[57]

The allotments were completed early in 1797.[58] Through the spring of 1797 quicksett hedges were planted and protective post and rail fences erected, but it was another year before the award was completed, on 13 February 1798.

Sneinton, like Cotgrave, was a formal enclosure, sorted out between landlords and organised in conjunction with the tenants. It was a clean-cut business in which little opposition was encountered; indeed, the biggest threat to law and order seems to have been posed by the speed at which fields were laid out and fences erected to protect the quicksetts. On 14 April 1797 Sanday complained to Pickin that he needed more rails, 'for it will be impossible to do without them, for one person wants to mow his piece, and another wants to eat his, so that if we have not rails to separate them we shall be all confusion'.[59]

In Nottingham itself enclosure of the open fields that surrounded the town was first proposed in the 1780s.[60] Subsequently it was resisted until 1845 by the freemen, who objected to the loss of their common rights, using a series of spurious claims as to the advantages of retaining the open fields. The enclosure act was finally passed in 1845, but it was another 20 years before the commissioners were able to bring all the vested interests together to agree the terms of the award.[61]

VI

Opposition to parliamentary enclosure as measured by Tate's methodology seriously underplays the likely extent of popular opposition, while highlighting minor issues: Wilford, for example, appears in Tate's list of opposed enclosures simply because one

---

57 NUMASC, M 3320/38.

58 NA, M 3321/1.

59 NA, M 3321/8.

60 Paul Elliott, 'The politics of urban improvement in Georgian Nottingham: The enclosure dispute of the 1790s', *TTS*, 110 (2006), pp. 87–102.

61 NA, CA 7751; 8 & 9 Victoria, cap. 7 sess. 1845, 'An Act for inclosing lands in the parish of St Mary, in the town and county of the town of Nottingham'; J.V. Beckett and K. Brand, 'Enclosure, improvement and the rise of"New Nottingham", 1845–67', *TTS*, 98 (1994), pp. 92–111.

man, John Bird, owner of just 40 acres, refused to sign the petition 'because he had not the naming of a commissioner and surveyor'.[62] While the absence of opposition in some areas, notably the Trent Valley, is explicable in terms of the nature of tenure and farming, the *extent* of opposition elsewhere cannot be measured purely through the formal records of parliamentary enclosure. In many Nottinghamshire parishes enclosure was not the straightforward process envisaged by Tate. For many people enclosure represented a threat to their livelihood that provoked them into taking some sort of opposition.

Popular opposition to enclosure cannot adequately be measured via counter-petitions to parliament or evidence of bills being dropped. Following Neeson's lead in her study of Northamptonshire, we have to look elsewhere. In doing so we run into difficulties. The loss of the Midland assize circuit records and the absence of quarter sessions order books for Nottinghamshire make any discussion of prosecutions for offences committed by opponents of enclosure difficult. Enclosure commissioners' minute books are also few and far between. Consequently we depend heavily on newspaper evidence. Although the oldest established local paper, the *Nottingham Journal*, dates from the 1770s and established some claim to county-wide coverage, the extent to which it was able to fulfil this role is uncertain.

Perhaps it is sufficient to point to the time taken in some enclosures to move from act to award as an indication of stubborn non-compliance, foot-dragging and even mischief-making, if not of outright opposition. Nottingham took 20 years but much smaller communities also took many years to reach an agreement. Ordsall took from 1800 to 1813 and Bilborough and Strelley from 1808 until 1828. Was the lateness of enclosure in other parishes, such as, for example, Norwell, a silent testimony to long and bitter opposition from freeholders, small farmers, squatters, cottagers and others who saw their livelihood being eroded? The loss of commissioners' notebooks is particularly unfortunate from this perspective.

Most studies of enclosure in Nottinghamshire since Tate wrote have tended to concentrate on field patterns and farming practices.[63] But this is not necessarily the full story. Parliamentary enclosure, at least in its early phase, was predominantly a phenomenon of the Midland counties, which had traditionally practised mixed husbandry, and in which the commons must have played much less of a role as a result. In the longer term squatters were squeezed out by the loss of grazing rights as surviving commons and other areas were stinted in order to increase the acreage under permanent pasture. Even in Laxton, famous because it was never enclosed, the commons were residual by the eighteenth century.[64] In these circumstances,

---

62   J. Newton, 'The middle ground: the experience of the farming community of Wilford, Nottinghamshire, *c.*1700–*c.*1870', unpublished MA dissertation (University of Nottingham, 1999), p. 20.

63   A. Cossons, 'Early enclosures in Beeston', *TTS*, 62 (1958), pp. 1–10; P. Lyth (ed.), *Farms and fields of Southwell: a study of enclosures* (Nottingham, 1984); F.N. Hoskins, 'Matlock House Farm: a post-enclosure farm', *TTS*, 78 (1974), pp. 68–75.

64   J.V. Beckett, *A history of Laxton: England's last open field village* (Oxford, 1989), pp. 107–14; Philippa Venn, 'Exceptional Eakring: Nottinghamshire's other open field parish', *TTS*, 94 (1990), pp. 69–74.

where commons were relatively unimportant, the number of claimants to common rights was likely to have been small. In such parishes only minimal popular opposition was to be anticipated. We might also expect to find different types of enclosure: prior to 1793 parliamentary enclosure was often designed to increase the acreage of permanent pasture, as in the case of Orston in the Vale of Belvoir.[65] In later years, when bread grain output was at a premium because of war, the emphasis came to be on agricultural efficiency and the creation of ring-fenced, predominantly arable, farms.

We can now see that both Chambers and Tate relied too much on official documentation when it came to understanding attitudes towards enclosure. Chambers was primarily interested in the agricultural impact of enclosure and the outcome in terms of tenure and ownership. Tate believed that the administrative records told a tale that was rather more comprehensive than we now accept. Today the historian of enclosure needs to look further than the parliamentary record. If in Nottinghamshire the reward is more meagre than we might have hoped, there is not much doubt that popular resistance to enclosure was more extensive than Tate assumed, at least in the areas of the county where extensive common and waste survived and common rights were still being exercised.

---

65 P. Barnes, 'The adaptation of open field farming in an east Nottinghamshire parish: Orston, 1641–1793', *TTS*, 101 (1997), pp. 125–32.

Appendix:
Opposition to parliamentary enclosure in Nottinghamshire

Unopposed (proprietors unanimously in favour)

Place	Act	Award	Place	Act	Award
West Leake	1742	-	Sneinton	1796	1798
West Leake	1754	-	Weston	1796	1803
Barton & Clifton	1759	1759	Bunny	1797	1798
Carlton-in-Lindrick	1767	1768	Keyworth	1798	1799
Farndon	1767	1769	East Leake	1798	1799
Lenton & Radford	1767	1768	Harworth	1799	1804
Ruddington	1767	1767	Newark	1800	1803
Burton Joyce & Bulcote	1768	1769	Wysall	1800	1801
Epperstone	1768	1770	Harby & Broadholme	1802	1804
Blidworth	1769	1770	Cropwell Bishop	1802	1804
Hucknall Torkard	1769	1771	Dunham	1803	1815
Normanton-on-Soar	1770	1771	Tollerton	1803	1806
Scaftworth	1772	1773	Widmerpool	1803	1804
Cromwell	1773	1773	Sutton on Trent	1803	1808
Brinsley	1775	1775	Worksop	1803	1817
Flintham	1775	1777	Alverton	1804	1810
Scrooby	1775	1777	Gotham	1804	1804
Screveton	1776	-	Blidworth	1805	1812
Sutton Bonington	1776	1777	Plumtree	1805	1807
(St Michael) Kersall	1778	1778	Barnby	1807	1809
Ollerton	1778	1779	Elton	1807	1809
Elkesley	1779	-	Annesley	1808	1809
Cropwell Butler	1787	1788	Gamston	1808	1809
Trowell	1787		Skegby	1808	1823
Radcliffe-on-Trent	1787	1790	Strelley & Bilborough	1808	1828
North Collingham	1790	1798	West Markham	1808	1808
Cotgrave	1790	-	Eaton	1809	1814
Lambley	1792	1792	Pinxton	1812	1829
Syerston	1792	1795	Spalford & Wigsley	1813	1817
Orston & Thoroton	1793	1797	Headon	1815	1818
Sutton-in-Ashfield	1794	1801	Edwinstowe	1818	1821
Upton	1795	1798	Walesby	1821	1825
East Bridgford	1796	1801	Sturton	1822	1828
Gateford & Shireoaks	1796	1797	Norwell	1826	1832
Lenton & Radford	1796	1799			

Opposed or in some way disputed

Place	Act	Award	Place	Act	Award
Everton	1759	1761	Costock	1760	1761
Staunton	1759	1760	Hawksworth	1760	1761
Upper Broughton	1760	1761	Hayton	1760	1762
North & South Clifton	1760	1761	Misson	1760	1762
Coddington	1760	1762	Carlton-on-Trent	1765	1766

Opposed or in some way disputed

Place	Act	Award	Place	Act	Award
Lowdham	1765	1766	Kirkby-in-Ashfield	1795	1814
Tickhill	1765	1766	North Leverton	1795	1801
Wilford	1765	1766	South Leverton	1795	1801
Balderton	1766	1768	East Stoke & Elston	1795	1801
Rempstone	1768	1769	Woodborough	1795	1798
Mattersey	1770	1773	Gringley-on-the-Hill	1796	1801
Misterton & Stockwith	1771	1775	Lenton & Radford	1796	1799
North Muskham	1771	1773	Weston	1796	1803
Stapleford and Bramcote	1771	1772	East Leake*	1798	1799
Laneham	1772	1774	Harworth*	1799	1804
Cottmore & Radley	1774	1775	Clarborough Moorgate	1799	1806
Finningley	1774	1778	Grassthorpe	1799	1801
Greasley	1774	1775	Tuxford	1799	1804
West Retford	1774	1776	Normanton-on-Trent	1800	1808
Sutton Bonington	1774	1775	Ordsall	1800	1813
(St Anne's) Hickling	1775	1776	Ranskill	1802	1805
Normanton by Southwell	1775	1776	Styrrup & Oldcotes	1802	1807
Sutton cum Lound	1775	1778	Cropwell Bishop*	1802	1804
Beckingham	1776	1779	Walkeringham	1802	1806
Clarborough Welham	1776	1778	Sutton-on-Trent*	1803	1808
Bleasby	1777	1780	Worksop*	1803	1817
Farnsfield	1777	1780	Blidworth*	1805	1812
Halam & Edingley	1777	1781	Plumtree & Clipstone*	1805	1807
Winthorpe	1777	1778	Beeston	1806	1809
Calverton	1779	1780	Barnby*	1807	1809
Scarrington & Aslockton	1780	1781	Elton*	1807	1809
Cropwell Butler	1787	1788	East Markham	1810	1816
Radcliffe-on-Trent*	1787	1790	Spalford & Wigsley*	1813	1817
Arnold	1789	1791	Blyth	1814	1819
Whatton	1789	1790	Warsop	1818	1825
Clayworth	1790	1792	East Drayton	1819	1825
Eastwood	1791	1793	Walesby*	1821	1825
Basford	1792	1797	Sturton*	1822	1828
Gedling	1792	1796	Norwell*	1826	1832
Granby & Sutton	1793	1799	Morton & Fiskerton	1836	1842
Willougby-on-the-Wolds	1793	1799	Nottingham	1845	1865
Caunton	1795	1795	Selston	1865	1879

Sources: W.E. Tate, *Parliamentary land enclosures in the county of Nottingham during the 18th and 19th centuries (1743–1868)*, Thoroton Society Record Series V (Nottingham, 1935), pp. 183–6; Margery Brown, 'Aspects of parliamentary enclosure in Nottinghamshire', PhD thesis (University of Leicester, 1995), pp. 206–8; W.E. Tate, *A Domesday of English enclosure acts and awards*, ed. M.E. Turner (Reading, 1978).

Note: opposition is counted in this table in its broadest form, i.e. the bill was contested, the bill was not carried when first introduced, proprietors were not unanimous in desiring enclosure. Places marked * appear in this list as well as the unopposed list because, while the bill that went through was unopposed, an earlier bill was dropped, indicating that there was some opposition. In the case of East Leake, bills of 1781 and 1786 were dropped but the 1798 bill passed unopposed.

Chapter 7

The rise and fall of a Peak District yeoman family: the Bagshaws of Hazlebadge, 1600–1942[*]

Alan G. Crosby

The land acquisition and management strategies of major estates have been extensively studied by historians, drawing upon the heritage of family and estate collections so important in the holdings of local record offices and fundamental to those of great houses. However, comparable analysis for yeoman families, the smaller freeholders who proverbially were the backbone of English rural society, is far more difficult. They rarely have significant archives of their own and it is unusual for coherent documentary evidence to be continuous over several generations. Their landholdings are less likely to be mapped and surveyed, and the absence of an estate steward means that the accounts, correspondence and journals that can be so valuable in reconstructing the management of major estates are unlikely to exist. To identify and analyse their landholdings, the augmentation or diminution of their estates, their wider economic activities and their provision for future generations requires research in a variety of sources that are often not specific to the family and whose survival may be haphazard. David Hey saw long-resident yeoman families as a force for continuity and stability in the countryside, a perspective he explored in his last book, *The grass roots of English rural history: local societies in England before the Industrial Revolution* (2016). 'The core groups of families who remained rooted in their "country" are the ones that shaped local culture and passed on their traditions'.[1]

This paper attempts to piece together such evidence for the Bagshaw family of Hazlebadge, near Tideswell in the High Peak, seeking to show how they arrived in the township at the end of the sixteenth century and steadily built up a portfolio of freehold and leasehold properties that complemented their main holding, the tenancy at will of Hazlebadge Hall, held from the dukes of Rutland. The evidence for diversification of their economic interests beyond farming is considered, as is the social position

*   I am greatly indebted to Lord Edward Manners of Haddon Hall for most generously granting access to his archive material relating to Hazlebadge and permitting me to use it in this paper. As will be apparent, without these documents the research could not have been undertaken. I am most appreciative of the patience and kind assistance of Lord Edward's house manager, Ruth Headon, in helping to make the documents available for study. The staff of the Derbyshire Record Office in Matlock were unfailingly helpful, and I also thank Peter Foden, archivist to the duke of Rutland at Belvoir, for his advice about the archival research. My warm thanks, too, to Richard Hoyle for his valuable comments on the draft of the paper.

1   *The grass roots of English rural history. Local societies in England before the Industrial Revolution* (London, 2016), p. 3.

that their increasing prosperity warranted. The penultimate section recounts the rapid collapse of the estate that had been amassed over two centuries, destroyed by drink and financial recklessness in the early decades of the nineteenth century.

David Hey was convinced of the importance of family history and advocated a close relationship between it and local and regional history. This is, in part, a study of my own family history. The Bagshaws were my direct maternal ancestors, and I discussed them several times with David Hey, talking with him not only about the family history in general but also about their distinctive locative surname (always a subject of special interest for David), their status as locally significant freeholders as well as tenants at will of the dukes of Rutland, and their economic diversification into, for example, lead-mining. David was enthusiastic and encouraged me to write up my researches, but I never imagined that, so very sadly, the results would appear in a posthumous tribute to that great man.

In 1815 my grandfather's great-grandfather was the last but one male Bagshaw to be born at Hazlebadge Hall, but an oral tradition of illustrious forebears was passed down, via lives spent in abject poverty in Ardwick in Manchester, to the later twentieth century, when I first heard the stories. My research over the years confirmed almost all of what I was told, the anecdotes fitting convincingly into the archive-based account I pieced together. When my great-uncle Leonard Bagshaw went to Hazlebadge Hall in 1949 he was not allowed across the threshold or even through the gate, but an old farm labourer to whom he chatted remembered elderly people in *his* childhood saying that 'Old Squire Bagshaw was the last of the line and he was a right one', a phrase which speaks volumes and is amply supported by the account in this paper.

A key to the exploration of the fortunes of small landowners is the character, and development, over time, of tenure in their particular area. This may be clear and well-documented: for example, a comprehensive overview of the landholding position in the Royal Forest of the Peak, including tenurial arrangements, has been given by Derek Brumhead.[2] However, Hazlebadge lay just outside the bounds of the Forest and is not covered by the systematic and wide-ranging evidence afforded by the Duchy of Lancaster records that Brumhead used. Even the archives of the Manners family of Haddon Hall, whose forebears held the lordship since the early fifteenth century and who still hold it six centuries later, are discontinuous. This exercise has therefore been akin to doing a jigsaw puzzle with no picture as a guide and numerous pieces missing. I hope that David would have enjoyed it.

I

Although rare elsewhere, Bagshaw is a familiar surname in the Peak District, not least because it is that of a local firm of estate agents and auctioneers. The word itself means 'the small wood where badgers live', but, as David Hey emphasised, the etymology is largely irrelevant in such cases, for this is a classic instance of a minor place-name giving rise to a distinctive locative surname. Bagshaw is a small

---

2   Derek Brumhead, 'Land tenure in the Royal Forest of Peak in the sixteenth and seventeenth centuries', *Transactions of the Lancashire and Cheshire Antiquarian Society*, 96 (2000), pp. 79–94.

hamlet, of only a dozen houses even today, tucked into a narrow side valley just east of Chapel-en-le-Frith. The available evidence, perhaps confirmable by future DNA analysis, strongly suggests that most of those with the surname (or its frequent variant, Bagshawe) are descended from one couple who lived in that insignificant place in the early thirteenth century.

References in deeds and in the records of the forest courts of High Peak indicate that by the late fourteenth century the surname had spread from its place of origin westwards to Chapel-en-le-Frith and nearby Ridge; north-west towards Hayfield and Glossop; south-east to Wormhill and Tideswell, where a significant concentration was developing; and eastwards to Castleton, Hope, Bradwell, Abney, Hucklow and Eyam. For example, the 1327 lay subsidy records four men called *de Baggeshaugh* living in Chapel-en-le-Frith (which included Bagshaw), but the 1381 poll tax lists *Ricardus de Bageshagh* at Castleton, four men and a woman with this surname in Eyam and two in Bowden (Glossop).[3] There were close connections with the administration of the royal forest of High Peak: thus, in 1331 Nicholas Baggeshawe was one of the four foresters of Hopedale, and two other men with this surname were listed among the 'regarders' who kept watch on the ground.

During the nineteenth century attempts were made to compile a definitive pedigree of the Bagshaw(e) families, focusing particularly on William Bagshaw of Ford Hall near Chapel-en-le-Frith (1679–1755), a celebrated dissenting minster popularly known as 'the Apostle of the Peak'. Such efforts were the special enthusiasm of W.G. Bagshawe, a Sheffield solicitor and genealogist, who accumulated a large collection of documents, transcripts, notes and pedigrees that are now divided between the John Rylands Library in Manchester and Derbyshire Archives in Matlock. His reconstructions of the different branches were based on archival research but, though generally reliable for the seventeenth century onwards, are unavoidably speculative for earlier centuries.

More recently the late Professor Roy Newton of Sheffield University undertook a monumental family reconstruction project aiming to demonstrate the inter-connectivity of the many clusters or branches of the surname. His work, privately published in three volumes, argued that all the better-documented lines of the family could ultimately be linked together in descent from Thomas Baggeshagh of Bowden near Hayfield, named in the lay subsidy of 1327.[4] Although Newton makes reference to the Bagshaws of Hazlebadge, he provides no detail and does not explicitly suggest any identifiable genealogical connection to his main tree, but the available evidence points to their descent from the branch of the family that lived at Abney in the later sixteenth century.

---

3   Carolyn Fenwick (ed.), *The Poll Taxes of 1377, 1379 and 1381*, Records of Social and Economic History 27, 29 and 37 (London, 1998–2005), vol. i, pp. 95–113.

4   R.G. Newton, 'The remarkable Bagshaw(e)s, part 1: how slowly they spread from their origin', *Derbyshire Family History Society Branch News*, 56 (March 1991), pp. 23–6; R.G. Newton, *A new consolidated Bagshaw(e) genealogy* (privately pub., 1997: copy in Derbyshire Local Studies Library, Matlock).

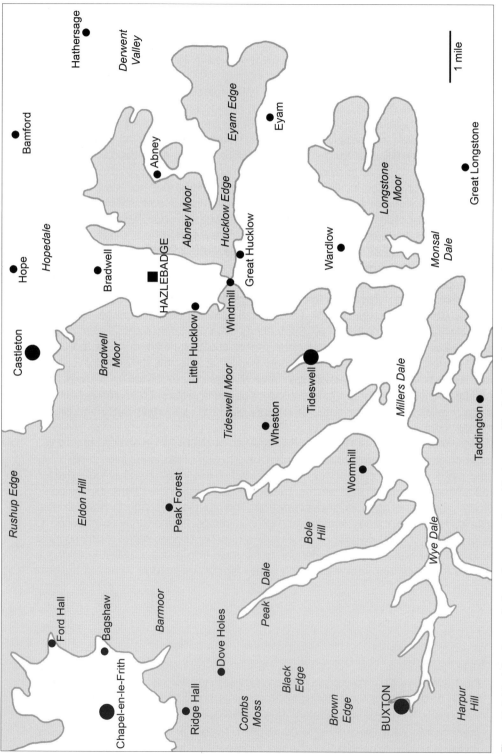

Figure 7.1. Hazlebadge and other places mentioned in the text. Shaded area is land over 1000 feet.

II

The small township of Hazlebadge is immediately south of Bradwell and two and a half miles north of Tideswell, and historically was part of the large parish of Hope (Figure 7.1). It covers only 822 acres, with no documentary or archaeological evidence of a nucleated settlement.[5] In 1801 the population was 77 and by the end of the century only 40. The focus of the township is Hazlebadge Hall, 700 feet above sea level beside the Bradwell–Tideswell road, at the upper end of the impressive limestone gorge called Bradwell Dale. The present house, bearing the date 1549 on the west gable, is the cross-wing of a once-larger building. Beside it are substantial stone barns of late seventeenth- or early eighteenth-century date.[6] On the east side of the township is the steep west-facing scarp slope of Bradwell Edge, Bleak Knoll and Abney Moor, composed of gritstones and shales rising to 1357 feet, while the western part of the township rises more gently to the limestone plateau at almost 1100 feet. Links between Abney and Hazlebadge were very close. In the late sixteenth century Abney Moor, on the high plateau to the east, was not yet appropriated to individual manors or townships. The moor was said to be 'parcell of the Mannor of Hasselbache', and it was claimed that the tenants of Hazlebadge had right of common there and on waste extending into other townships. Disputes over boundaries and intercommoning were not finally settled until 1804.[7]

Hazlebadge was exclusively the freehold property of the dukes of Rutland and their forebears from 1421, when the manor was sold by Johanna de Strelley to Richard Vernon. In 1565, on the death of Sir George Vernon, the 'King of the Peak',[8] the manor was bequeathed, with other Derbyshire estates, first to his wife Maud, and then to his daughter Dorothy and *iure uxoris* to her husband John Manners (1527–1611), younger son of the first earl of Rutland. In 1641 their grandson John (1604–1679) inherited the earldom and in 1703 his son John was created duke of Rutland. The manor or liberty has remained with the family to the present day, although the freehold estates were sold in 1920.

III

The earliest known reference to a Bagshaw at Hazlebadge occurs in a rental of 20 March 1604, listing George Bagshaw as paying 18s 9d per annum for an unspecified

---

5   John Barnatt, *Reading the Peak District landscape* (Swindon, 2019), p. 49; there are numerous variant spellings of the name, but the Ordnance Survey has always used the form 'Hazlebadge'.

6   Clare Hartwell, Nikolaus Pevsner and Elizabeth Williamson, *Buildings of England: Derbyshire* (New Haven, CT, 2016), p. 448.

7   HHA, 4619 (bill of complaint, *c.*1590, Manners v Bradshawe); DRO, D7676/BagC/1644a+b; C.E.B. Bowles, 'Depositions in action for trespass brought by Henry Furness against Robert Eyre', *DAJ*, 23 (1901), pp. 87–9; 'The manor of Abney: its boundaries and court rolls', *DAJ*, 29 (1907), pp. 129–40.

8   S. T. Bindoff (ed.), *The history of Parliament. The Commons, 1509–58*, 3 vols (London, 1982), vol. iii, pp. 525–6.

Table 7.1
The Bagshaws of Hazlebadge, 1600–1830.

1	*George Bagshaw [of Abney] (I)*
	b. c. 1570, Abney
	d. 1624, Abney
2	*Roger Bagshaw*
	b. 1602, Abney
	m. 1624, Margaret Jonson
	Francis (1625); Ann (1627); Roger (1630); Elizabeth (1632); Margaret (1636)
	d. 1679, Hazlebadge
3	*Francis Bagshaw (I)*
	b. 1625, Abney?
	m. Margaret x
	George (c.1660); John (?); William (1672); Mary (?)
	d. 1695, Hazlebadge
4	*George Bagshaw (II)*
	b. c.1660, Hazlebadge
	m. 1683, Mary Middleton [daughter of Martin Middleton]
	Ellen (1685); George (1687); William (1690); Mary (1690); William (1692)
	d. 1743, Hazlebadge
5	*George Bagshaw (III)*
	b. 1687, Hazlebadge
	m. (1) 1714, Catherine Edge at Leek, Staffordshire [died 1716]
	Mary (1715); Ellen (1716)
	m. (2) 1719, Mary Wright (née Warrington) of Tideswell
	Martha (1720); Rebecca (1722); Sarah (1724); George (1726); Hannah (1727)
	d. 1763, Hazlebadge
6	*George Bagshaw (IV)*
	b. 1726, Hazlebadge
	m. 1755, Mary Howe
	Francis (1760); George (1762); John (1764); Catherine (1766)
	illegitimate children by Mary Fox: John Fox (1782); Joseph Fox (1785)
	d. 1791, Hazlebadge
7	*Francis Bagshaw (II)*
	b. 1760, Hazlebadge
	m. 1780, Ann Barnsley (died 1831)
	George (1780); Mary (1784); John (1786); Martha (1788); Elizabeth (1791); Joshua (1794); Francis (1796); Hannah (1799); Samuel (1801); William (1802)
	d. 1828, Hazlebadge
8	*George Bagshaw (V)*
	b. 1780, Hazlebadge
	m. 1809, Mary Banks Robinson
	Francis (1809); Ann (1811); Mary (1813); George (1815); Samuel (1817)
	d. 1850, Windmill, Little Hucklow
	[Samuel 1817 was the last Bagshaw born at Hazlebadge Hall]

property at *Hassellbache*.[9] He was the least of seven lesser tenants, the others paying between 24s and £3 18s 4d, while Richard Marshall, who held the main tenancy at will, paid £140 per annum. The details of the tenancy are unknown, but it was apparently renewed on 10 December 1604, when George, 'husbandman of Abney', leased a cottage and land for 21 years from Sir John Manners at the identical rent of 18s 9d.[10] A printed pedigree of Bagshaw of Abney includes one George Bagshaw, who would have been born in about 1570 and is probably the same person.[11] George was buried at Hope on 27 June 1624 and thereafter the direct male line of descent is clear through seven generations, summarised in Table 7.1. Connections between the families at Abney and Hazlebadge remained: for example, Margaret, widow of Roger Bagshaw, husbandman of Abney (*d.* October 1687), renounced her right to administer his estate and nominated his 'kinsman', George Bagshaw of Hazlebadge, to perform the task.[12]

In addition to the lease to George Bagshaw (I) there are three other leases with very similar provisions, all dated 5 or 10 December 1604, for cottages and closes in the lordship. Nine years earlier John Manners had leased all of Hazlebadge 'except the Mannor place' to his servant Roger Rooe for seven years at a yearly rent of £8, but, as noted above, by 1604 the main tenancy at will was held by Richard Marshall at £140 per annum. This, together with the 1604 leases and their near-identical predecessors, implies the emergence of a closer management for this separate outlying property.[13] John Manners followed in a family tradition of exerting close control over his estates. Sir George Vernon, his father in law, had been legendary for the expansionist acquisition of rights, manors and freehold properties, and for maintaining a tight grip over his tenants. In this part of the High Peak there was latent, and sometimes overt, social and economic tension over issues such as land acquisition, enclosure and mining rights, and the organised nature of the 1604 leases may perhaps be seen in this context – as a way of asserting control in a tense social environment.[14]

The 1604 lease to George Bagshaw (I) was of a cottage and a one-third share in two closes called 'Stanloe and Coploe'. A detailed rental of 1636 shows that the Hall demesnes had by then been divided between 33 tenants at will. In addition, there were seven tenements held by lease, apparently the same as those leased in 1604. This remained the situation in 1645. The 1636 rental includes among the seven leaseholds one let to Roger Bagshaw at 18s 10d per annum and thus clearly the same tenancy as in 1604. In 1645 Roger Bagshaw was still leasing a tenement at 18s 10d. His lease was renewed on 28 March 1646, when the cottage and closes of 'Stannlowe

---

9   HHA, Hazlebadge, item 4.

10   HHA, 4592.

11   DRO, D743/Z/F/2.

12   Separate references are not given for probate records: all are at Staffordshire Record Office and available on www.findmypast.co.uk.

13   HHA, 4251, 4445, 4591 and 4592 (Dec. 1604 leases); 4446 (1595 lease).

14   Andy Wood, *The politics of social conflict: the Peak Country, 1520–1770* (Cambridge, 1999), pp. 245–7, 121.

& Copplowe' were let for 21 years at the customary rent.[15] Roger was then described as 'of Abney', implying that, although he and his father had leased the property for at least 50 years, the family had not yet shifted formally to Hazlebadge. However, Roger's probate documents of 1679 give Hazlebadge as his place of residence and his son Francis (I), in his will of 1685, described himself as 'of Haslebadge ... yeoman', although his probate inventory (of February 1695) refers to him as 'of Coplodale', a hamlet just a mile south-east of Hazelbadge Hall.

During the second half of the century a major advance in the status and fortunes of the Bagshaws of Hazlebadge can be identified. A rental of 1692, drawn up three years before the death of Francis (I), names 42 tenancies with Francis heading the list, paying £68 8s. He is also in ninth place for another tenancy, paying £14 7s: a total of £82 15s per annum. His will indicates what had happened, as he left 'unto George Bagshawe my sonne one shilling and I will hee to have the tenant right of Hasolebadge hilles and Barne flatt'. Although he was not yet the occupier of the Hall and was living at Coplowdale, Francis had taken on a sizeable tenancy at will, relating to at least 48 acres lying north-east of Hazlebadge Hall and below the slope of Abney Moor. The starting date of this tenancy is unknown: no rental survives for Hazlebadge between 1653 and 1692, and there is no known deed. The 1653 rental states that 'the greate hills' were then leased to Henry Brand and Adam Kirk, who also held 'the house, garden & yardes'.[16] Roger and Francis Bagshaw are not mentioned, but that rental is an incomplete draft that omits the 'tenements at lease'. All we can conclude is that the tenancy of this large property was acquired sometime between 1654 and 1685.

In his will Roger Bagshaw (died 1679) describes himself as 'yeoman', which can be contrasted with the words 'of Abney, husbandman' used of him in the 1646 lease. Too much emphasis should not be placed on the terminology, but there is an implicit enhancement of status. The will makes no specific reference to property, and his inventory was valued at just £43 12s 6d. The probate records of Francis (I) (died 1695) are much more informative. His will not only refers to the tenancy at will of Hazlebadge Hills and Barn Flatt but also reveals the augmenting of landholdings by the purchase of freehold properties adjacent to the liberty of Hazlebadge. The manor had no private freehold, and the acquisition of additional land there depended solely on the leasing policies of the Haddon Hall estate. The Bagshaws could not invest the profits of farming by the purchase of land within the manor (or in the building of a new house), so they had to look for opportunities outside it. There was the possibility of acquiring land after enclosure had taken place in adjoining townships. The later seventeenth century was a period of active private enclosure in this part of Derbyshire and two bequests in the 1685 will highlight this. The commons at Little Hucklow abutted Coplowdale and the Hazlebadge boundary, and Francis was clearly aware of their potential. He left 'unto William Bagshawe my sonne all that ... inclosed ground [called] Newland lieinge and beinge within [Little Hucklow] together with all that barne and beast house adioyneinge to the said close by north the which I bought of Adam Grant'. This property was different from that, worth £8, listed in a supplementary

---

15   HHA, Hazlebadge, bundle 2, 1645 and 1646 rentals; 4503.

16   HHA, Hazlebadge, bundle 2, draft rental of Hazlebadge, 1653.

inventory as 'the incrouchment taken of the Comin belonging to Little Hucklow which he had of Adam Pointon deseased'.

A considerable farming estate was developing, as the main inventory for Francis Bagshaw indicates. It refers to 123 sheep valued at £46; five kine, two bullocks and five calves (£34); a horse with its gear and saddle (£3); and hay, corn in the barns, oatmeal, wheat and malt (totalling £13). The total value of this inventory was £128 5s, but the supplementary one reveals extensive money-lending activities using the profits of farming: he had provided a mortgage of £100 to William Pointon, together with loans of £10 to Edward Hall of Abney, £5 to Hugh Bradwell of Abney and £13 6s to Daniel Heaps and Joseph Woolley. The overall inventory total was almost £265 (six times the value of his father's just 16 years earlier). Francis thus built upon the foundation his father had laid, rising to become a very substantial yeoman farmer.

This upward trajectory was reinforced by his son George (II), born in about 1660. He died at the end of 1743 and his will specifies numerous monetary payments to family members (including 14 named grandchildren) totalling £323 3s. The inventory suggests that, as an old man in his early 80s, he had already handed over control to his eldest son, but it also points to the continuing importance of money-lending: debts by bill and bond of £100 were due to him, and he had lent a further £34 to Miles and Elias Marshall of Bradwell.

The will itemises a series of properties and gives valuable information about their acquisition. From the duke of Rutland he held the tenantright of a dwellinghouse, garden, barn, two shippons and the close called Intack at Coplowdale, which he left to his grandson Francis Bagshaw (II). A superb 1725 survey of the duke's estates, undertaken to improve rent income by identifying those holdings where payments had lapsed, describes this property.[17] It records George Bagshaw senior as 'Tenant at will to a house of 3 bays, stone built and slated, with a barne and stable of 3 bays, stone built and thatched in good repair'. The associated estate totalled 27¼ acres. The tenancy at will of Hazlebadge Hall was already held by his eldest son George and so is not mentioned in the will. That his entry into his tenancy took place in the lifetime of George sen. [George II] is demonstrated by the same survey, which states that George Bagshaw jun. [George III] (then aged 38) was 'Tenant at will to a house of four bays, a barne, stable & cowhouse of five bays, all stone built and slated in good repair'. This house is Hazlebadge Hall. The tenancy (including the 48-acre Hazlebadge Hills) now totalled fractionally over 299 acres, almost four times the size of the next largest farm in Hazlebadge lordship. By the mid-1720s, therefore, the Hazlebadge Hall estate and Hazlebadge Hills were consolidated as one exceptionally large entity, which was not subject to further reorganisation. A comparably detailed survey of 1792 shows that the estate at Hazlebadge totalled 303 acres, the small difference being accounted for by improvements in areal measurement.[18]

George (II) was highly acquisitive, using connections by marriage and kinship to further a strategy of building up freehold to supplement the 300-acre Hazlebadge

---

17   HHA, 'A survey of the mannors and lordships in the county of Derby belonging to His Grace John, Duke of Rutland, 1725'.

18   HHA, Survey of the estates of His Grace the Duke of Rutland (1792).

estate. For example, he left lands in Bradwell to his grandson George Bagshaw (IV): Eden Tree Close; 2½ acres in a common close called Moor Furlong; a parcel of 'Three Half Acres' called Great Piece in the Long Meadow; a little pingle called Eden Tree Pingle; and a barn and shippon in Tofts Fold, 'all which said Premises I Purchased from my Father in Law Martin Middleton'.[19] His grandson George Torr was given a life interest in 'All that Land which I purchased from his Father Gervas Torr'. Most of these properties can be tentatively identified from later mapping and surveys, and the purchase of other land, not itemised in the will, can also be traced: in April 1693, for example, when his father Francis was still alive, George purchased two closes called 'Myrey Holme and Myrey Holme Layes' and the stretch of Bradwell Water running between them, paying Ellis Oldfield £60 for the property.[20] George also actively exploited the availability of rented property in the Bradwell area, to be worked in conjunction with the Hazlebadge estate. In April 1704, for example, he agreed to lease from Adam Bagshaw the elder of Wormhill, gentleman, a parcel of common in Bradwell of about 'one hundred Forrest Acres', for 20 years at £10 a year. This lay west of Bradwell village, adjoining the commons of Castleton to the north. It complemented the grazing land of Hazlebadge Hills to the east, and was adjacent to several freehold parcels that George already owned.[21]

Further lands were acquired by George (II)'s son George Bagshaw (III) and are identified in his will, made in December 1760. Some of these were more distant from Hazlebadge. His daughter Mary, wife of Thomas Slinn, was bequeathed the life interest in a messuage, barn and cowhouse in Wheston near Tideswell, and her sister Ellen Barnsley a life interest in other lands and tenements in Wheston. On the expiry of the life interests all these properties were to go to their brother George (IV). The estate at Wheston was actively managed: thus, in 1758, George (III) acquired from Robert Middleton a close there called Annett Close adjoining his existing property in exchange for a close called Westa abutting Middleton's estate.[22] George (III) left his son-in-law Thomas Slinn, Mary's husband, and their two sons Robert and George 'all my estate in the lands and tenements at Hathersage Booths which I purchased from the said Thomas Slinn'. The rationale for this odd procedure is unclear, and there are no Slinn wills to provide further detail, but it seems possible that Thomas Slinn was financially insecure and that the purchase of his land by his father-in-law was a way of bailing him out. The return of the land by the will might therefore have, in effect, cancelled a loan. That Mary Slinn was given a life interest in a property independent of her husband perhaps reinforces the conclusion that Thomas was not to be trusted.

Furthermore, George (III), like his father, augmented his freehold and tenantright properties by taking out leases – he left to his son George (IV) 'that farm or tenements at the Upper Moor of Bradwell which I lease for a certain number of years yet to come from Henry Eyre of Rowtor esquire'.

---

19 Pingle is an East Midlands dialect term meaning a small enclosure, usually long and narrow.
20 DRO, D7676/BagC/2292, 'Abstract of the title of Mr George Bagshaw and others … to two closes or parcels of land called Mirey Holme and Mirey Holme Lees … at Bradwell' (April 1831).
21 SA, OD/1351.
22 DRO, D7676/BagC/2212.

Despite these family connections, there is little to suggest that the Bagshaws acquired freehold property by inheritance from anyone other than their own father or grandfather. The only clear exception concerned the acquisition of two tenements at Haigh, on the edge of Glossop, 16 miles to the north-west. In 1698 Nicholas Warrington of Haigh, yeoman, left these to his daughter Mary Wright. She was married to Timothy Wright of Litton near Tideswell, but when he died in 1716 she retained the Haigh property, which did not pass to her stepchildren by Timothy's first wife. In 1719 she married, as his second wife, George Bagshaw (III) of Hazlebadge and brought with her the two tenements, but in 1724 she and George sold them to her brother John, a yeoman of Hayfield. This was logical: John could manage the property far more conveniently, and the sale relieved George of dealing with a holding that was geographically distant from and irrelevant to the Hazlebadge estate.[23]

Successive generations therefore regarded the acquisition of freehold land as an investment and as a means of providing an inheritance for junior male descendants. Younger sons and grandsons were bequeathed smallholdings and lesser properties, sometimes for life and sometimes outright. The use of the device whereby holdings were given as a life interest, with the obligation that they would eventually revert to the senior male line, emphasises that this was a rationally organised policy rather than random gift-giving. Furthermore, the smaller tenantright estate at Coplowdale in Hazlebadge, with freehold additions immediately adjacent in Little Hucklow, was employed as a specific provision for a younger son or grandson. Thus George (III) left the tenancy to his grandson George Barnsley (when it was then called Grant Intack). In the late seventeenth century Francis Bagshaw (I) had acquired the land immediately adjoining this in Little Hucklow. This was added to the farm in Hazlebadge and was subsequently managed separately from the Hazlebadge Hall estate. A 1776 survey of Bradwell itemises George's holdings in the open fields and meadows: there were 14 separate parcels of land totalling 8a 3r 31p (probably of customary measure), an average size of just over three-quarters of an acre and all acquired piecemeal during the previous half century. Most of the smaller parcels of freehold land in Bradwell, like the outlying properties at Wheston and Hathersage Booths, were held by tenants – thus Abraham Ibberson was the occupier of the Bagshaw-owned smallholding in Bradwell that bore his name.

As noted, the Hathersage Booths property reverted by bequest to the Slinn family on the death of George (III) in 1764, while George Barnsley acquired the Coplowdale tenantright estate, but all the other properties were still in the hands of George Bagshaw (IV) when he died in 1791. He bequeathed to his disabled son George 'all my freehold closes lands and tenements at Copladale in the possession of John Heely'.[24] Mary Fox, widow, was to receive the rents and profits of closes in Bradwell called Balgy Crofts, in the possession of Isaac Moltby, and of a tenement in the possession of Robert Cooper, for the upkeep of her two sons John and Joseph Fox, who at the age of 21 were to inherit the properties outright. The reason for this

---

23   DRO, D7676/BagC/2930.

24   The nature of George's disability is never spelled out, but from the way the provision for him is described in the wills of George IV (his father) and Francis (his brother), some form of mental incapacity is implied. He died at the age of 62.

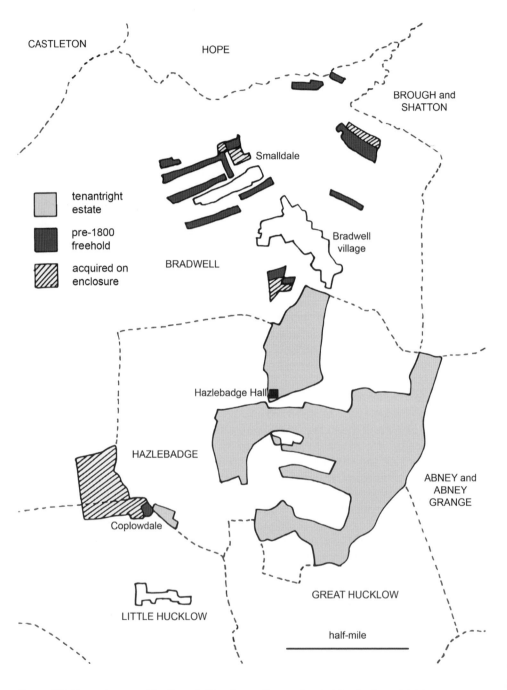

Figure 7.2. Property owned by Francis Bagshaw either as freehold or by tenantright.

bequest is not stated, but, unsurprisingly, the parish register shows that George was the father of the two boys. George left 'all other freehold lands and tenements ... with all my estate in Bradwell, and all my estate in Wheston, Tideswell and Little Hucklow' to his eldest son Francis (II), as well as the 'tenant right of that part of farm or tenement called Haslebadge Hall which I now occupy under the Duke of Rutland'.

The final stage in the acquisition of land came in the early nineteenth century, when, as a freeholder in Bradwell and Little Hucklow, Francis Bagshaw benefited from the enclosure of the two townships. At Bradwell, as in many other townships in the White Peak, parliamentary enclosure differed from the conventional model.[25] Earlier piecemeal enclosure within the open fields had created a fragmented pattern with surviving unenclosed strips or bundles and irregular patches of common meadow, militating against the creation of large geometric fields. The new enclosures tended to be small and abutted older enclosures of the same freeholder. By the award of 1819 Francis Bagshaw was allocated 11a 2r 05p in six allotments scattered among the open fields, together with 23a 1r 38p of the former Berristall Common, at the south-western corner of Bradwell township, adjacent to Little Hucklow and Hazlebadge.[26] At Little Hucklow the pattern of enclosure was less complicated, but the principle of making allotments immediately adjacent to a freeholder's existing inclosures likewise applied, even where the ancient enclosures were over the boundary in Hazlebadge lordship. In 1814 Francis received three allotments together containing 10a 2r 35p.[27]

IV

At the end of the eighteenth century Francis Bagshaw had an estate of around 500 acres, spread across five townships and, as the foregoing outlines, acquired over two centuries (Figure 7.2). His family had consolidated its position, becoming locally the chief tenants of the Rutland estate and purchasing or renting a range of additional properties. Their wills and inventories demonstrate a rapidly increasing prosperity in the middle decades of the eighteenth century, giving an evolving social position that can be identified in various sources. The 1658 Easter Roll for the parish of Hope provides a useful starting point: a 'full census of all the householders of this extensive parish', it named 606 householders. There were six contributors from Hazlebadge, of whom Edward Oldfield paid 1s 6d and John Slater and Francis Bagshaw 1s 4d each. In the parish as a whole 56 paid more than Francis, giving a measure of his standing as a middle-ranking yeoman, while 24 others paid the same amount. Martin Middleton, whose daughter Mary would marry Francis's son George, paid 1s 10d in Bradwell, including customary token sums for cows, calves, horses and sheep, while another of the same rank was Roger Bagshaw of Abney, who paid 1s 3d and had cows and sheep as well as ploughland.[28]

---

25   John Barnatt and Ken Smith, *The Peak District: Landscapes through Time* (Bollington, 2004), ch. 7, esp. 82–5.

26   DRO, D1828/A/PZ/3/1, Hope, Aston, Bradwell and Thornhill enclosure award and map.

27   DRO, D1828/A/PZ/2/1, Little Hucklow enclosure award and map.

28   J. Charles Cox, 'Easter Roll for the parish of Hope for the year 1658', *DAJ*, 11 (1889), pp. 15–30.

Because they were not freeholders in Hazlebadge, the Bagshaws did not qualify for the county franchise for their main estate, but they were eligible to vote by virtue of freehold elsewhere. The poll book for High Peak Hundred in the December 1701 general election shows that George Bagshaw voted, while in 1734 he qualified because of property in Bradwell. There is no entry for Bagshaw of Hazlebadge in the poll books for the 1656 and 1689 general elections, or for 1768.[29] As freeholders and prominent tenants under the dukes of Rutland, the Bagshaws occupied a locally significant social position, albeit one less elevated than that of their distant cousins at Ford Hall and Ridge Hall. Between 1708 and 1755 James Clegg of Chapel en le Frith, a dissenting minister and doctor, kept a diary in which on 15 April 1742 he recorded that 'I was at home til afternoon, Mr Bagshaw of Hazelbatch din'd with us, I walked up to the Fair on business, met with Mr Fletcher there and spent some time with him and other good friends.' George Bagshaw was visiting Chapel Fair on agricultural and, perhaps more importantly, social business. He was familiar with, and part of the social circle of, the professional classes in and around the small market town.[30]

Another potential measure of relative social position is the amount of Land Tax paid, although the unchanging sums contributed by each township do not precisely reflect changes in individual rankings.[31] In 1787 Hazlebadge was assessed for £8 13s in Land Tax, of which George Bagshaw (IV) paid £2 14s 1d and his cousin George Barnsley, whose daughter Ann had married George's son Francis seven years before, paid 11s 7d for the tenantright estate at Coplowdale. In Bradwell in the same year George Bagshaw paid 10s 2½d, his contribution being in respect of seven separate holdings all occupied by tenants. In 1800 Bradwell contributed £20 16s 4d and Francis Bagshaw paid £1 8s 3d of this, for properties let to 14 different tenants. This reflected the acquisition of scattered parcels of land, a strategy his father and grandfather had pursued in the previous 50 years as an investment producing rent income.

The titles used for individuals are notoriously prone to self-flattery, or deliberate downgrading by external observers, but they help to indicate social mobility. As noted earlier, Roger Bagshaw was described as a husbandman in 1646 and a yeoman in 1679, and for the next hundred years the latter was the most usual description – although in 1742 James Clegg referred in his private diary entry to 'Mr Bagshaw', using the courtesy title for a gentleman. By the end of the century a further public progression had been achieved. In September 1791 Francis Bagshaw of Hazlebadge was among those issued with a licence to kill game,[32] an indicator of superior status and marking his place among the gentry and clergy of the county (even though his estate was largely held as a tenancy). This upgrade was emphasised by a lease that

---

29 DA, 208 (poll book for 1701 general election); D215 Z/Z 1, 'A copy of a poll taken for the County of Derby, the 16th, 17th, 18th, and 20th Days of May, 1734'; D258/34/5/1 (poll sheets for the 1656 general election); D258/24/27/1 and 2 (two copies of poll books for the 1689 election).

30 Vanessa S. Doe (ed.), *The diary of James Clegg of Chapel en le Frith, 1708–55*, 3 vols, Derbyshire Record Society 2, 3 and 5 (Chesterfield, 1978–81), vol. ii, p. 456.

31 All material relating to the Land Tax is taken from the returns for High Peak Hundred available on microfilm at the DRO.

32 *Derby Mercury*, 15 September 1791.

he granted in 1799 as 'Francis Bagshaw of Hazlebadge ... Gentleman'.[33] Another indicator of social status and gentlemanly pursuits was that in 1813 John Farey's *General view of the agriculture and minerals of Derbyshire* included 'Bagshaw, Francis, of Hazlebadge in Hope, near Tideswell' in 'An alphabetical list of those persons who contributed their assistance and information towards the contents of this ... volume'.[34]

However, his gentlemanly status was marginal and, as a minor freeholder, he never quite made the grade: his death notice in 1828 describes him ambivalently as 'Mr Francis Bagshaw, of Hazlebadge, yeoman'.[35] By farming perhaps 500 acres he was able to aspire to the rank of gentleman, but the enduring tenancy at will was unquestionably a constraint. Indeed, Hazlebadge Hall itself was not rebuilt or improved after the late seventeenth century. The Bagshaws had no incentive to do so and the Rutland estate was likewise unmotivated. The house became steadily more old-fashioned, visually and functionally, and signally failed to complement the social aspirations of its occupants.[36] That, significantly, could also be said of Haddon Hall itself. In the eighteenth century its decaying and neglected medieval character was sharply and unfavourably contrasted with the smart and fashionable appearance of its arch-rival, Chatsworth.

A different measure of social position was the role played within the local community, but here Hazlebadge, with its very small population and absolute dominance by the dukes of Rutland, offered no opportunity, while in Bradwell there were numerous freeholders, a strongly independent-minded group of free miners and only a modest Bagshaw landholding. There is no evidence that members of the family ever held lesser county office or served in such roles in the High Peak hundred. Nevertheless, there are glimpses of an aspiration to act as patrons of the community. For example, George Bagshaw (II), in his will of 1743, adopted a long-familiar and by then very old-fashioned form of *post mortem* patronage: 'I likewise give and bequeath to all poor persons who shall come to my house on the day of my funeral to each of them two pennies.' This kindness was matched by a longer-term commemoration:

> I likewise give and bequeath the rents, issues and profits of a certain piece of land called the Calf Patch within the Liberty of Little Hucklow and now in the possession of Hugh Pierson, to be distributed in beef for ever, among the poor of the neighbourhood for ever at Christmas Eve, at the discretion of my son George Bagshaw and his heirs male for ever.

There seems to be no further trace of this thoughtful gesture.[37]

---

33   University of Manchester Library, GB 133 BAG/13/3/47.

34   John Farey, *General view of the agriculture and minerals of Derbyshire*, 2 vols (London, 1813), vol. ii, p. xiii.

35   *Derby Mercury*, 27 August 1828.

36   I am grateful to Richard Hoyle for discussing this with me.

37   For example, it is not mentioned in the *Digest of the Reports made by the Commissioners of Inquiry into Charities ... County of Derby* (1841).

V

Although farming was central to the prosperity of the Bagshaws of Hazlebadge, successive generations understood the potential of diversification. Building a complete picture of these activities is impossible, as the documentary record is so fragmented, but a number of interests can be demonstrated. One, already considered, was money-lending; another was involvement in minor industrial enterprises. In September 1699 George Bagshaw (II) and Samuel Bennett of Hope agreed with John Calver, steward to the duke of Rutland, to take a lease on a water cornmill and kiln for seven years at £10 per annum.[38] The fate of this venture is unknown, but it was an overtly speculative decision on the part of both men, as the mill was at Alport by Youlgreave, ten miles south of Hazlebadge Hall. It had no connection with farming at Hazlebadge and can have been of interest only for the potential profit involved. Almost precisely a century later, in June 1799, George's great-grandson Francis Bagshaw (II) leased two small parcels of land called The Close and Far Bradwell Lee, with the Bradwell Brook running between them, to Hugh and Isaac Hill of Bradwell, cotton manufacturers, for 21 years at an annual rent of £5. The lease hinted that the brothers would erect a cotton mill on the land, the water wheel and other machinery being explicitly mentioned.[39] In April 1812 these properties were among those described in a mortgage deed as being in the possession of Hugh Hill, with 'a manufactory thereon'.[40]

Potentially more important than these opportunities, though equally difficult to reconstruct from fragmented evidence, was involvement in lead-mining and lead-smelting. Hazlebadge was on the southern edge of the Bradwell lead field, by the eighteenth century among the most productive in the Peak District. A series of veins trended roughly east–west across the liberty, their exploitation being regulated by the private barmote court of the dukes of Rutland. The mining records for Hazlebadge are scanty because it was a private jurisdiction, but those that survive provide insights into the Bagshaw interest, particularly in the decades around 1800.[41] The limited seventeenth-century sources do not refer to the family, although others connected with them by marriage are mentioned. Thus, in January 1645 Martin Middleton, father in law of George (II), was among those who illegally sank a shaft into 'two meeres of ground lying in hasslebadge' and took ore from it.[42] C. Heathcote, the historian of the industry, lists Francis Bagshaw as being involved in 1785 in an unnamed mine in Intake Dale, south-west of Hazlebadge Hall, while in 1778 George Barnsley, his cousin, was involved in the Farmers Venture Mine on Nether Water Farm, where he

---

38   HHA, Alport item 1.

39   University of Manchester Library, Special Collections, BAG/13/3/47.

40   DRO, D7676/BagC/2292.

41   The Bagshaws of Hazlebadge did not give their name to Bagshaw(e) Cavern, the erstwhile showpiece cave at Bradwell discovered during mining operations in 1807. It was named for their distant relative, Sir William Chambers Bagshawe.

42   Quoted in C. Heathcote, 'A history and gazetteer of the lead mines within the private liberty or lordship of Hazlebadge, Derbyshire, 1292–1947', *Mining History: The Bulletin of the Peak District Mines Historical Society*, 19/5 (Autumn 2016), p. 2.

held the tenantright under the duke of Rutland.[43] Barnsley discovered the lead vein there while quarrying for limestone, and in 1779 formally took possession when he

> freed a Founder Meer in the Dale or Hollow Close which he gave the name Farmers Venture.[44] 6 Meers at the East End of the 6 Meers as first allowed ranging up the hill Eastwardly – And he having in his tryal some appearance of another vein he had 6 meers south and the same north.[45]

A verdict of the Hazlebadge barmote court in April 1812 relating to the state of repair of the belland yards, the walled enclosures around mine-workings that prevented animals from grazing on the toxic waste heaps, noted that those on 'Mr Bagshaw's Graunt Hedge [property]' and his farm at Broomhill Mine did not require immediate attention, suggesting that there was further otherwise undocumented mining on the Hazlebadge estate.[46]

Within the liberty of Bradwell, where he held freehold property, Francis was more actively involved in exploiting lead reserves. In 1808 'Mr Francis Bagshaw gave one dish of ore to free a 2nd Taker Meer North West from the Founder Shaft at Never Fear in a Pipe called Moorfurlong Old Pipe at Smalldale Head'. Eight years later he 'gave one dish or ore to free a Founder Meer in an Old Vein West of Hearne Stone Lane Head called Wooden Stile'.[47] Moorfurlong Pipe extended north-westwards from Bradwell village across Smalldale in the direction of Castleton, passing through an area of commonland and open fields where Francis held a number of enclosed parcels. Immediately north of Smalldale was an area much disturbed by older mining operations and given the unflattering epithet of 'Dirty Half Acres'. Others were trying their luck in that area of the township, making use of the mining custom whereby anybody could stake a claim in another's land: in 1806 Christopher Jackson gave the customary dish of ore 'to free a Founder Meer in an Old Vein for the mine called Union Venture lying in the North Side of Dirty Half Acres ... in Mr Bagshaw's Fields'.[48]

Lead-smelting was a lucrative opportunity for local landowners. By the mid-eighteenth century the older method of using 'bole hearths', with the draught provided

---

43   *Ibid.*, p. 23.

44   This arcane terminology refers to the procedure, carefully regulated by and enacted at the barmote court, whereby the discoverer of a lead vein could stake a claim to work it [to 'free a Founder Meer'] on payment of a dish of ore to the mineral owner, in this case the duke of Rutland. A 'meer' was a length of vein, which in the private mining liberty of Hazlebadge was 28 yards. The original 'founder meer' could be extended if the vein was followed further. The dish of ore was proof that this was a genuine discovery, and was quite distinct from subsequent royalty payments.

45   *Ibid.*, p. 23.

46   DRO, Wagstaffe Mining Collection, D1289/BL/104.

47   C. Heathcote, 'A history and gazetteer of the lead mines within Bradwell liberty, Derbyshire, 1216–1890', *Mining History: The Bulletin of the Peak District Mines Historical Society*, 17/5 (Summer 2010), pp. 62, 68.

48   Heathcote, 'Bradwell liberty', p. 59, citing Chatsworth Archives (Barmasters' Collection), 215, 26 July 1806.

by water-powered bellows, was being superseded by the cupola system, operating on the reverberatory principle using closed furnaces. A major problem hitherto had been that the fuel and ore were mixed, requiring the use of expensive charcoal because the sulphur in mineral coal produced impurities in the smelted metal. In the cupola system the ore and the fuel were separated, allowing the use of coal, readily available in Derbyshire. This was more efficient and greatly increased production, but required a more substantial building to accommodate the process. Cupola furnaces appear to have been introduced to Derbyshire in the 1730s by Richard Bagshawe (another distant relation) and by the 1770s had largely eclipsed the older methods.[49]

Over half a century ago Willies suggested that information about the Bradwell cupolas was very limited, although he identified four sites.[50] The Bradwell Land Tax assessment for 1820 records that James Furness paid 2s 2d for a 'cupola', and in his will of 1825 George Barnsley, father in law and cousin of Francis (II) Bagshaw, left to his three sons and his daughter Ann Bagshaw equal shares in 'The Cupiloa situate on Bradwell Hills with all the tools and apurtenances thereunto belonging … which said premisis I hav[e] let to Messrs Furnis for a number of years yet to come'. Ann Bagshaw died in 1831 and left her quarter share of 'All that Cupola or smelting mill with the premises thereto belonging situate at Bradwell now in the occupation of Mr James Furniss' to be subdivided into three smaller equal shares, one each for Elizabeth, Rachel and Isabella Furniss, the daughters of her daughter Mary Furniss, when they attained the age of 21. James Furniss, the smelter, was therefore not only George Barnsley's tenant but also his grandson-in-law.

VI

The 1820 Land Tax returns show that Francis Bagshaw farmed some Bradwell land himself, but also had 11 tenants including his son George (V), himself a smallholder. However, George is not named in the 1827 return, having been replaced by George Fox, his brother-in-law, who had married Hannah Bagshaw in 1819.

The financial disintegration of the estate can be traced to 1812. Francis, although (or probably because) he could describe himself as a 'gentleman', was a spendthrift. An abstract of title to the two parcels of land at Mirey Holme and Mirey Holme Lees in Bradwell recites the sequence of transactions by which the estate was first mortgaged and then changed hands.[51] Francis, though not the freeholder of the Hazlebadge Hall estate, borrowed heavily on the security of his tenancy at will. In April 1812, 'having immediate occasion for £600', he mortgaged the two closes to George Gosling of Chesterfield at 5 per cent interest. In October 1814 some £200 was repaid, but in mid-September 1816 a further mortgage was agreed, this time between Francis Bagshaw and Thomas Marriott of Marple, Cheshire. It was required because Gosling had called

---

49   Lynn Willies, 'The introduction of the cupola "for smelting down lead" to Derbyshire', *Bulletin of the Peak District Mines Historical Society*, 4/5 (June 1971), pp. 384–94.

50   Lynn Willies, 'Cupola lead-smelting sites in Derbyshire, 1737–1900', *Bulletin of the Peak District Mines Historical Society*, 4/1 (1969), pp. 100–101.

51   DRO, D7676/BagC/2292.

in the balance of £400 together with interest. Bagshaw requested Marriott to 'advance him the sum of £700' in order to pay Gosling and to 'supply his other occasions', and this was duly done, subject to a bond for £1400. Shortly afterwards Marriott levied a fine against Francis and Ann Bagshaw on 'two messuages, two Barns, two Stables, two shippons, two curtilages, two gardens, 100 acres of Land, common of pasture for all cattle and common of turbary … in Little Hucklow and Bradwell', indicating that all the freehold estate was now encumbered.

In November 1821 it was stated that the £700 actually belonged to the late Moses Hadfield of Newton in Manchester, to whom Marriott was nephew and executor. By then Francis Bagshaw had borrowed a further £200 from the Hadfield estate, bringing the total capital loan to £900. Meanwhile, in 1819 he had made his will, which perhaps reflected the incipient crisis – and the associated family breakdown – in that it leaves only a cash sum to his heir and makes no mention of the real estate or the Hazlebadge tenancy. He provided for the maintenance of his disabled brother George; left £200 to his son George (V); left a lifetime interest in the estate to his wife Ann; and required that on her death everything should be equally divided between his eight children. He died on 21 August 1828 aged 68, having acquired a legendary reputation for drunken and eccentric behaviour:

> Bull and bear baiting were very popular in Derbyshire at one time, and Bradwell Wakes never passed without one or the other of them, often both [held] in some open space, either the Town Gate or the Town Bottom … the bull was tied to a post securely fixed in a stone let into the ground. At a given signal dogs were let loose on the bull, and betting was made on the dogs, the one that could pin the bull by the nose being declared the winner … Sometimes the bull might break loose, when the spectators would take to their heels helter skelter for their life to elude him. But one of the most exciting scenes was witnessed at one of these bull baitings about the year 1820. There was the bull, the dogs … but no post. Among the spectators was old Frank Bagshaw, of Hazlebadge, who stepped into the breach. Running into the ring he cried 'Tey him me; tey him to me'. They tied the bull by the tail to poor Bagshaw, and when the dogs were set at the brute it darted off, dragging Bagshaw at its tail up Bradwell Brook, a deplorable spectacle.[52]

He died with his £900 mortgage debt still unpaid. His brother George had predeceased him, as had his children Francis and Mary, leaving Ann and the six surviving children to deal with the tangled finances. As stated in a legal opinion at the time, 'Francis Bagshaw was considerably involved, and he had granted mortgages upon the whole of his property by the time of making his will.' And his son George (V) had more than his father's debts: he had debts of his own.

In March 1830 George (V) raised a further mortgage of £270 (at 5 per cent) from Thomas Gregory of Eyam, necessitated because he was facing an action for

---

52   Seth Evans, *Bradwell: Ancient and modern. History of the parish and of incidents in the Hope Valley and District* (1912), pp. 45–6.

debt for £540. The freehold estate was fully mortgaged and in any case was held by George's mother Ann for her lifetime, so the new loan was on the security of his future inheritance. Thomas Marriott, however, now wanted the £900 repaid, so a remortgage covering the full sum was arranged in May 1830 at 4.5 per cent, the lender being Josiah Birley, farmer of Wardlow. In late November 1830 William, one of the younger Bagshaw brothers, borrowed £81 from a consortium of moneylenders, also on the security of future inheritance. It was fully repaid in February 1831, but in mid-December 1830 Samuel, the third remaining brother, 'being in the immediate want of money and by reason of the said Ann Bagshaw being yet living, no sale of the hereditaments … could then be effected', had borrowed £50 from Thomas Gregory. He increased this by £10 in February 1831 and another £20 in April, making a total of £80, none of which was repaid. Meanwhile, it was stated that George was further in debt to the tune of £110 to William Kenyon of Bradwell, victualler, for 'meat, drink and lodging found and provided for him [by] William Kenyon'. As he already owed £270 plus interest to Thomas Gregory, the only solution was for George to convey to Kenyon the three one-eighth shares in the freehold properties that he would soon inherit on the death of his mother, unless the debt of £110 could be repaid. Ann died in late February 1831 and her will was proved on 26 March 1831. The debt was not repaid, the mortgage to Birley now encumbered the entire estate, and the edifice collapsed.

The beneficiary was George Fox, the ambitious former lead-miner and husband of Hannah Bagshaw. In November 1830 Ann Bagshaw made her will and appointed Fox 'of Bradwell' as joint executor. However, when he proved the will in mid-March 1831 Fox described himself as 'of Hazlebadge, farmer'.[53] It seems certain that, at the beginning of 1831, when Ann was still alive, he secured the tenancy at will of the Hazlebadge Hall estate. Although specific proof is lacking, he presumably also bought out the interests of the various mortgages and of his brother in law, so that the estate was no longer encumbered and he enjoyed unchallenged possession. In 1841 he and Hannah were living at the Hall with their six children and in 1851 he was described as a farmer of 230 acres. This 'usurpation' of the tenancy of course ended the tenure of male Bagshaws at Hazlebadge, but it is important to note that it actually kept the farm within the extended family. Fox's brother in law, feckless and dissolute George Bagshaw, was clearly incapable of taking on the tenancy, while the younger Bagshaw brothers had shown themselves to be bad financial managers, albeit on a less spectacular scale. Fox was manifestly competent to take over, and it is evident that he rose to the challenge. George Bagshaw, abandoned by his family, died in 1850 aged 70 at Little Hucklow, when he was described as a pauper labourer, but the Hazlebadge Hall estate stayed in the hands of the Fox family as tenants of the dukes of Rutland for almost another century.

During this period it was sometimes worked with the adjacent Hazlebadge Farm, sometimes separately. George Fox died in February 1875, having long retired from running the farm. His son Samuel had predeceased him in 1866, and the 1871 census lists Samuel's widow Margaret (aged 46) as head of the household at Hazlebadge Hall, and not her father in law George. In that year she was described

---

53   The transfer of the tenancy has not been traced in the Haddon Hall Archives.

148

as a farmer of 180 acres but in 1881 she farmed 250 acres – the tenancy, under the management of a formidable woman, was apparently subject to changing geographical definitions.

VII

In March 1920 a grand sale of many of the Derbyshire properties of the duke of Rutland, totalling 14,500 acres, was held in Chesterfield.[54] The 254½ acre Hazlebadge Hall Farm was sold to the sitting tenant Thomas Fox, the son of Samuel and Margaret, who in 1881 had farmed the 45-acre Hazlebadge Farm immediately adjacent to the Hall. The sale catalogue refers to a 'Yearly Lady-Day Tenancy', but the real story is more complicated, because the property was let at an 'apportioned rent of £174 per annum'. This indicates that the ancient tenancy at will had not been enfranchised, either voluntarily or statutorily under the Copyhold Acts 1852 and 1894, but had been subdivided with the rent apportioned *pro rata*. The particulars list six other lots with apportioned rents and these, together with Hazlebadge Hall, amounted to 306a 2r 4p, the size of the area confirming that this was the ancient tenantright estate. The aggregate rent for all seven subdivisions was £225 10s per annum, or about 15s per acre, a figure sufficiently low to explain why there had been no incentive on the part of George, Margaret or Thomas Fox to demand enfranchisement.[55]

The tenancy at will therefore survived until the beginning of the 1920s, shortly before it would have been compulsorily abolished under the Law of Property Act 1922. It had surely been both a benefit and a liability to the Bagshaws and the Foxes – a benefit because it guaranteed that rent payments would, with inflation, reduce inexorably in real terms, a liability because improvements and enhancements to the farm were ever more difficult to achieve and unlikely to be sought. Several generations of the Bagshaws were acquisitive, entrepreneurial and conscious of their status and lineage. Latterly, though, those qualities seem to have been lost as financial mismanagement and decadence eroded their robust and hard-headed approach. Under George Fox and his daughter in law the initiative was regained, but conservatism and perhaps inertia eventually resurfaced. In 1939 the widowed Thomas Fox, aged 87, was still the farmer at Hazlebadge Hall, living there with two unmarried sons aged 59 and 58 and three unmarried daughters, one aged 55 and twins of 45. Thomas and his wife Ann had had no other children: their line was destined to come to an end.[56]

The elder son, Spencer Fox, died in hospital in Sheffield on 17 March 1941, an event that may have sealed the fate of the house and estate. On 21 January 1942 Hazlebadge Hall and its farm were sold by auction. The sale notice describes it as an excellent sheep and dairy farm of about 240 acres, with a three-stall stable and indoor accommodation for a total of 53 cattle, as well as piggeries and barns. The stone-

---

54 DRO, D504/113/1 pt. 2 (sale catalogue, 1920).

55 I am very grateful to David Towns, Head of Agriculture, Estates and Rural Property at Muckle LLP, Newcastle-upon-Tyne, for discussing the enfranchisement question with me.

56 1939 Register <https://www.findmypast.co.uk/transcript?id=TNA/R39/5936/5936F/008/08>, accessed 19 September 2020.

built, rough-cast and slate-roofed house had four bedrooms, and its centuries-old role as a working farmhouse is indicated by references to a dairy and a wool store.[57]

The property was purchased by the Rowarth family, who already owned the neighbouring Hazlebadge Farm, bringing to an end over 350 years' occupation by the Bagshaw and Fox families. Thomas Fox outlived his eldest son, dying in November 1943 at the age of 91. The surviving son, Samuel Bagshaw Fox, and his three spinster sisters moved into a new property, The Bungalow, a couple of hundreds of yards away on the opposite side of the Tideswell road.

Samuel died there in August 1962, to be followed by his sisters Helen Ann (in the cruel winter of 1963) and Hannah Elizabeth in July 1965. And then there was one … the last of the family, Margaret Kate Fox, died in August 1969 in a nursing home in Chesterfield. Hazlebadge Hall and the combined farms are now owned by E.S. Rowarth & Sons Ltd.

---

57   *Derbyshire Times and Chesterfield Herald,* 16 January 1942.

Chapter 8

The food production campaign in the First World War: the Derbyshire War Agricultural Committees, 1915–1919[*]

Nicola Verdon

On 29 May 1919 members of the Ilkeston District War Agricultural Committee met at the town's Rutland Hotel for the final time. Under an edict issued by the Board of Agriculture in the spring of that year, the County and District agricultural committees across England and Wales were to be disbanded and their work transferred to newly created committees of the county councils.[1] The Ilkeston District Executive Officer, Mr Frederick S. Ogden, a local surveyor and estate agent, took the opportunity to deliver a report that reflected on the role and achievements of the committee.[2] It had, he argued, dealt with 'every variety of circumstance arising in connection with agriculture during the War' and watched over the interests of farmers in connection to labour supply ('a matter in which the military authorities had been extremely difficult to deal with'), the cultivation of land and cropping – through which an additional 2,400 acres of grassland had been brought under arable production in the district – and the provision of horses, machinery, tools, seeds and additional sources of labour, such as prisoners of war and threshing gangs. The committee had kept farmers informed about the latest developments and shielded them from the volley of orders and directives 'showered upon them', as he put it, from Whitehall. Ogden was confident that their work had left firm foundations on which the new committees could build during peacetime. He concluded,

> To the agricultural committees belongs the honour of a notable achievement, in the organization and bringing to a successful conclusion of the gigantic food production campaign, a campaign into which, though so many things were against his interest, the farmer entered wholeheartedly for the safety of the country and the feeding of its people.[3]

---

[*] All citations to the records of the County War Agricultural Committee are to records held at the Derbyshire Record Office.

1 John Sheail, 'The role of the War Agricultural and Executive Committees in the food production campaign of 1915–1918 in England and Wales', *Agricultural Administration*, 1 (1974), p. 153.

2 Ogden had been invited to become a member when the Derbyshire War Agricultural Committee was first set up in 1915, probably, as he put it, 'on the grounds of my membership of the Agricultural division of the (then) Surveyors Institute'. D331/1/28, letter, F.S. Ogden to J. Sheail, 14 June 1972.

3 D331/1/27, Assorted documents and miscellaneous papers relating to the War Agricultural Committee, 1915–19, Meeting of Ilkeston District, 29 May 1919.

Committee members – 'gentlemen whose interests were in, and knowledge and experience of, the land' – were thanked for their work, aided, as Ogden noted, by the presence of the 'pleasantest relations' among them. In his absence, the tact and acumen of the long-serving chair of the committee, Charles Crompton, councillor and JP of Stanton Hall, were acknowledged as central to his success in promoting 'the work of the committee and the interests of the agriculturalist'.[4]

The self-proclaimed achievements of the Ilkeston district can be set against those for Derbyshire as a whole. In 1917, when government intervention gathered pace, farmers in the county were given two main tasks: to plough and sow 30,000 acres more than in 1916 (mostly on newly broken-up land) and to maintain the maximum output of food crops on existing arable. In April 1918 the Board of Agriculture wrote to congratulate the Derbyshire Executive Committee on being the first county in England to reach its plough-up quota. Farmers had been persuaded 'to set aside hitherto accepted principles of husbandry and adopt methods required by a war emergency programme' in order for this to succeed.[5] In a county more suited to dairy farming than arable production, this chapter will explore how this policy was implemented. Unlike after the Second World War, when the government required all agricultural committees to deposit their records centrally (these are now in The National Archives), the records relating to the First World War committees were largely destroyed or lost. Those that survive are patchy, but in Derbyshire Record Office there is a good deposit of material, albeit fragmentary, that has been little utilised and allows us to piece together an overview of how a national policy was implemented at the local level. How were the targets met? Who ran the committees and what do they tell us about the operation of power relations at the local level? Did farmers enter 'wholeheartedly' into the scheme? Behind the achievements of the plough-up campaign was a series of disputes and tensions, between the centre and locality and within the localities themselves, that show that success in Derbyshire was far from straightforward.

I

In 1914 farming was emerging, bruised but intact, from decades of depression. While those who farmed crops on the heavy claylands of the south-east of England were the worst affected, farmers who concentrated on meat, dairy, fruit and vegetables had fared better. Derbyshire was predominately a dairy county, providing milk for urban populations and, to a lesser extent, cheese and butter. It was dominated by small family farms, with an average size of 49 acres.[6] Some 40,000 acres of formerly arable land had been laid down to permanent grass in the county between the 1870s and the beginning of the war (Table 8.1). Before the plough-up campaign, therefore, arable

---

4   *Ibid.*

5   D331/1/27, Quarterly report of the Derbyshire War Agricultural Executive Committee, 15 December 1917.

6   BPP, 1919, Cmd 25, Board of Agriculture and Fisheries. Wages and conditions of employment in agriculture, II, Report of investigators, South Derbyshire, p. 62.

Table 8.1
Agricultural statistics of Derbyshire in 1874 and 1915.

	1874	1915	+/- change
Total acreage under crops and grass	501,528	483,125	-18,403
Permanent grass	361,852	402,412	+40,580
Total arable:	139,676	80,713	-58,963
Wheat	33,125	18,752	-14,373
Barley	13,264	4,105	-9,159
Oats	24,952	19,912	-5,040
Beans	2,032	146	-1,936
Potatoes	3,203	2,058	-545
Horses	18,693	20,211	+1,518
Cattle	144,565	152,087	+7,522
Sheep	275,483	140,677	-134,806
Pigs	41,197	30,641	-10,556

Source: D331/1/22, Agricultural statistics of Derbyshire, comparative acreage in 1874 and 1915.

formed one-sixth of the total acreage under grass and crops. The number of cattle increased slightly over the same period, but sheep numbers halved.

At the start of the war there was little concern over food production nationally and any possible disruption to supply lines was downplayed, despite Britain's heavy reliance on imported foodstuffs: around 80 per cent of wheat and flour, 40 per cent of mutton and lamb and 30 per cent of beef and veal consumed in Britain were produced abroad. Domestically, the harvest of 1914 was brought in without too much trouble, aided by warm weather and an adequate supply of labour. Total wheat production in 1914 showed an increase compared with the average of the previous ten years, and yields per acre of wheat, barley and oats were better in 1914 than they had been in 1913.[7] Some unease was beginning to be felt by 1915, however. In the autumn of that year the Milner committee (set up by the new president of the Board of Agriculture, Lord Selbourne) recommended that wheat production should be expanded through a series of deficiency payments.[8] War Agricultural Committees (WACs) should be set up via county councils to organise the supply of local labour and examine food production in their localities. Their establishment was not mandatory, they had no statutory powers and, overall, a 'business as usual' attitude prevailed.[9]

The agricultural committees began to take shape locally towards the end of 1915. In November Derbyshire County Council appointed the existing agricultural sub-committee to be the WAC for the county, with powers to add to their number. Following

---

7   Nicola Verdon, *Working the land: a history of the farmworker in England from 1850 to the present day* (London, 2017), pp. 123–4; P.E. Dewey, *British agriculture in the First World War* (London, 1989), Table 2.7, p. 16.

8   Explained by Dewey, *British agriculture*, p. 25.

9   Dewey, *British agriculture*, p. 27.

a Board of Agriculture requirement that both a central Executive Committee (EC) and District Committees (DCs) should be convened, six district committees were created, for Derby, Chesterfield, Ilkeston, Ashbourne, Bakewell and Chapel-en-le-Frith. At first, the work expected of the Committees was somewhat unclear. As Mr Jenkyn Brown, director of Education for Derbyshire, told a meeting of farmers in December 1915, 'the Board of Agriculture itself did not know exactly what could be done'.[10] Topics such as labour supply and how to increase the home supply of food formed part of the early discussions, but there was uncertainty about the role Derbyshire could play in this. Mr J.R. Bond, organiser of Agricultural Education in Derbyshire, told a meeting at Cromford in late November that this county was 'not much affected by war', beyond higher grain and cattle cake prices, and, even if it had been a wheat-growing county, he would not, 'on account of the shortage of hands, advise the ploughing up of grassland. This was a grazing county, and the pastures and meadows were the principal crops'.[11]

As part of this initial, somewhat hesitant intervention in the agricultural sector, counties were also encouraged to set up Women's Committees, attached to the WACs. This was in light of Board of Trade estimates that showed the number of women working on the land in England and Wales had declined by 16,000 between July 1914 and July 1915.[12] In February 1916 this voluntary step became compulsory and by the summer of that year 63 Women's War Agricultural Committees (WWACs) were in existence across England and Wales.[13] In Derbyshire each district WAC had appointed a Women's Committee by April 1916 with the remit of increasing the number of resident village women working on the land. To promote this, a register of women willing to work in agriculture was established. Although all rural women, whatever their social background, were encouraged to participate in work on the land, a Board of Agriculture circular stated that 'by far the largest and also the most suitable source of labour for the farmer's need' was working-class village women, 'the wives and families of the male labourers and other residents'.[14] In Derbyshire arrangements were also made for a number of women to receive a three-week training course at the Midland Agricultural and Dairy College, Kingston-on-Soar, and prominent local landowners, including Captain Fitzherbert Wright, MP, of Yeldersley Hall, Ashbourne, offered to train women on their farms.[15]

The real shift towards greater state control took place in the autumn of 1916, when a series of issues coincided to reveal the pressures the agricultural sector was coming under. The home-grown wheat crop of that year was substantially less

---

10 *Derbyshire Advertiser and Journal*, 11 December 1915.

11 *Derbyshire Advertiser and Journal*, 3 December 1915.

12 BPP, 1918, Cd. 9164, Employment of women. Report of the Board of Trade on the increased employment of women during the war in the United Kingdom, pp. 13–14. See Nicola Verdon, '"Left out in the cold": village women and agricultural labour in England and Wales during the First World War', *Twentieth Century British History*, 27 (2016), pp. 1–25.

13 Pamela Horn, *Rural life in England in the First World War* (Dublin, 1984), p. 120.

14 Imperial War Museum, LAND 1/38, Circular letter to the Women's Farm Labour Committees, December 1916.

15 *Derbyshire Advertiser and Journal*, 15 April 1916.

than that of 1915, and potatoes, oats and barley showed little, if any, improvement. Inflation had rocketed and food importation became more expensive and challenging: four million tons of shipping was lost in a six-month period as the German U-boat campaign expanded. There was also growing concern about labour shortages in agriculture: rates of volunteerism had been high among farm workers and although skilled workers were protected from conscription, the designation of skilled labour was disputed and the needs of the war machine continued to draw labour off the land. Although the figures are contested, contemporary estimates stated that agriculture lost around a third of its workers during the war.[16] In Derbyshire, labour losses may have been even more pronounced: it was estimated that of the 7,763 men recorded as agricultural labourers in the 1911 census, around 3,500 had left by the end of 1916, while other men had taken work in the mines or munition factories.[17] The start of 1917, with David Lloyd George newly installed as the coalition prime minister, therefore saw the beginning of a much more targeted and organised food production policy.

This food strategy took several directions. A new administrative structure was developed to frame and manage policy. In December 1916 Rowland Prothero became the president of the Board of Agriculture, and on the first day of 1917 a new Food Production Department (FPD), attached to the Board of Agriculture, was appointed. A plough-up policy was launched, to increase the acreage of land committed to arable production and assist farmers to cultivate their land more effectively. This was to be implemented through County War Agricultural Committees (CWACs), a remodelled version of the earlier WACs. As their name implied, these were also organised on a county basis. They were to consist of between four and seven persons and were held responsible for ensuring that central government policies were implemented at the local level.[18] To assist them were numerous sub-committees to oversee cropping, issue orders and organise labour supplies.

In Derbyshire the central EC met at St Mary's Gate in Derby, chaired by Brigadier-General Harry Chandos-Pole-Gell. J.R. Bond became its chief executive officer. This was an onerous position that carried responsibility for coordinating the work of the different branches and effectively implementing government policy, and it needed men who had comprehensive prior knowledge of the county.[19] The choice of agricultural educational organisers such as Bond to take this role was therefore judicious. Costs for office accommodation and secretarial assistance were funded by the FPD. In Derbyshire sub-committees for Labour, Supplies, Finance, General Purposes, Machinery, District Representatives, Compensation, Hay Purchases, Milk Prices and the Farm Survey were established. In the quarter ending September 1917 the EC met 13 times and its sub-committees 33 times.[20] Two additional District

---

16 Verdon, *Working the land*, pp. 130–2.

17 BPP, 1919, Cmd 25, II, Report of investigators, North Derbyshire, p. 57.

18 Dewey, *British agriculture*, p. 92.

19 Sheail, 'War Agricultural and Executive Committees', p. 147.

20 D331/1/27. The Labour sub-committee met 13 times and Supplies six. The rest met once or twice. A reorganisation in the middle of 1918 streamlined the committees into five – Cultivation, Labour, Supplies, Horticulture and Finance.

Committees, Sudbury and Swadlincote, were added to the existing six. The powers of the central EC were devolved to the District Committees (each with its own Executive Committee). These reported weekly or fortnightly to the county Executive Committee, had the services of a full- or part-time officer and every parish or group of small parishes had representation on the district body.

The network of agricultural committees was the conduit between the farmer and the government departments whose activities and instructions impacted their daily working lives. They were, as Prothero later put it, the Board of Agriculture's 'agents in each county' and relied on the energy, efficiency and leadership skills of those who gave up their time to steer them.[21] Unlike their earlier incarnation, the CWACs were given powers of compulsion under the Defence of the Realm Act: they could inspect land, issue orders to plough up, remove inefficient farmers and take over land themselves if necessary. Farmers had the right to appeal decisions, but only to the EC that had issued them.[22] These powers were implemented with two key objectives: firstly, to improve land and increase the harvest of 1917 and, secondly, and most importantly, to extend the area of arable for the 1918 harvest. The network of administration to oversee food production and its new powers enhanced the role of both the EC and the DCs. As John Sheail argued, state policy 'could only be implemented through local committees with an intimate knowledge of conditions on each holding'.[23] The September report of the Derbyshire EC recognised the authority vested in it:

> The Committee is becoming the regular channel of communication between the farmer and the several departments whose activities affect his business; and, by the incidence of national requirements and the farmers' difficulties, the War Agricultural organization is being made increasingly responsible for the agricultural welfare of the County.[24]

A similar reorganisation of the Women's Committees took place in early 1917. In addition to their ongoing work in rallying and coordinating the work of local women, the WWACs took control of recruiting, training and placing recruits to the newly created Women's Land Army (WLA) at the local level, and for appointing organising secretaries, welfare officers and group leaders to oversee the work. Miss Ethel B. Jackson of Stubben Edge Farm in Ashover was the original county organiser for Derbyshire. The Women's Executive Committee met once a week in Derby, while Selection Committees, who interviewed and selected recruits for the WLA, were established in Derby (chair Miss M. Meynell), Ilkeston (chair, Miss Smith) and Chesterfield (chair, Mrs Peck). An additional centre at Burton-on-Trent interviewed prospective recruits for

---

21 Lord Ernle [R.E. Prothero], *The land and its people: chapters in rural life and history* (London, 1925), p. 180.

22 Dewey, *British agriculture*, p. 172.

23 Sheail, 'War Agricultural and Executive Committees', p. 145.

24 D331/1/27, Report of the Derbyshire War Agricultural Executive Committee for the three months ending 15 September 1917.

Derbyshire and Staffordshire. Miss Jackson reassured farmers that there was 'no fear of the women of Derbyshire funking work even under disagreeable conditions', and she asked farmers to 'Give us a helping hand and we shall be able to do a good deal more for you than we have done in the past.'[25]

II

One of the first edicts issued under this new structure came in January 1917 when each District Committee was asked to undertake a survey of all farmland in their area, to determine the state of farming and what land was available to plough up. Surveyors were authorised by the Board of Agriculture to enter farms and fields. This first survey was directed to the harvest of 1917. In June the ECs were then informed of their ploughing quota for 1918, targets based upon the proportion of arable to grass in each county in 1875. In Derbyshire the original quota of 35,000 was shaved down to just under 30,000 acres. This triggered a more detailed survey aimed at the 1918 harvest. By the middle of September most districts had managed to chart much of their area for this second survey – Ashbourne had surveyed 397 out of 460 farms, Swadlincote 203 out of 210 and Sudbury 225 out of 280. Others had done less well, with Chapel-en-le-Frith in the High Peak managing only 337 out of 850 farms.[26]

The Ilkeston district was comprised of around 360 farms in 28 parishes. Its survey is the only one for the county that survives. It recorded the name and address of occupier, name and address of landowner/agent, a description of the holding, the 1917 land area, livestock and labour (men including the occupier, women excluding indoor servants and boys), the area of grass to be ploughed by August 1918, the assistance required in order to achieve this and some general remarks.[27] These comments reveal the problems faced by many farmers. Virtually none had any assistance that could be spared, and many were short of labour. A farmer of 43 acres at Barrowash and Ockbrook could not 'undertake any more with the labour that he has'. The 133-acre Scotland Farm in the same parish was 'short of labour', with the land 'getting full of thistles'. Although Emma Land's 46-acre grass farm in Denby was reported 'in good condition', she had 'neither hands nor implements'. Some farmers complained of their sons being enlisted and the impact this had on completing work. At Dale Abbey it was recommended that Joseph Beeston's son, an infantryman, 'be recalled to manage and work the farm as his father is aged and unable to cope with it'. At Stanley farmer Hartshorn had been 'willing to plough four acres but his son has been taken in the army and he is now unwilling', while at Cottage Farm, Breaston, the farmer was willing to plough an additional 14 acres to the eight already completed 'if could have help of his son … who has been serving since September 1914'. Although the occupation of 'farmer' was protected from conscription, as Hilary Crowe has shown for the West Ward of Westmorland, on small family upland farms it was often the (elderly) father

---

25 *Derbyshire Times and Chesterfield Herald,* 8 September 1917.

26 D331/1/27, Report of the Derbyshire War Agricultural Executive Committee for the three months ending 15 September 1917.

27 D331/1/21, Survey of Farms, 1917.

who was given this designation, leaving the sons, who were physically fitter and did much of the work, liable to being called up.[28]

Other farms in Ilkeston were short of manure, of implements, of horses or of all three, and the survey shows that the agricultural depression of the late nineteenth century had left a legacy of dilapidated drains and fences that was difficult and costly to correct quickly. One occupier in Draycott was noted as 'willing to plough four acres of an eight-acre meadow providing a fence is put up'. He also required 'a horse, manual labour and implements'. The tenant of the 147-acre Church Farm in Sandiacre required 'mechanical cultivation, considerable labour and also financial aid to get it into anything like condition'. The scattered nature of many holdings and difficult access were also cited as impediments. At Denby the 31-acre farm of Benjamin Seals was described as 'A useful grass farm, well kept, but a long way from hard road, could not get thrashing done'. The 65-acre Land End Farm in Marlpool was a 'Very scattered holding: not suitable for arable'. Back in Breaston, it was deemed 'almost impossible' to get manure onto arable land 'owing to the state of this road in winter and the severe gradient of a portion of it'.

Although many of the comments in the remarks section were positive – farms were well maintained and farmers willing to comply with the plough-up orders – some show frustration at the lack of attention given to 'filthy' or 'wasted' land. It was recommended that 30 acres of a 117-acre farm in Stanton-by-Dale 'should be broken up at once … a complete waste of land. Covered with thistles and docks. Very badly farmed', while at the 60-acre Brook farm in Denby it was noted, 'Wheat crop spring sown is very bad, full of rubbish'. Herbert Smith of Church Farm, Sandiacre, mentioned before, was castigated for his holding being in a 'shocking state' and a special report was commissioned for this farm. William Faulkes, who farmed 65 acres in the same parish, was accused of neglecting his land. The surveyor noted pointedly, 'He has plenty of labour and ought to improve it'. The 16½-acre holding farmed by R.L. Nursall in Sandiacre was condemned as follows:

> In pitiable condition. Full of weeds and no attempt has been made to eliminate them. He has ample labour if used intelligently. He has also a large field in Risley parish: been in his possession 3 years and already depreciated badly – It was in excellent condition when he took it. He has 10 acres which ought to be ploughed. A good deal of it barren. A very strong line ought to be taken with this man.[29]

The results of the survey of farms, which detailed the quota of plough-up demanded for each district in the county and the area promised, was debated at a meeting of the chairmen and secretaries of the District Committees in Derby in October 1917. As Table 8.2 shows, progress was patchy at best. Three districts had identified around four-fifths of their quota but six had failed to reach half. Swadlincote had pledged just 14 per cent of its quota. There was considerable complaint in some districts at

---

28   Hilary Crowe, '"Murmurs of Discontent": the upland response to the Plough campaign, 1916–1918', in Richard W. Hoyle (ed.), *The farmer in England, 1650–1980* (Farnham, 2013), p. 281.

29   All quotes taken from D331/1/21, Survey of Farms, 1917.

Table 8.2
Survey of farms, as of 30 September 1917.

District	Quota of ploughing on the basis of 30,000 acres in 1915 (% of acres)	Acres promised voluntarily	Percentage of land required that was promised voluntarily
Ashbourne	2,212 (4.7)	1,754	79
Bakewell	3,544 (4.5)	2,937½	83
Chapel-en-le-Frith	2,497 (3.7)	1,167½	47
Chesterfield	10,203 (9.2)	3,200	31
Derby	5,616 (6.3)	2,584	46
Ilkeston	1,930 (5.9)	796	41
Sudbury	1,471 (4.9)	885	60
Swadlincote	2,476 (9.4)	347	14
County	29,949 (6.2)	13,671	45

Source: D331/1/27, Meeting of the Chairmen and Secretaries of the District Committees, 16 Oct. 1917.
Note: Headings as in the original document.

the level of the quotas set, with wrangling over the totals between the EC and the District Committees. Ashbourne farmers protested at their original tariff of 2,830 acres against 1,170 for neighbouring Sudbury, claiming it would be 'suicidal' to plough up heavy and unsuitable grassland.[30] Moreover, these were only the acres promised: in the Ilkeston district, for example, only 99 of the 796 acres that it was promised would be ploughed had been so by October 1917.

At this stage the policy of conversion to arable was based on the voluntary consent of both landowner and tenant farmer. Both were issued with a number of reassurances. For landowners there were protections for loss of value that the ploughing of grassland might mean for their estates. There was a recognition of the necessity of maintaining the milk supply, with sufficient grass retained to provide proper grazing for dairy stock. Farmers were told to find land that could be ploughed without affecting the summer output of milk or that would impede the movement of stock.[31] It was stressed that crop failures should be treated as a 'national liability' rather than as a personal loss to the farmer, and a system for financial claims was set up.[32] In addition, the Corn Production Act, which passed into law on 21 August 1917, guaranteed prices for wheat and oats and fixed a minimum payment for agricultural labourers under the mechanism of an Agricultural Wages Board. Government guarantees that labour, horses, machinery and supplies would be made available to assist in the plough-up campaign were also made.

---

30   *Derbyshire Advertiser and Journal*, 23 June 1917.
31   D331/1/28, Derbyshire War Agricultural Committee, Instructions to Parish Survey Committees, May 1917.
32   Sheail, 'War Agricultural and Executive Committees', p. 149.

The EC acted initially 'on the principle that people are better influenced by what they are taught to think than by what they are ordered'.[33] Even so, these results were clearly disappointing. Farmers were blamed for failing to realise the gravity of the situation, and the parish farm surveyors castigated for setting a poor example by not ploughing their own quota. District chairs were asked to report on activities in their area and while some, notably Ashbourne, Bakewell and Sudbury, believed they could meet their quotas without interference, compulsion was urged in other regions. This frustrated Mr German, the chair of Swadlincote District Committee. He 'emphatically protested' that his district could only contribute 1,000 acres to the scheme and that several difficulties, including a significant amount of existing arable, labour shortages and fields with timber that needed removal, had impeded progress.[34] He repeated these arguments the following month, in November 1917, where he also informed the EC that 'his committee and surveyors would not apply the necessary pressure'. He was told by an exasperated Captain Fitzherbert-Wright 'that difficulties were being met with in every district' and 'apparently Swadlincote was exceptional in not being able to overcome them'. Captain Boyd, the Board of Agriculture's sub-commissioner for the district, was dispatched to manage the problem.[35]

While the Derbyshire EC had initially hoped that the appeal to patriotic duty would be enough to induce farmers to comply with the plough-up order, by the autumn of 1917 the tone and tactics hardened. At the EC meeting in October it was 'resolved to resort to compulsory measures'.[36] General Chandos-Pole-Gell began a circuit of the county, where he attended District Committees and meetings of local farmers to emphasise the urgency of the situation. Addressing a meeting of farmers in Belper in early November, he argued that the voluntary effort had been given a 'fair trial' but as the results had 'not come up to expectation', it was time that 'compulsion under the Defence of the Realm Act must be put in force'. He went on,

> The full amount of land allotted to each district must be taken in hand and dealt with at once … Remember the sacrifices which have been made, and are being made, by our soldiers overseas … I know that you have had your difficulties but they are not insurmountable … Do not consider for one moment as to whether you have been told to plough more than your share, or that your neighbour has not been told to plough enough. Get to work at once on your own allotted task, and the more land you can put under arable cultivation over and above your allotted task will be a lasting memorial to you as having done your duty and your best for your country in her time of need. All forms of compulsion are abhorrent to Englishmen, but when necessity drives there can be no alternative, and the order for compulsion has gone out, and I give it to you now.[37]

---

33   D331/1/27, Report of the Derbyshire War Agricultural Executive Committee for the three months ending 15 September 1917.

34   D331/1/27, Meeting of the Chairmen and Secretaries of the District Committees, 16 October 1917.

35   D331/1/27, Meeting of the Chairmen and Secretaries of the District Committees, 27 November 1917.

36   D331/1/27, Meeting of the Chairmen and Secretaries of the District Committees, 16 October 1917.

37   *Derbyshire Advertiser and Journal*, 9 November 1917.

The turn to compulsion led to the EC making more demands on farmers. They deferred a decision on whether to compile a Roll of Honour or a blacklist of farmers as an incentive to follow orders. But they warned farmers that they would not be able to avoid the ploughing-up of scheduled land or the legal consequences should they fail to do so, and asserted 'that the whole war agricultural organization of the County is bent on the execution of the whole task'.[38] While the general organisation and execution of the scheme was done centrally by the executive in Derby, it was managed by the district committees, whose membership was dominated by local farmers. While, as Peter Dewey argues, the government felt that farmers were more likely to take advice and requests from fellow farmers, there was anxiety among members of District Committees that they were being put in the uncomfortable position of essentially being asked to spy on their neighbours. At a meeting of the district chairmen and secretaries in October 1917 a letter was read from Mr John Deakin of Coton-in-the-Elms 'stating his opposition to criticizing neighbours' farms', a task he thought 'should be the duty of a stranger'. Other districts concurred with this sentiment. However, General Chandos-Pole-Gell, in the chair, believed that 'On the contrary ... it was the duty of the parish representatives ... to report on farms locally'.[39] These tensions were similar to those found by Crowe in Westmorland, where farmers were also suspicious of providing information to people within their own farming circle (a 'delicate duty'). This, she argues, produced an atmosphere where farmer could turn against farmer, some reporting their neighbours for failures of cultivation and others accusing committee members of using their position to protect their own interests.[40] Back in Derbyshire, the Executive Committee showed sympathy for the farmers' position. They understood 'how unpleasant it must be for a farmer to inspect and perhaps criticize his neighbour's farm and for a District Committee to be the medium of enforcing measures they may personally regret ...'. Given the extensive flow of communication between the centre and the localities, they were also mindful that a farmer might 'become embittered by the cumulative effect of the numerous and frequently unfair attacks on him by the plethora of food orders and their administration'. However, the firm line was unshakeable: the EC was to 'exercise such supervision and pressure where necessary to ensure that the work promised ... is actually performed'.[41]

III

The most pressing issue for farmers, and the largest brake on progress with ploughing and sowing across the autumn and winter of 1917–18, was a shortage of labour. Deficient at the start of the war, the new focus on arable production exacerbated an already unstable situation. Many farmers complained that neither new land nor old land was of any use without adequate labour. Mr. W.J. Cutts, president of Derbyshire Farmers' Union, warned in the middle of 1917:

---

38   D331/1/27, Quarterly report of the Derbyshire War Agricultural Executive Committee, 15 December 1917.

39   D331/1/27, Derbyshire WAEC, Meeting of District Chairmen and Secretaries, 10 October 1917.

40   Crowe, '"Murmurs of Discontent"', pp. 286–7.

41   D331/1/27, Quarterly report of the Derbyshire War Agricultural Executive Committee, 15 December 1917.

> We have been like voices crying in the wilderness since the war began, and it now looks as though retribution is going to come. We don't wish to cast any reflection on the Government, but it is unforgettable that the farmer has been starved, the land has been starved, and it is just possible that, in its wake, the people will be starved. And if it were not for the disaster it will bring, it will serve the authorities right.[42]

In January 1917 the government called up a further 30,000 men from agriculture for military service, but in June of that year an agreement between the War Office and the Board of Agriculture established that no more full-time agricultural workers should be called up for military service without sanction from the CWACs. Between July 1917 and January 1918 1,496 exemption applications from Derbyshire farm workers were received. Of these, 1,056 (70 per cent) were exempted to remain on the farms where they were presently employed, 145 were exempted to move to or assist on other farms and 89 were exempted subject to conditions of ploughing; 196 applications (13 per cent) were refused and 10 deferred.[43] A government investigator found complaints of labour shortages 'universal' across the county in early 1918 and the situation in some districts 'deplorable', with skilled labour 'in most parts unobtainable'.[44] During the final stages of the military push exemptions for men aged 18 to 23 were withdrawn and in May 1918 the CWACs were issued with orders to identify a further 30,000 men for the army, with Derbyshire required to find 550.[45] One appeal, from Elizabeth Titterton of Rock Farm, Middleton by Youlgreave, near Bakewell, sent in June, is interesting for a number of reasons, highlighting the difficulties faced by widow farmers, the extra labour undertaken by the family in the absence of the eldest son, the unsatisfactory nature of substitute labour and the way the system fuelled resentment in the community:

> Gentlemen will you kindly reconsider the case of Titterton Bros. I am the mother and have been a widow 24 years so it will give you some idea what the struggle was for me. In fact I am almost crippled with rheumatism through working to bring them up. My three sons have worked early and late to plough extra. The eldest of the three has been in France nearly two years as a signaller with the R.G.A. [Royal Garrison Artillery] and is doing good work in that respect. Now we have got used to the extra work his absence causes to take another of my sons and tenant off a 2 hundred acre farm is simply cruel. No substitute can work as they have worked and take the place of my son and the land going so far off. Now I can mention 2 farms close by where five and six worker on the farm and the man got off until October [sic]. Hoping to have a favourable reply.[46]

---

42   *Belper News*, 25 May 1917.

43   D331/1/27, Report of the Derbyshire War Agricultural Executive Committee for the three months ending 29 January 1918. See also Scott Lomax, *The Home Front: Derbyshire in the First World War* (Barnsley, 2016), p. 91.

44   BPP, 1919, Cmd 25, II. Report of investigators, North Derbyshire, p. 57.

45   *Derbyshire Courier*, 1 June 1918. In the event these men were not needed.

46   D557/3/6, Petition from Elizabeth Titterton of Rock Farm, Middleton by Youlgreave, 13 June 1918.

The most common source of substitute labour was soldiers. The War Office made soldier labour available from the summer of 1915, although they were initially met with distrust, as most were unskilled and unaccustomed to farm work. The selection process gradually improved, and in the spring of 1917 around 40,000 soldiers were at work on farms across England and Wales, including 21,000 skilled ploughmen, lent for eight weeks.[47] Derbyshire farmers had posted 874 applications for soldier labour by May 1917, with most fulfilled. Further requests for ploughmen had to be turned down, however, as those category A men released for spring tillage had been sent back to their regiments.[48] At their September 1917 meeting the EC reported that 500 applications for labour had been received during the hay harvest, 'but unfortunately the class of labour available was not satisfactory'.[49] As many men were unskilled in farm work and given the heavy applications for labour – around 30 per week in that autumn – a distribution centre at Derby was organised to provide training. In October it was reported 'that some of the soldiers including those sent for training were not working well' and the EC were asked to 'repeat their request for the return of skilled agricultural labourers from the Army to carry out the 1918 programme'.[50] The following month the request had become more specific: that 'Derbyshire men be sent to Derbyshire if possible'.[51] This wasn't necessarily fulfilled: a farmer at Morley complained to the Ilkeston District Committee that 'instead of a skilled ploughmen being sent he had got a man who was a London barman'.[52]

If soldier labour gradually came to be accepted, the reception for women workers was much more hostile. The push to engage local village women via a registration system in the middle of the war was met with reluctance. This was for several reasons. In the Peak districts of north Derbyshire, where small hill farms were worked predominately by family members with some hired labour 'living in', the employment of 'outside' women's labour was not usual. Women were not considered to possess the correct skills or physical endurance for much farm work. In the mining districts of the county, high male wages were said to discourage women from seeking paid work outside the home. At a meeting of the Chesterfield District WAC in March 1916 two invited speakers, Miss Beardsley and Mrs Davies of the Nottingham and Northampton Labour Exchanges, were barracked when they outlined the valuable work women could and were doing on farms across this country and in Europe. One committee member 'ventured to suggest that if women were put to turnip thinning there would be more weeds than turnips left', 'whilst one farmer from Palterton predicted that the register for women workers in this mining district would generate 'nil' response and women's labour on farms would 'be a failure'.[53] A report on the operation of the

47   Verdon, *Working the land*, p. 146.
48   *Derby Daily Telegraph*, 17 May 1917.
49   D331/1/27, Report of the Derbyshire War Agricultural Executive Committee for the three months ending 15 September 1917.
50   D331/1/27, Meeting of the Chairmen and Secretaries of the District Committees, 16 October 1917.
51   D331/1/27, Meeting of the Chairmen and Secretaries of the District Committees, 27 November 1917.
52   D331/1/19, Minute Book of the Derbyshire WAC, Ilkestone, 1915–19, Report, 6 December 1917.
53   *Belper News*, 17 March 1916.

WWACs in August 1916 seemed to confirm this, finding that the attitude of farmers in Derbyshire was 'not favourable' and the training courses at the Midland Agricultural and Dairy College at Kingston-on-Soar had 'not been taken advantage of'. The district WACs, it concluded, with the exception of Bakewell, had failed to 'treat the employment of women seriously'.[54] Indeed, the Bakewell WAC had written to the County Council back in February 1916 'to give what assistance and encouragement they could towards helping in any way to secure and register any available women who would be willing to undertake agricultural work', given the 'likelihood of a serious shortage of men in the near future ...'.[55]

In the second phase of the war, when the focus turned to training and employing full-time women workers for the Women's Land Army, progress was still sluggish. By the end of the summer of 1917 there had not been many requests for large numbers of women workers. In January 1918, when only 41 WLA recruits were at work in the county, it was still reported that 'Derbyshire farmers are slow in coming forward to apply for this labour'.[56] In response to a government call in May 1918 for 30,000 more women to work on the land, a recruiting committee was formed, with a county target of 800. A public meeting and rally were held in Derby Market Place and Guildhall. With only 77 WLA members at work in Derbyshire at this time, and an additional 60 women in training, farmers were urged to take their share in the scheme by training recruits, employing them after training and advertising the system to their fellow farmers. As Mrs Armistead, chair of the Recruiting Committee, urged, 'The girls are volunteering splendidly, even giving up high wages to work on the land and we will do our share in helping them if the farmers will meet us half-way'.[57] Overall Derbyshire accounted for around 300 members of the WLA, which at its height in September 1918 totalled 16,000 nationally. Although some reports of women workers were complimentary, noting they were doing 'unobtrusive work, often in isolation and discomfort without which our food war could not be won', generally speaking the custom of the county remained, as one report put it, 'against women's labour'.[58] The nature of farm production, the lack of decent accommodation and the shorter hours and better pay in munitions and other war work did not stimulate high levels of either demand or supply for full-time women land workers in the county.

The number of prisoners of war (POWs) working in Derbyshire was also small. In March 1918 it was reported that 'increasing use' was being made of prisoner labour, with 35 recently arrived in Ashbourne and 'doing satisfactory work in hedging and ditching in the neighbourhood'. Ashbourne had made further applications for this source of labour, as had the Sudbury and Chesterfield districts.[59] Forty-three POWs

---

54 *Summary of the work of the Women's War Agricultural Committees from their Inception to the end of August 1916* (1916), p. 16.

55 D2478.PC.13, Bakewell District WAC. Recruitment of women to agricultural work, 9 February 1916.

56 BPP, 1919, Cmd 25, II. Report of investigators, North Derbyshire, p. 57.

57 *Derby Daily Telegraph*, 16 May 1918.

58 *Derbyshire Advertiser and Journal*, 28 September 1918; BPP, 1919, Cmd 25, II, Report of investigators, North Derbyshire, p. 57.

59 *Derby Daily Telegraph*, 14 March 1918.

were at work in the Ilkeston district in September 1918 and at the end of the year 30 German POWs were working in five peripatetic gangs following threshing machines in the Chesterfield area.[60] The Ilkeston District executive officer described the work that these men did as 'valuable' and 'admirable' and lamented the curtailment of POW labour in 1919 'as much labour needs to be done'.[61]

The Executive Committee was also responsible for hiring out horses, tractors and machinery to those in most need. Machinery was housed at depots in various parts of the Districts from which a farmer could hire them. The system was not altogether straightforward, however. Tractors provided some assistance, but the terrain of the county impeded their widespread use. The EC noted in December 1917 that the 'quality performance' of tractors was 'disappointing' and the number in use in the county peaked in November 1918 at just 27.[62] The ploughing scheme, whereby teams of horses were hired out, was criticised for not suiting north Derbyshire conditions, was prohibitively expensive at 30s per acre and was 'encumbered with heavy administrative procedure'.[63] In early 1918 there were six two-horse teams on hire, with 23 ploughs, 50 harrows, six cultivators, five rollers and 61 whippletrees available. The EC also had possession of four threshing machines, but they could not be utilised 'for want of drivers and engines'.[64] In November 1918 the threshing sub-committee noted that in many instances some machines had 'much more work than they can reasonably be expected to accomplish on the first round, whilst others are not fully employed'.[65] Despite the schemes for provision of labour, horses and machinery, the burden of work fell largely on family members who remained on the farms of Derbyshire during the war.

IV

In August 1917 the FPD instructed CWACs to issue plough orders to all land ploughed since the start of that year, whether under voluntary or compulsory action, in order to protect tenant farmers' rights to compensation.[66] By the end of March 1918 Derbyshire had issued 4,883 orders, the largest number of them, 1,439, in the Chesterfield

---

60 D331/1/19: Minute Book of the Derbyshire WAC, Ilkestone, 1915–19. Report, 28 February 1919; D331/1/27, Derbyshire Agricultural Executive Committee Quarterly Report, 21 December 1918.

61 D331/1/27, Ilkeston District, Report on farming conditions to the Derbyshire Agricultural Committee, 20 May 1919; D331/1/19, Minute Book of the Derbyshire WAC, Ilkestone, 1915–19, Report 28 February 1919; Report 17 April 1919.

62 D331/1/27, Quarterly report of the Derbyshire War Agricultural Executive Committee, 15 December 1917; Derbyshire Agricultural Executive Committee Quarterly Report, 21 December 1918. According to Sheail there were 3,925 tractors hired out nationally in October 1918. Sheail, 'War Agricultural and Executive Committees', p. 151.

63 D331/1/27, Meeting of the Chairmen and Secretaries of the District Committees, 27 November 1917.

64 D331/1/27, Report of the Derbyshire War Agricultural Executive Committee for the three months ending 29 January 1918.

65 D331/1/30, Derbyshire Agricultural Executive Committee, 13 November 1918.

66 Sheail, 'War Agricultural and Executive Committees', p. 149.

Table 8.3
Progress of plough-up schedule in Derbyshire, March 1918.

District	Quota (in acres)	Acreage ploughed	No. of orders	% of task completed
Ashbourne	2,212	3,070.7	426	139
Bakewell	3,544	4,165.0	753	118
Chapel	2,497	3,148.8	655	126
Chesterfield	10,203	10,477.1	1,439	102
Derby	5,616	5,711.7	839	102
Ilkeston	1,930	2,093.8	293	108
Sudbury	1,471	1,982.2	268	135
Swadlincote	2,476	1,968.9	210	80
Total	29,949	32,618.2[1]	4,883	109

Source: D331/1/27, Derbyshire War Agricultural Committee Meeting of Chairmen and Secretaries, 26 Mar. 1918.

Note: [1] The ms reads 32,636.2.

district, followed by Derby with 839, Bakewell with 753 and Chapel-en-le-Frith with 655. Swadlincote saw the fewest number, 210, although that district had ploughed only 80 per cent of its 2,476-acre quota (see Table 8.3).[67] Farmers contested many of the orders and claimed, among other things, that they were being asked to plough up fields unsuitable for arable cultivation. Arthur Skevingham wrote to Frederick Ogden in July 1917 arguing that, as he farmed less than 20 acres, 'I do not see that I should be compelled to plough or allow it to be ploughed', that he could not look after arable land as 'we have more now than we have labour for' and finally that the land was 'worth double the rent as a grass field than it would be if it was arable'.[68] On the whole the committees dismissed such interventions, and were willing to take action to force farmers to comply. In addition to the plough-up orders, 32 warning notices and eight cultivation orders had been served by January 1918.[69]

The first prosecutions for non-compliance came to court in Derby in May 1918. The first concerned three orders issued in January and February to George Spencer, who farmed 244 acres at Kirk Langley near Derby (17 acres of which had been arable before the war). The orders were to plough five plots of land totalling 30 acres, and he was given three weeks (the usual term) to carry out the work. Spencer had ploughed 16 acres but had written to the District Committee stating that 'he had ploughed as

---

67 D331/1/27, Derbyshire War Agricultural Executive Committee, Meeting of Chairmen and Secretaries, 26 March 1918.

68 D331/1/29, War Agricultural Committee Cultivation Sub-Committee report and papers, letter from Arthur Skevingham to Frederick Ogden, 3 July, 1917.

69 D331/1/27, Derbyshire War Agricultural Executive Committee, Meeting of Chairmen and Secretaries, 29 January 1918.

much land as he could attend to, and could not work harder than he was doing'. He was assisted by two sons and had not made any application for labour, horses or implements, partly because he lacked accommodation on the farm. In his defence in court Spencer claimed that he had no objections to the orders in principle and 'he always endeavored to carry them out to the best of his abilities'. Under cross-examination he stated one field was not ploughed as this would prevent his cattle having access to other fields. The second case, against James Foster of Trusley, was similar in nature. His was a 44-acre pasture farm on which a notice to plough 11 acres had been served in mid-February. Foster claimed that, although he did not wilfully disobey the order, the land was unsuitable as ploughing it would prevent access to other fields. In both cases the bench felt obliged to convict, but being the first cases and with acknowledged difficulties, offered some leniency. Both farmers were fined 40s. A third case, John Poyser of Shardlow, was thrown out of court on account of mistakes made by the committee in identifying land in his occupation.[70]

As well as prosecution, ECs could authorise landowners to terminate tenancies and could take over farms themselves, either directly or by placing another farmer on the land. This was a last resort, however, and only done in extreme circumstances: nationally the ECs took over 27,287 acres of badly farmed land, just 0.5 per cent of the total area of crops and grass in Britain.[71] In Derbyshire ten tenancies had been recommended for termination by early 1918.[72] One that caused ongoing concern was Scotland Farm, a tenanted farm worked by the Heath brothers in the Ilkeston parish of Ockbrook. This case shows how severe a measure tenancy closure was considered and the reluctance to pursue this to a conclusion. In the 1917 survey of farms Scotland Farm was recorded as a 133-acre farm, 112 being pasture and 21 arable. It possessed two work horses, 23 milk cows and 19 other cows. We have already seen that at this time it was deemed short of labour, its land choked with thistles. The Cultivation sub-committee made several visits to the farm during the winter of 1917–18. After a visit on 12 November they reported: 'The arable land is deplorably foul throughout and bears evidence of gross neglect and mismanagement'. Wheat still lay on the ground, oats had not been thatched down, some hay had not been cut and the cut hay had not been gathered in. The farm as a whole was 'deplorable ... going from bad to worse'. The case was considered 'hopeless' and they recommended 'that the tenancy should be terminated at once, and the farm either put into the hands of an energetic and capable tenant or be taken over by the committee and worked with a good bailiff'.[73] A new inspection in late January found there had been 'practically no improvement since first visit' and by February the Ilkeston DC unanimously decided that the farm should be taken over by the Executive 'and that we are to find a good tenant at once'. Still time was granted, however. In April the farm continued to be 'very carefully' watched; a supervisor's report noted that it was still unsatisfactory

---

70   *Derby Daily Telegraph*, 3 May 1918; *Derbyshire Advertiser and Journal*, 4 May 1918.

71   Dewey, *British agriculture*, pp. 179–80.

72   D331/1/27, Derbyshire War Agricultural Executive Committee, Meeting of Chairmen and Secretaries, 29 January 1918.

73   D331/1/29, Cultivation Sub-Committee, Report upon Scotland Farm, Ockbrook.

and 'If the cultivation order was not carried out at once an order would be issued to terminate the tenancy forthwith'. In May there was some 'confidence' the order would be carried out. By the end of June, however, the committee recommended 'that the tenancy be terminated in September next'. An inspection in August 1918 noted a general improvement at the farm, with two German POWs engaged. The following month, however, the case was taken out of the committee's hands and the farm was reported as being for sale.[74]

V

The last two years of the war saw the acreage under temporary and permanent grass fall and that under tillage increase nationally, although there were regional differences in the extent of agricultural land-use change. Across Britain as a whole, tillage rose by 2.13 million acres between 1916 and 1918 (that is, just over 20 per cent of the 1916 level), with wheat increasing by 33.4 per cent, barley by 10.1 per cent, oats by 30.8 per cent and potatoes by 43.9 per cent. Crop yields on the new tillage nearly matched those for land already in production. These changes were accompanied by a fall in the output of the dairy and livestock sectors.[75] The spring of 1918 saw the successful completion of the plough-up campaign in Derbyshire. In March 1918 it was reported that all districts had gone beyond their ploughing quota, apart from Swadlincote, which had reached 80 per cent of its target. In all, 32,636 acres had been broken up across the county (Table 8.3). Looking back at the campaign, the Ilkeston DC noted that, despite 'very many difficulties, not the least of which has been the abnormal wet weather experienced, the results must be considered excellent on the whole, and fully justifying the line taken'.[76]

But the success of the campaign was achieved at a price. In Derbyshire there was a need to maintain the milk supply while increasing the amount of land devoted to arable production in line with government targets. The CWACs had no authority to intervene in milk and meat production and 'while they could direct a delinquent farmer to cultivate his fields in accordance with the rules of good husbandry', they held no power 'to require him to attend to the livestock departments of his business in corresponding manner'. Moreover, in a county focused on dairy production, the emphasis on arable during the war had led to areas of the county being farmed in a manner that was 'both detrimental to the holding and against the interests of food production'.[77] Substitute labour was largely unskilled, had to be trained and housed, and its use in Derbyshire was mainly restricted to soldiers. Nor was the terrain suited to the new farm machinery that became available during the war. Crowe argues that, for Westmorland, the success of the 'centrally imposed production targets involved

---

74 D331/1/19, Minute book of the Ilkeston District War Agricultural Committee, 12 September 1918.

75 Dewey, *British agriculture*, p. 207.

76 D331/1/19, Minute book of the Ilkeston District War Agricultural Committee, 28 February 1919.

77 D331/1/27, Report of the War Agricultural (County Executive) Committee for the quarter ending 21 December 1918.

both heavy physical and psychological costs' to the land and its farmers.[78] The same applies to Derbyshire.

All ploughing orders were rescinded in early 1919. As the administrative machinery of the agricultural committees was wound down over the following months, fears about labour shortages and state protection of agriculture were expressed in Derbyshire. Little autumn cleaning and sowing had been possible because of the wet weather and infestations of wire worm, spring sowing had been delayed and work was much in arrears. In February 1919 the labour situation was said to be 'as awkward as it has ever been', with little prospect for improvement, as POW labour was gradually withdrawn under a protracted repatriation process, soldiers who had been working on farms were sent back to their units to be demobilised and men discharged from the army failed to return to agriculture.[79] Of 600 soldiers withdrawn from agriculture in Derbyshire, only 129 had re-engaged for farm work by March 1919.[80]

Anxieties over the future were shared between the key men who had operated the committees during the war. In March 1919 J.R. Bond wrote to F.S. Ogden of his fears of 'an almost complete relapse of all control of food production'.[81] Ogden in turn repeated this warning in a letter to Councillor Crompton in May, where he expressed his 'chagrin' at 'the complete collapse of the work of the committees for the benefit of agriculture, particularly after the hopes held out, and the rosy pictures painted by those in authority some short time ago'.[82] The final EC report in March 1919 ruminated on the conditions needed to stimulate progress in British farming in the future, including 'proper conditions for the employment of additional labour, skill and capital', alongside 'a guaranteed market and prices based on costs of production ...'.[83] Within a couple of years this entreaty rang hollow. Amid a severe economic downturn the government abolished guaranteed prices for wheat and oats and disbanded the Agricultural Wages Board, effectively ending the state control of agriculture established during the war and abandoning the farmers (and labourers) who had fulfilled their national duty, often under adverse circumstances, in a time of emergency.

---

78   Crowe, '"Murmurs of Discontent"', p. 267.

79   D331/1/19, Minute book of the Ilkeston District War Agricultural Committee, 28 February 1919.

80   D331/1/27, Quarterly report of the Executive Committee for the period ended 31 March 1919.

81   D331/1/27, Letter, J.R. Bond to F.S. Ogden, 3 March 1919.

82   D331/1/27, Letter F.S. Ogden to Councillor Crompton, 19 May 1919.

83   D331/1/27, Quarterly report of the Executive Committee for the period ended 31 March 1919.

Chapter 9

Boundary settlements
and overlapping jurisdictions:
marginal communities and Little Londons*

John Broad

Historians of rural England, whether intent on constructing regional, county or village histories or undertaking micro-studies of rural communities, constantly demarcate their work using boundaries of one type or another. It is the political and administrative divisions – parish, hundred (by whatever name) and county – that form the framework of English local history, even though many of the typologies of 'pays' and of agricultural regions transcend them. We tend to take for granted these political and administrative divisions. However, the very clear units of the pre-1974 world of 'historic' counties and their subdivisions that constrain much rural and local history are largely a product of the reforms of the second half of the nineteenth century, which culminated in the reorganisation brought about by the County Councils Act of 1888 and the setting-up of rural district and parish councils in 1894. These created a hierarchical structure in which civil parishes sat within rural district councils, which in turn were subordinate to the county council.[1]

This chapter seeks to dig beneath the familiar hierarchical model established by those two Victorian acts to look at the realities of boundaries and their place in rural society. It briefly discusses the origins of these ancient divisions, concentrating on the period 1500 to 1834. It outlines how the Victorians moved us to that now familiar pattern of 'historic' counties and civil parishes enshrined in the Victoria County History. It uncovers a world in which a significant proportion of boundaries overlapped one another, parishes were divided between counties and between hundreds, and hundreds themselves overlapped county boundaries. It encompasses changing ideas about overlapping jurisdictions and different kinds of property rights. Above all, the chapter examines the uncertainties about certain places that could allow them to dispute jurisdictions and claim special status and exemptions from duties and taxation of various kinds. Not surprisingly, in a time of rural population expansion before

---

*   This paper has been much improved by the comments of Max Satchell, Steve Hindle, Richard Hoyle and Heather Falvey, and of participants in seminars at the Cambridge Group for the History of Population and Social Structure, University of Cambridge and the Localities and Regions seminar at the Institute of Historical Research.

1   The subject of how, why and when local boundaries of all kinds were demarcated, mapped and later reconfigured is a subject of a separate paper provisionally entitled 'Making English local boundaries: Victorian dilemmas, solutions and failures'.

1700, the colonisers of commons and wastes found places of uncertain jurisdiction particularly attractive. The evolution of such settlements over time, using the example of Little Londons, is the focus of this chapter.

I

Some boundaries have origins that stretch back to pre-Conquest times. Roman roads still form parish or county boundaries along some of their routes: for instance, Watling Street on the Leicestershire–Warwickshire border and much of the Berkshire–Hampshire boundary east of Silchester. Anglo-Saxon charters often contain perambulations that historians have painstakingly rediscovered and reinterpreted in the modern landscape. These were estate boundaries, but over time some at least became parish boundaries, particularly where, in the eleventh and twelfth centuries, manorial lords founded their own churches and carved out parishes from the territories established by the minster churches of the pre-Conquest era. By the end of the twelfth century a pattern of parishes had been established that remained largely intact until the new creations of the nineteenth century, the product of rapid urbanisation.[2] Where village desertions took place in the late medieval period, the parish church frequently continued in use through to the eighteenth century at least.[3]

In the early nineteenth century there were approximately 9,500 parishes in England and Wales. Parishes were ecclesiastical entities onto which civil responsibilities had been rather haphazardly grafted as manorial jurisdictions waned. They were used to raise national and local taxation and for first-line responses to crime and disorder, welfare provision and highway maintenance. However, they were fragmented in many ways. While in southern England a majority of parishes were administered as single entities, plenty had chapelries within them that provided an alternative place of worship and community. Others contained two villages that administered themselves discretely in civil matters. In northern England the existence of large parishes covering tens of thousands of acres, normally divided into townships with their own chapelries and autonomous civil functions, was not unusual. Large parishes also existed in other upland areas of England and Wales, and sporadically in lowland forest, fen, marshland and heathland areas.

Most of England and Wales came within the parish system but over a quarter of a million acres, an area roughly the size of Bedfordshire, was outside it and regarded as 'extra-parochial'. These 556 extra-parochial districts arose in the Middle Ages when lords, especially monastic bodies, were granted exemption from tithes. Tithes were the signature feature of a parish from the outset. After the dissolution of the monasteries the crown granted lay figures ex-monastic lands that retained the tithe exemption and

---

2   Michael Reed, 'Anglo-Saxon charter boundaries', in *Discovering past landscapes* (London, 1984), p. 263; Steven Bassett, 'Boundaries of knowledge: mapping the land units of late Anglo-Saxon and Norman England', in Wendy Davies, Andrew J. Reynolds and Guy Halsall (eds), *People and space in the Middle Ages, 300–1300* (Turnhout, 2006), pp. 115–42.

3   John Broad, 'Understanding village desertion in the seventeenth and eighteenth centuries', in R. Jones and C. Dyer (eds), *Deserted villages revisited* (Hatfield, 2010), pp. 134–9.

remained outside the parish system. The same applied to a small number of peculiar jurisdictions, such as royal chapels and palaces and the inns of court. Historians tend to imagine that extra-parochial areas were small anomalies, but 74 exceeded 1,000 acres and four over 5,000 acres; the largest, Exmoor, was over 20,000 acres.

Before the mid-nineteenth century local government units were also fragmented in many other ways. The smallest divisions – parishes, townships and extra-parochial areas – all existed within uncertain parameters. In a surprisingly large number of cases their boundaries were only roughly known and certainly remained unmapped until the nineteenth century, particularly where considerable areas of low-value rough grazing lay between the parish settlements and was shared as common pasture. This sharing, known as 'inter-commoning', has been researched in northern England in both the Pennine uplands and in poorly drained lowland areas such as the mosses and meres of Lancashire.[4] It was also common in royal forests right across the country. Inter-commoning is well documented for the New Forest and for Bernwood, Whittlewood and Salcey in the south Midlands, as well as for pre-drainage fenland areas. In fact, inter-commoning continued widely across England through the early modern period, certainly well beyond the sixteenth century. For instance, the boundary between Badby and Newnham, south of Daventry in Northamptonshire, was divided in 1506 by the abbot of Evesham, but inter-commoned lands were still shown as such on early twentieth-century Ordnance Survey maps.[5] The process of its elimination is poorly documented in most places, as it was left to private agreement, though some enclosure acts made provision as part of the process.[6] Even in the mid-nineteenth century there remained about 250 places across England and Wales where modern mapping exercises have been unable to determine their boundaries.[7]

Many parishes with well-defined boundaries were fragmented by the existence of outlying areas surrounded by other parishes. Sometimes this reflected ancient estate boundaries with outlying areas, for instance at Dauntsey, Christian Malford and Bremhill in Wiltshire.[8] However, the existence of such detached portions often reflected the enclosure of previously inter-commoned land. This might have involved only one or two detached parts, but some involved interwoven areas. The process of eliminating inter-commoning is often obscure. Some Yorkshire examples make the point well. The township of Calton, east of York, including Stamford Bridge, inter-commoned with the adjoining townships of Wilberfoss and Full Sutton, a right granted in the thirteenth century in exchange for extinguishing common rights over

---

4   William D. Shannon, 'The survival of true intercommoning in Lancashire in the early-modern period', *Agricultural History*, 86 (2012), pp. 169–91; Angus J.L. Winchester, *Discovering parish boundaries*, 2nd edn (Princes Risborough, 2000).

5   M.W. Beresford, *History on the ground: six studies in maps and landscapes*, rev. edn (London, 1971), pp. 49–50.

6   See my forthcoming paper 'Making English local boundaries'.

7   These places are amongst the 290 listed in the Campop file 1851EngWalesParishandPlace Anomalies.xls. Some of the places listed here are small urban parishes and precincts in ancient towns, but the majority represent land shared between two or more parishes.

8   Reed, 'Anglo-Saxon charter boundaries', pp. 287–97.

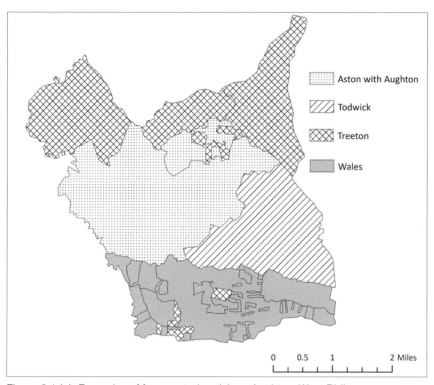

Figure 9.1 (a). Examples of fragmented parishes, Aughton, West Riding.

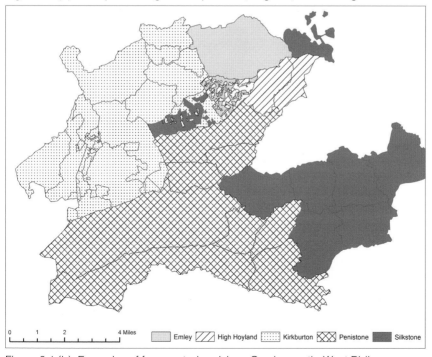

Figure 9.1 (b). Examples of fragmented parishes, Cumberworth, West Riding.

9.1 (c). Examples of fragmented parishes, Blore, Derbyshire/Staffordshire.

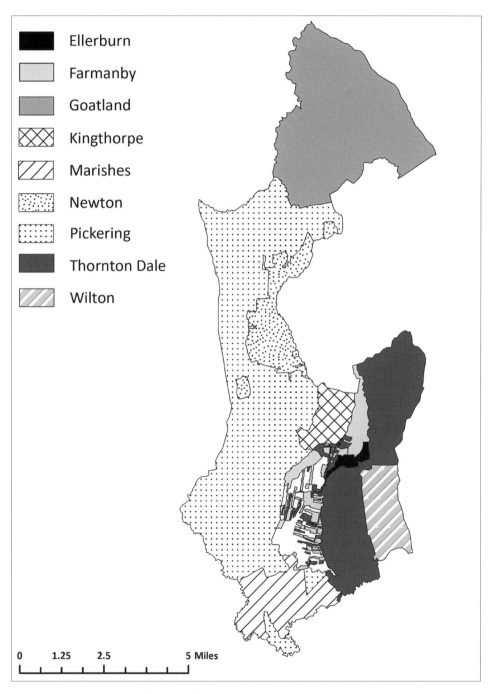

Figure 9.1 (d). Examples of fragmented parishes, Thornton le Dale and Ellerburn, North Riding.

other land. Piecemeal enclosure took place in Calton in the sixteenth and seventeenth centuries and was completed by parliamentary act in 1760, but the division of the intercommoned land is never explained in the VCH account.[9] In David Hey's home countryside, Dronfield's land included enclaves in Staveley in 1844, while, south-east of Rotherham, Treeton parish had land intermingled with Aston with Aughton, and then beyond Aston. Aughton had detached lands intermingled with the township and parish of Wales. It is highly likely that these represented the division of previously inter-commoned land (Figure 9.1 (a)).

Multiple fragmented parishes were largely the result of ensuring that the quality and value of soil was fairly divided between the interested parties. At its most extreme, there are parishes with 30 or more intermeshed detached parts. Striking examples are at Cumberworth in West Yorkshire (Figure 9.1 (b)), where the township's two halves were divided between four parishes, the Peak district pastures around Blore on the Derbyshire–Staffordshire borders, near Ashby de la Zouch in Leicestershire (Figure 9.1 (c)) and on land divided between Thornton le Dale and Ellerburn near Pickering in the North Riding (Figure 9.1 (d)).[10]

Other examples show these complications spanning county boundaries. Finningley, adjoining Doncaster airport, lies on the borders of the West Riding and Nottinghamshire. Auckley common, the northern section of the parish with many 'Peat Holes' shown on the 1850s Ordnance Survey map, had multiple parts, split between both counties, and their sub-divisions, the Soke of Doncaster and Bassetlaw (Holland) hundred (Figure 9.2 (a)). Just to the south of the Leicestershire example, and on the borders of Warwickshire, lay a large area of inter-commoned land that was reapportioned between parishes without fragmentation. However, at the point where five parishes met there was an extra-parochial place called No Man's Heath (Figure 9.2 (b)). On a map showing just parish boundaries, this division of lands is simple and straightforward. But if we overlay the pattern of county boundaries it instantly becomes more complex. No Man's Heath itself lies right on the border between Warwickshire and Leicestershire, and today lies in the Warwickshire parish of Newton Regis. However, in 1851 the parishes abutting lay in four different counties: Warwickshire, Leicestershire, Staffordshire and Derbyshire. One parish, Clifton Campville, was itself divided between Staffordshire and Derbyshire.[11]

Historians have known about the complications of parish boundaries and detached portions for a long time but have usually regarded them as quaint and largely irrelevant features. This underestimates the situation. In 1873, when a House of Commons Select Committee considered questions of modifying local government

---

9   VCH *East Riding*, vol. iii, pp. 147–58.

10   The most accessible detailed map of English parish boundaries is Tim Cockin, *The parish atlas of England* (Barlaston, 2017). This paper made use of it, but is based primarily on the GIS database CGKO (Cambridge Group – Kain and Oliver) held at the Cambridge Group for the History of Population and Social Structure, and the encyclopaedic knowledge of it provided by Dr Max Satchell.

11   David Brown, 'The relationship between local elites and central government: the Victorian attempts to "reform" No Man's Heath', *Journal of Victorian Culture*, 2 (1997), pp. 42–70.

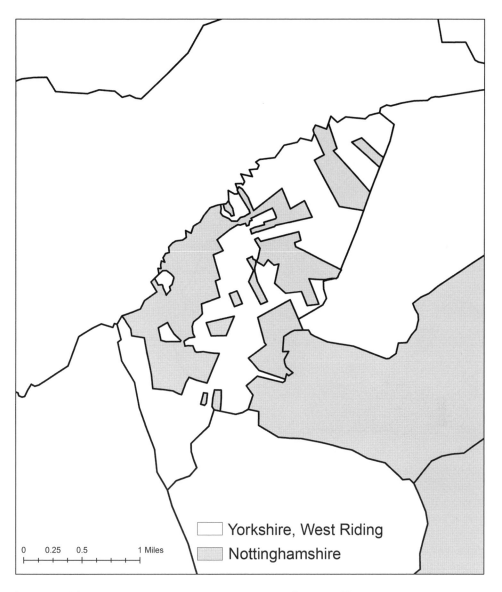

Yorkshire, West Riding
Nottinghamshire

0   0.25   0.5   1 Miles

Figure 9.2 (a). Parishes split between counties, Auckley Common, Finningley
(West Riding/Nottingham)

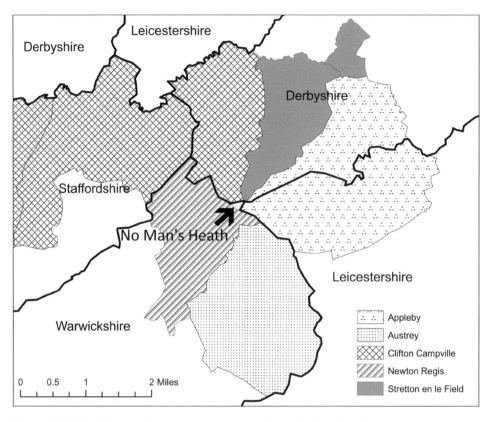

Figure 9.2 (b). Parishes split between counties, No Man's Heath, where five counties meet.

boundaries, research was presented showing that 1,294 parishes had detached areas entirely surrounded by other parishes, and that, while 834 of these involved only a single detached area, the remainder had anything from two to more than ten parts. This is almost certainly a significant under-estimate of the numbers for two reasons. Firstly, it represents a significant change from the position in 1851, as we know that there was much simplification in the intervening 20 years. None of the extreme cases shown in the maps in Figure 9.1 above are listed in the 1873 report. I would suggest that in 1851 somewhere between a quarter and a third of parishes included detached areas. As it is, comparison of the table in the 1873 report with Ordnance six-inch and 25-inch mapping of the 1880 and 1890s in various sample areas can demonstrate that many detached areas were omitted from the report.[12]

---

12   BPP, H.C., 308 (1873). VIII, 1 Report from the select committee on boundaries of parishes, unions and counties. The table is on p. 195. Late 1890s Ordnance Survey maps of the Bedfordshire parishes of Holwell and Shillington show more than four detached parts, but in the table Bedfordshire is shown with only three parishes with detached parts, and just one of them with more than a single outlier.

Parish boundaries were complex enough but the position with hundred and county boundaries compounded these complexities. Pre-1832 counties included numerous detached areas, sometimes at a great distance. County Durham had two large outlying areas in north Northumberland – Norhamshire and Islandshire. The early medieval origins of these outliers link them to the bishop of Durham's part in border defence against the Scots. The hundred of Amesbury in Wiltshire included the townships of Farley, Diddenham and Broad Hinton in four parishes 40 miles away in Berkshire in Windsor Forest – Wokingham, Swallowfield, Hurst and Shinfield.[13] (The Wokingham enclaves also abutted the Hampshire–Berkshire border.) One of the anomalies associated with the special status of the Cinque port of Sandwich in Kent was that Brightlingsea, across the Thames estuary in Essex, was technically in Kent. One of the most enduring was the town of Dudley in the West Midlands, which until 1974 remained a detached part of Worcestershire lying in Staffordshire. The township of Coleshill in the Chilterns was part of Hertfordshire, but entirely within Buckinghamshire.

To detached parishes at a distance from the county we can add the phenomenon of parishes near county boundaries being bisected by the boundary line. When Peter Kitson mapped the parishes and chapelries of England that had parish registers in 1813–18, he found 180 places out of 11,401 straddled two counties. Wiltshire had nine parishes shared with one of Somerset, Hampshire, Dorset or Berkshire. Five Oxfordshire parishes had segments in Northamptonshire, Buckinghamshire, Gloucestershire or Warwickshire. In Shropshire 15 parishes were similarly divided, not only with Herefordshire, Staffordshire or Worcestershire but crossing the national border with Wales in Flintshire, Denbighshire or Montgomeryshire. No part of England and Wales did not have instances of this phenomenon. County boundaries themselves were not always well delineated, as David Hey's own foray into this field showed.[14] Although hundreds (and their variants and divisions, ridings, tithings, rapes, and wapentakes) were increasingly irrelevant to local administration by the nineteenth century, they too were bisected by county boundaries, and themselves divided parishes.

This maze of overlapping boundaries and jurisdictions was considerably simplified by government action between 1832 and the end of the century but the process has never been completed. In 1980 there were still 402 special-purpose local authorities and three kinds of rate.[15] That process of rationalisation is discussed in detail elsewhere, but the main bones of it are as follows. The mapping of parish boundaries was taken forward during tithe redemption in the 1840s, while the Ordnance Survey's substantial detailed mapping in the 1870s and 1880s included a series devoted to parish boundary details.[16] The process of dealing with outlying parishes in other counties began with parliamentary reform in 1832, when the County

---

13 For the changing county boundary of Berkshire, and the enclaves within it, see Joan Dils and Margaret Yates (eds), *An historical atlas of Berkshire*, 2nd edn (Reading, 2012), pp. 6–7.

14 David Hey, 'Yorkshire's southern boundary', *Northern History*, 37 (2000), pp. 31–47.

15 J.R.S. Booth, *Public boundaries and Ordnance Survey, 1840–1980*, ed. R.A.G. Powell (Southampton, 1980), p. 1.

16 E.J. Evans, *The contentious tithe: the tithe problem and English agriculture, 1750–1850* (London, 1976); R.J.P. Kain and R.R. Oliver, *The tithe maps of England and Wales: a cartographic analysis and*

Boundaries Act (2 & 3 Will. 4 c. 64) moved most, but not all, parishes surrounded by other counties into that county for electoral purposes. Policing and judicial powers were transferred by the Counties (Detached Parts) Act of 1839 (2 & 3 Vict. c. 82) and County Police Act of the same year (2 & 3 Vict. c. 93). This was followed by their transfer for remaining purposes in 1844 (Counties (Detached Parts) Act 1844 7 & 8 Vict. c. 61). Nevertheless, the Ordnance Survey Act of 4 & 5 Victoria, which required the mapping of county boundaries, specifically excluded changes to subsidiary boundaries – 'City, Borough, Town Parish, extra-parochial and other exotic places or any property rights'.[17] Extra-parochial areas were dealt with by the Extra-parochial Places Act of 1857, which turned them into civil parishes with overseers of the poor, but its provisions for merging with an adjoining parish were, like so much legislation affecting local jurisdictions in England and Wales, effectively voluntary. It was soon deemed ineffective and a further measure in 1868 required extra-parochial areas to merge with the adjoining parish with which they shared the longest common boundary. In 1873 the Select Committee on Boundaries was explicitly told that now 'there can be no extra-parochial places'.[18]

The Select Committee was established after failed attempts to legislate for the tidying up of parish boundaries. Mechanisms already existed to do this under the 1867 Poor Law Amendment Act, which in cl. 3 made provisions for the owners of parishes with outlying and intermixed parts to rearrange them under the supervision of the Poor Law Board, with later confirmation by parliament.[19] However, relatively few changes came forward in succeeding years and it was not until the passing of the Divided Parishes Act of 1876 that central government became proactive in pushing through boundary changes. The successor to the Poor Law Board, the Local Government Board, was empowered to hold enquiries and make orders to amalgamate divided parishes, or even constitute new ones, powers reinforced in 1882.[20] Parishioners could still appeal the decision, which was, as before, subject to parliamentary scrutiny. The changes were published in the *London Gazette*. Before the reform of local government was enacted, a major effort was made to undertake a thorough remodelling of boundaries to ensure that Poor Law and Sanitary Union boundaries did not straddle two counties. A Boundary Commission, which was created in 1887 and reported the following year, proposed significant transfers of parishes between counties. However, its proposals offended too many local interests and were quickly dropped. When local government was remodelled in 1888 and 1894, the framework of poor law and sanitary unions stood outside it, and the process of creating ring-fenced local entities remained far from complete.

---

county-by-county catalogue (Cambridge, 1995). TNA class OS 27 is devoted to parish boundary maps. In Bedfordshire boundary maps for all but eight parishes survive.

17   Statute 4 & 5 Vict. c. 30 cap. 12.
18   Statute 20 Vict. c. 19; 31 & 32 Vict. c. 122 cap. 27; BPP, H.C., 308 (1873). VIII, 1 Report from the select committee on boundaries of parishes, unions, and counties, para. 40.
19   Statute 30 & 31 Vict. cap. 106.
20   Statute 39 & 40 Vict. cap. 61; 45 & 46 Vict. cap. 58, 'Divided parishes and poor law amendment act, 1882'.

II

Nineteenth-century administrative changes modified the patchwork of boundaries and outliers but failed to complete the process. This was ultimately irrelevant unless these phenomena significantly affected how people acted and where they lived and worked. In practice people used the blurring of jurisdictions and uncertainties in boundaries in all kinds of ways. Religious dissenters used boundaries to avoid persecution in the seventeenth century. Coleshill, then in Hertfordshire, was a township divided in several ways. Part lay in the parish of Amersham, the remainder in the parish of Beaconsfield, both Buckinghamshire parishes. The Beaconsfield section lay within the hundred of Burnham and county of Buckinghamshire, but the Amersham portion was assigned to Dacorum hundred, Hertfordshire. In the mid-seventeenth century, when nonconformist meetings were illegal, Jordans Farm, just across the Hertfordshire boundary, became a regular meeting place for a Quaker group. The Upperside Meeting, as it became known, took place in the house of Thomas Ellwood, the poet, diarist and friend of John Milton. It was where William Penn, founder of Pennsylvania, worshipped and was buried. In the 1680s a Meeting House was built there. Its position straddling a county boundary gave it greater security when anti-conventicle laws were enforced by JPs who had jurisdiction only within a single county.[21]

The small market town of Buntingford in Hertfordshire seems to have benefited from its position astride four parish boundaries, and also the diocesan boundary between London and Lincoln, to promote its commerce and accommodate religious dissent. It was not an original medieval market foundation but 'a bastard settlement, surrounded by the legitimate markets of Braughing, Buckland, Chipping (on the manor of Pope's Hall), Collier's End, Corneybury, Puckeridge and Standon' and 'was a settlement which possessed the right to hold its own market, but which did not exist as a civil, manorial or parochial entity'.[22] Its local rivals withered away as its unregulated environment attracted a variety of trades and textile workers. Its religious configuration facilitated nonconformist communities when dissent was punishable in the sixteenth and seventeenth centuries. Layston's parish church and vicarage lay not in Buntingford town but a mile away on the site of the deserted medieval village. Dissenters gathered in the town and built a Baptist chapel. However, it was the other side of Ermine Street, in Throcking parish and Lincoln diocese. The early seventeenth-century incumbent of Layston, Alexander Strange, tried to counter growing dissent by building an Anglican chapel in the town (dedicated in 1628), close to the dissenters' chapel but on the Layston side of the boundary.[23] In Buntingford, border uncertainties fostered both commerce and religious dissent.

---

21 J. Chenevix Trench, 'The houses of Coleshill', *Records of Buckinghamshire*, 26 (1983), pp. 61–109; Beatrice Saxon Snell (ed.), *The minute book of the monthly meeting of the Society of Friends for the Upperside of Buckinghamshire, 1669–1690* (High Wycombe, 1937), pp. ix–xix; Julian Hunt, *A history of Coleshill* (Much Wenlock, 2009), pp. 6–15, 25–32.

22 Mark Bailey, 'A tale of two towns: Buntingford and Standon in the later middle ages', *Journal of Medieval History*, 19 (1993), pp. 357, 361.

23 Steve Hindle, *On the parish? The micro-politics of poor relief in rural England, c.1550–1750* (Oxford, 2004), pp. 326–7; Heather Falvey and Steve Hindle, *'This Little Commonwealth'. Layston parish*

County boundaries were important because the writ of constables and justices of the peace who enforced the law was explicitly limited by numerous English statutes to a single county. The consequences of this were exploited by those who worked at the margins of the law. The site of Tunbridge Wells was open countryside until the seventeenth century, and the chalybeate springs that made its fame were located adjacent to the county border between Kent and East Sussex. Here, shops, reading rooms and libraries, an Anglican chapel and a marketplace developed on 'The Parade', now known as the Pantiles, which was the social centre of the pre-railway settlement. Sarah Baker constructed the town's first theatre there in 1802 on a site that straddled the county boundary, with the stage in Sussex and the auditorium in Kent, causing jurisdictional problems and thwarting theatre censorship. Any attempt to enforce the law could be evaded by moving from one part of the building to the other. When in the mid-nineteenth century the building became the Corn Exchange, the position became a means of evading the enforcement of trade regulations.[24]

County boundaries were also used by rural gangs engaged in poaching, deer-stealing and smuggling to evade attempts at suppression. The notorious 'Black Act' of 1723, passed to deal with deer-stealing gangs in southern England (known as 'Blacks' because they blacked their faces) who had made bold raids in Windsor Forest and on parks on the Surrey–Hampshire borders, specified that a local call to action, or 'hue-and-cry', applied only within a single county. It failed when used in Hertfordshire to deal with Col. Gore's stolen deer in 1727. His deer park was close to the Hertfordshire–Buckinghamshire border, near Tring, as well as Bedfordshire, providing an easy escape for the poachers.[25] In Windsor Forest the poaching gangs were particularly common in the Wiltshire enclave parishes of Wokingham, Hurst, Swallowfield and Shinfield, surrounded on most sides by Berkshire but outside the jurisdiction of the Berkshire JPs.[26]

Parish and county borders also attracted settlements on their margins and often on 'waste' of limited agricultural value, communities that grew up in the post-medieval era and particularly in periods of rapid population growth. Until the late seventeenth century this reflected relatively slow urbanisation in England. London grew spectacularly, while the major provincial centres (such as Bristol, York, Norwich and Newcastle) grew at the same rate as country towns and villages. Towns of 5,000 or more outside London had a virtually unchanged share of the population. England's population more than doubled between 1520 and 1700, creating demand for almost half a million new houses in the countryside. While existing villages could accommodate some of this by sub-dividing existing plots or indeed some larger older houses, perhaps a third

memorandum book, 1607–c. 1650 and 1704–c. 1747, Hertfordshire Record Society 19 (Hitchen, 2003), pp. xv–xvi, also p. xl.

24   John Colbran, *Colbran's new guide for Tunbridge Wells, being a full and accurate description of the Wells and its neighbourhood … within a circuit of nearly twenty miles …* (Tunbridge Wells, 1840), pp. 125–6.

25   John Broad, 'Whigs and deer-stealers in other guises: a return to the origins of the Black Act', *Past and Present*, 119 (1988), p. 70.

26   E.P. Thompson, *Whigs and hunters: the origin of the Black Act* (London, 1975), pp. 70–72, 88–9, 110.

of new families looked to marginal areas. In long-enclosed areas with few open-field systems, such as the south-east of England, there was much less common waste and pasture than elsewhere. In the Rape of Hastings in East Sussex David Martin and his colleagues have mapped the sites of cottages in the early modern period. There are some clusters on commons but a high proportion were built by the roadside, taking in thin strips of land on the verges.[27] In open-field midland England the availability of common waste varied widely but many parish-edge settlements developed. In upland areas of northern and western England common waste was relatively plentiful, of low monetary value and accessible for settlement.

Parish edges, particularly those on county boundaries or where parish-edge lands were inter-commoned and split between jurisdictions, were particularly attractive to those without housing. It was easy to squat on these marginal lands because manors did not police settlers and by the seventeenth century the overseers of the poor often preferred to turn a blind eye to families building their own houses. If they were prevented from doing so they might expect the parish authorities to find accommodation for them and, until the latter part of the century, little attempt was made to prevent incomers gaining settlement. Manorial lords claimed ownership of the soil subject to common rights but had plenty of reasons for turning a blind eye to squatter encroachments on poor and under-used land. If settlers became permanent they could be retrospectively fined and then added to the rental. In Shropshire James Bowen found that in the manor of Prees the rise of squatting between 1579 and 1673 increased annual manorial income by almost 23 per cent.[28] Most squatter houses of this kind were built by the families who lived in them. Part of the reason was that rural housing for less well-off people was never profitable in the past. Individuals – both larger landowners and small village freeholders – built cottages to rent. The income from the house (at least before it aged and needed repair) was greater than they could get from letting the site out as agricultural land.

New communities on parish wastes and margins appeared in every era. In the sixteenth century, particularly after 1570, new cottage settlements in royal forests such as Bernwood and Arden, in the Northamptonshire forests and in Wiltshire were commonplace.[29] David Hey vividly detailed the new settlements on the waste of Myddle in Shropshire, while Tupling's work on the Tudor industrial development

---

27   David Martin *et al.*, *Early-modern housing in the eastern High Weald, 1570–1750* (Burgess Hill, 2018).

28   James P. Bowen, 'Cottage and squatter settlement and encroachment on common waste in the sixteenth and seventeenth centuries: some evidence from Shropshire', *Local Population Studies*, 93 (2014), p. 17; James P. Bowen, 'The struggle for the commons: commons, custom and cottages in the sixteenth and seventeenth centuries', in J.P. Bowen and A.T. Brown (eds), *Custom and commercialisation in English rural society: revisiting Tawney and Postan* (Hatfield, 2016), pp. 96–117.

29   John Broad and R.W. Hoyle (eds), *Bernwood: the life and afterlife of a forest* (Preston, 1997); V.H.T. Skipp, *Crisis and development: an ecological case study of the Forest of Arden, 1570–1674* (Cambridge, 1978); P.A.J. Pettit, *The royal forests of Northamptonshire: a study in their economy, 1558–1714*, Northamptonshire Records Society 23 (Northampton, 1968); Buchanan Sharp, *In contempt of all authority: rural artisans and riot in the west of England, 1586–1660* (Berkeley, CA, 1980).

of Rossendale in Lancashire demonstrates how the valley was rapidly settled by textile workers.[30] In the fens Joan Thirsk, Margaret Spufford and, most recently, Steve Hindle have shown the expansion of population as new families exploited the wetland resources.[31] Elsewhere Margaret Spufford explored the poverty of the squatter settlements of Croxton and Offleyhay in Eccleshall, Staffordshire.[32] Richard Parrott's survey of Audley in Staffordshire in 1733 describes lightly wooded heathland north-west of Stoke-on-Trent on which cottages had sprung up on small freehold plots, common land and disputed land, occupied by men working in a wide range of non-agricultural trades, but not in the potteries. Parrott recorded the history of the area plot by plot going back a hundred years or more, and his survey shows that, although most new cottages were permanent, and might be enlarged and improved, others were pulled down and the land put to other use.[33]

In some places divided parishes with outliers played their part. Layston parish in Hertfordshire, which we met earlier when discussing Buntingford, was sliced in half by Wyddial to the north, while Wyddial contained four Layston enclaves until 1883. Layston's border with Little Hormead to the east included enclaves along the London–Cambridge road that paralleled Ermine Street, where a settlement developed with inns, the Dogs Head in le Pott in 1608 and the Bell in 1659. By 1806 a substantial settlement of 32 houses called Hare Street had developed.[34] Later nineteenth-century Ordnance Survey maps show a post office and a Methodist chapel, the whole settlement athwart an area where five detached portions of Layston parish intermingled with Little Hormead land.[35]

Juniper Hill in Cottesford (Oxfordshire) sprang up in the eighteenth century when the parish built houses for the poor on waste lands that were intermingled with the adjoining parish of Hethe. The settlement was also adjacent to the county boundary with Northamptonshire. This became the community that Flora Thompson fictionalised (with considerable licence) as *Lark Rise*.[36] It was one of many settlements

---

30 David Hey, *An English rural community: Myddle under the Tudors and Stuarts* (Leicester, 1974); G.H. Tupling, *The economic history of Rossendale* (Manchester, 1927).

31 Margaret Spufford, *Contrasting communities: English villagers in the sixteenth and seventeenth centuries* (Cambridge, 1974); Joan Thirsk, *Fenland farming in the sixteenth century* (Leicester, 1953); Steve Hindle, 'Power, poor relief, and social relations in Holland Fen, *c.* 1600–1800', *Historical Journal*, 41 (1998), pp. 67–96.

32 Peter Spufford and Margaret Spufford, *Eccleshall: the story of a Staffordshire market town and its dependent villages* (Keele, 1964); Margaret Spufford and James West, *Poverty portrayed: Gregory King and Eccleshall in Staffordshire in the 1690s*, Staffordshire Studies 7 (Keele, 1995).

33 Richard Parrott, *An accountt who hath enjoyed the severall estates in the parish of Audley and hamlet of Talk in the county of Stafford for 200 Years Last Past ... 1733.* ed. S.A.H. Burne (Newcastle, 1947). I would like to thank James Bowen for drawing my attention to this source.

34 HALS, 75772, DE/X107/T29 & 79909.

35 I have used the comprehensive range of Ordnance Survey maps available on Digimap (maintained by Edina at the University of Edinburgh). Specific references are not provided.

36 Flora Thompson, *Lark Rise to Candleford* (London, 1954); Barbara English, 'Lark Rise and Juniper Hill: a Victorian community in literature and in history', *Victorian Studies*, 29 (1985), pp. 7–34.

that developed from the waste in the nineteenth century. In Oxfordshire the borders of Wychwood forest were the site of two new communities, Freeland and Barnard Gate, both at the extreme edge of Eynsham parish. Barnard Gate attracted squatters because it was at one of the regulated forest entry points and gave access to its resources. There were only two houses in 1650, and a century later fewer than a dozen, but it then expanded to more than 50 during the nineteenth century.[37] David Brown's studies of late enclosures in the north Midlands give fascinating insights into the process. No Man's Heath, discussed earlier, was a tiny area of extra-parochial land on the borders of four counties (Derbyshire, Leicestershire, Warwickshire and Staffordshire). The late nineteenth-century local press stated that it had originally been a stopping place for gypsies, but no houses were erected until the turnpike built a toll house there around 1790. Settlers on its nine acres had no access to grazing. Their occupations included shopkeeping, beerhouses (one called the Four Counties) and cattle dealing. It became notorious as a place outside the law and a setting for prize fights. In censuses between 1861 and 1881 more heads of households there described themselves as farmers, tradesmen or artisans than as agricultural labourers.[38] In Kent an extra-parochial area north-west of Canterbury, Dunkirk, was the setting for the dramatically named 'last rising of the agricultural labourers' in the 1830s. Interestingly, it was the subject of a detailed and systematic social survey at the time, revealing a society that was not wealthy but full of trades and a multitude of enterprises. Indeed, as Reay points out, the leaders of the uprising came from the most prosperous and diverse township in the area, Hernhill.[39] In Hertfordshire the land around Harpenden Common was inhabited by poor labourers living in what an account of mid-nineteenth-century conditions there called 'the hamlets, or cottage colonies' of Bowling Alley, Chapel Row, Pimlico and Hatching Green.[40]

III

When gathering evidence of marginal or liminal settlements it is striking how frequently some of the names for such settlements recur in different parts of the country. There are four Pimlicos, four Juniper Hills, four Californias and 14 Dunkirks.[41] But the one

37   VCH *Oxfordshire*, vol. xii, pp. 116–17.

38   Brown, 'Relationship between local elites and central government', pp. 48–9.

39   Francis Liardet, *Riot in Kent. Report made to the Central Society of Education on the state of the peasantry* (London, 1838), pp. 22–46; Barry Reay, *The last rising of the agricultural labourers: rural life and protest in nineteenth-century England* (Oxford, 1990); Barry Reay, 'The last rising of the agricultural labourers: the battle in Bossenden Wood, 1838', *History Workshop Journal*, 26 (1988), p. 91.

40   Edwin Grey and E. John Russell, *Cottage life in a Hertfordshire village: 'how the agricultural labourer lived and fared in the late '60's and the '70's'* (St Albans [n.d.]), p. 17.

41   These place-names mainly suggest a combination of opportunity and social and economic diversity. Pimlico in London (originally in Hoxton) was, according to Ben Jonson (*The Alchemist*, act 5, scene 5) a place where 'Gallants, men, and women,/And of all sorts, tag-rag, been seen to flock here,/In these ten weeks, as to a second Hogsdon,/In days of Pimlico'. Dunkirk (in Flanders,

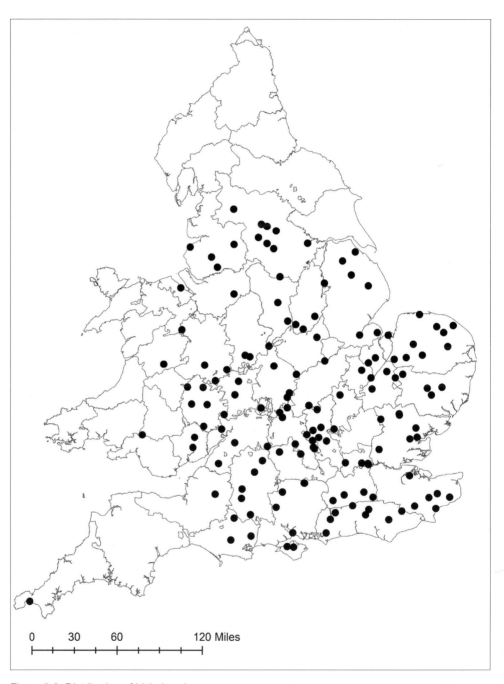

Figure 9.3. Distribution of Little Londons.

that occurs most often is Little London. The name is ancient, with several medieval examples of which the earliest is from 1270. Place-name experts are uncertain as to its derivation and meaning. Some have suggested that it is ironic, as London was so large and Little Londons are tiny. Two Yorkshire examples are possible contenders, yet the Little London in Yeadon township, in Guiseley parish, north-west of Leeds, which appears on maps of the 1850s as a small development of four or five roads, appropriately named London Street, Lombard Street and Back Lombard Street, was, according to local historians, so named because its developer was impressed with London after a visit.[42] In Mirfield, an area known as Little London City by 1850, which had been described a century earlier by Rev. Joseph Ismay as 'Near Lee Green Pits … poor, mean cottages among the pits, with coals about their doors' is a more likely candidate for irony.[43] Yet a search for the term in *Early English Books Online* finds it used in a variety of places to indicate a thriving commercial centre.

Another suggestion connects it to Welsh drovers and the cattle trade from the thirteenth century onwards, and links the proliferation of the name to the expansion of their activities, as their staging posts became known as Little Londons.[44] Some such settlements are spelt Llunon, a degraded rendering of Llundainfach, the translation of Little London into Welsh. However, the geography of known Little Londons makes this problematic. Locations in the sea off Cornwall, in the Isle of Man and on the Isle of Wight (twice) are unlikely stopping places for Welsh drovers, but their absence in the far north of England and in the south-western peninsular provides some basis of support. Overall, it seems inadequate to serve as an all-embracing explanation.

Little Londons are found widely distributed across England, as Figure 9.3 shows. The most northerly is in Long Preston, just south of Settle in the West Riding of Yorkshire. There are none in the North and East Ridings. The few in Wales are on the eastern side. There are hardly any to the west of Bristol on the south-western peninsular. That in Cornwall is, curiously, an uninhabited rock in the sea off Marazion. There are at least 140 settlements in England and Wales given this name. They share some distinctive characteristics. Firstly, they are small, mostly no more than a dozen or so houses and in at least one case just a single house. They have never had administrative recognition as a parish, township or other subdivision. Over half of them (73 out of 141) lie at the junction of two or more parishes or townships, either adjacent or close to the boundary, while 33 (23 per cent) straddle

---

long fought over by French, Spanish and Dutch) gained a reputation for piracy/buccaneering in the seventeenth century, and the French declared it a free port, open to all and sundry of all nations. California must be a nineteenth-century adoption, linked to the gold rush and the vast swings of fortune associated with it. Juniper Hill is less obvious, perhaps relating to juniper bushes flourishing on poor sandy soils – but juniper was also an essential ingredient of the gin that became such a popular drink from the late seventeenth century.

42   <https://www.a-history-of-rawdon.co.uk/little-london-13/>, accessed 26 April 2020.

43   Information from successive Ordnance Survey maps. See also <http://mirfield-2ndlook.info/ Reverend_Joseph_Ismay_1/>, accessed 25 April 2020.

44   This is fully explored at <http://www.llundainfach.co.uk/>, accessed 19 September 2020, which details most of the sites and expounds the thesis.

county boundaries. Many lie at some distance from their parish centre, in or near woodlands. However, there are others in towns, both large and small, where not infrequently they are found relatively close to the town centre or marketplace, but set back from it and accessible only by back roads. Another group are also isolated but are compact groups of houses away from the village houses, sometimes near a mine or quarry. The remainder are less easily spatially classifiable, but are most often found in isolated backwaters on road junctions.

A brief examination of each Little London in two English counties – Gloucestershire and the West Riding of Yorkshire – gives a better sense of the places. Gloucestershire has six Little Londons, three close to county borders. The smallest and most blatantly liminal place is in Haffield parish, literally astride the Herefordshire–Gloucestershire county boundary. Standing on a main road from mid-Wales to Gloucester, it is just a single house that has been known by that name since at least the eighteenth century. Little London in Aston Subedge parish consisted of a tiny group of houses on a common pasture. It lay just beneath the Cotswold edge on the Gloucestershire–Worcestershire border. The third lay in the town of Lechlade, important commercially in the early modern period as it was the highest point of navigation on the Thames, with wharves and malthouses close to the river. The town straddled the border between Gloucestershire and Berkshire, and parts of the town were under Berkshire's jurisdiction in the nineteenth century. Little London lay, as in several other urban settings, slightly away from the market centre but with easy access to it. Of the remaining three, Longhope on the edge of the Forest of Dean fits the cattle-droving stereotype best. It is a settlement round a small green on the borders of three parishes and close to the main drove road between south Wales and London. In Rodborough parish, not far from the Little London at Aston Subedge, Little London was a tight-knit group of houses close to ancient quarries on the customary woodland of Rodborough common. It fits with a different group of Little Londons, those that are apart from the village/township centre but with crowded housing on a small plot. Like Little London City in Mirfield and Scarrington in Nottinghamshire, it was swept away as slum property in the twentieth century. Finally, the Little London in Frampton Cotterell was a cluster of houses at a road junction on the outskirts of the village. This was an agricultural area to the north of Bristol in the nineteenth century, but with coal mines nearby.[45]

The eleven West Riding examples are also varied. Some have potential links to the livestock trade because they are adjacent to upland grazing on the moors and commons. The most northerly, at Long Preston, lies on a green road parallel with one main track from the valley up onto the moors, but close to where it is joined by a second track to a different moorland area. It predates the coming of the railways and certainly the construction of the cattle market at the railhead in the village below. A position in proximity to moorland, possibly at the boundary between it and early enclosures, characterises several other West Riding Little Londons lying in an arc

---

45   I have gained much from Dr Anthea Jones's knowledge of Gloucestershire and her work on the Lloyd George Land Valuation surveys of *c*.1909 <http://www.glos1909survey.org.uk/>, accessed 19 September 2020, which detected and pinpointed new Little Londons from the information in the indexes.

from Leeds to Huddersfield, including an extremely isolated farmstead in Bingley and another in Rishworth on a triangular plot besides the main road from Sowerby Bridge to Oldham. The Little London in Yeadon lies on uplands between Airedale and Wharfedale at the confluence of ways that in earlier times led up to Rombalds Moor, including Ilkley Moor. It is also well placed for main routes into Leeds and Bradford. The first houses, called Smithy Hill cottages, date from the 1750s, a clothier's house was built in the 1780s and six cottages to the south of it *c*.1800. By 1832 the settlement had grown to 14 properties. The name Little London appears on the Ordnance Survey map published in 1851, but London Street, Princess Street and Lombard Street are named on the 1838 tithe map.

The Little London in Mirfield can also be traced back to the mid-eighteenth century. By the time of the Ordnance Survey six-inch survey of 1855 it was a group of 20 or 30 houses in the countryside between a beck and Lee Green Road and was known as 'Little London City'. It was engulfed by new housing in late Victorian times and by the 1930s it had been redeveloped as Saville Place and the original name obliterated. If it was known as Little London before the mid-eighteenth century then it was nicely placed between various roadways that would have brought cattle down from Mirfield Moor. Another isolated rural Little London lies in Sitlington township of Thornhill parish, between Huddersfield and Wakefield on a back lane near woodland. In the late nineteenth century there were about 14 houses by Victoria colliery and the colliery railway, but it existed before either had been built in an entirely rural setting. Today its industrial past has gone; the houses are still there, but the name Little London is omitted from modern Ordnance Survey maps.[46] North-east of Halifax, Little London in Northowram was a group of ten or 12 houses on the side of Bleak Hill, near an old quarry. It remains as a row of five cottages, with a rather larger house adjoining. The history of the Little London just to the north of Leeds city centre is difficult to trace. It was there in the 1850s before the Carlton St barracks was built, but successive episodes of rebuilding have buried the original nature of the place, if not its name.

The three remaining West Riding Little Londons are slightly different. Little London in West Cowick township in Snaith parish near Goole is a group of six or seven houses just outside the village and the boundaries of Cowick Hall's South Park. In the 1850s it adjoined a brick yard and may have housed its workers. It lies on one route from the village out onto the low-lying floodplain of the rivers Don and the 'Dutch River', which in earlier times may have been common pastures. The Little London in Leathley also lies on the edge of the settlement, but as it was opposite the rectory it was hardly secluded. The final Little London lies on the routes south from Sheffield towards Dronfield, in Ecclesall Bierlow. On the earliest maps it was entirely rural, with a mill on the river Sheaf used to make scythes and hay and straw machinery and two or three houses straddling the county boundary between Yorkshire and Derbyshire. The arrival of the adjacent railway line, and of a range of industries including dye making

---

46 Information from successive Ordnance Survey maps. In particular, compare maps of the area from the 1850s and 1880s. The name is still acknowledged locally in the 2010 Sitlington Parish Plan. With thanks to Jane Housham for this information.

and metal working, with their attendant workers' houses, meant that the whole area had become heavily industrialised by the 1890s. Across the railway line but beside the main road, a small triangle of streets still carries the name Little London, but the original site consists of a dam and a couple of cottages.[47]

These Little Londons in Gloucestershire and the West Riding show how varied they could be. Apart from a tendency to be small and near parish and county boundaries, they have some common characteristics. The largest group has some affinity with the livestock trade. Those in Gloucestershire are plausibly linked to the Welsh droving trade, but those in Yorkshire seem more likely to be seasonal meeting places for farmers to sort their herds and flocks after removal from upland pastures on the moors. A second group are those in an urban setting, usually close to the centre and/or marketplace. Little Londons in Lechlade in Gloucestershire, and perhaps that in Leeds, are examples. This still leaves a few in the sample counties where the Little London designation has no obvious connotation: Sitlington in Yorkshire and Frampton Cotterell and Rodborough in Gloucestershire are candidates. The Rodborough instance may also be one example of isolated but dense pockets of housing at a distance from the village centre. Others include those at Yeadon, Mirfield and Scarrington in Nottinghamshire. Ultimately, however, so little of the history of Little Londons has survived that they preserve their mystery.

IV

Boundary uncertainties at parish, hundred and county level as much as unenclosed wastes and commons provided the space that enabled the English countryside to absorb a growing population in the sixteenth and seventeenth centuries, and then again in the late eighteenth. New communities on the waste developed across the whole period as the local dynamics of enclosure and landownership shifted opportunities. Lax management of unproductive and barely rentable lands by manorial lords and landowners allowed squatters to establish themselves with minimal disturbance. The declining ability of those with common rights to defend them from interlopers reinforced that tendency. Landlords might turn a blind eye to encroachments on the waste and commons but might impose rents when the communities became economically viable. A tolerance of cottages by overseers might allow the homeless and marginally poor an independent subsistence.

Historians have tended to assume that marginal settlements were poor, lawless and unruly, adopting the cultural label attached to them by contemporaries. Portrayals of Eccleshall and Headington Quarry and the reimagination of Juniper Hill as Lark Rise have all reinforced such a view.[48] However, as David Brown pointed out, these were

---

47 Information from successive Ordnance Survey maps. See also *Sheffield Directory and Guide* (1828), including under the place heading 'On the River Sheaf': William Webster 'hay and straw machine manufacturer, Little London'.

48 Spufford and West, *Poverty portrayed*; Raphael Samuel, '"Quarry roughs": life and labour in Headington Quarry, 1860–1920: an essay in oral history', in Raphael Samuel (ed.), *Village life and labour* (London, 1975); English, 'Lark Rise and Juniper Hill'.

the views of those whose primary interest was control – whether political, social or religious – rather than any objective assessment of wealth and poverty.[49] One reason why outlying settlements sprang up in new places was the gradual 'closure' of older outlets for population growth by parliamentary enclosure and central government's disafforestation of ancient royal hunting reserves.

The families that settled on the wastes and commons enclosed small plots, rarely more than an acre in size. Attempts to prosecute those with less than four acres between 1572 and 1775 were notoriously unsuccessful. Tiny plots provided basic garden vegetables and perhaps some grain crops, but were not the basis for economic survival. The economy of these settlements was the economy of makeshifts, in which produce from the plot and casual labouring were vital for survival but were not dominant components. Two other sources of income were important. One was the growing availability of employment in the secondary sector, industrial work of all kinds. Rural textile work expanded in the dales of Yorkshire and Lancashire and southwards into Derbyshire and Nottinghamshire, but was also important in regional economies from Devon, Wiltshire and Somerset to Norfolk, and less obviously in most counties. Industries such as brick and tile, fostered by the demand for housing, used the resources of the commons. Another vital component of the economy of the commons was livestock, and the failure to rigorously police their use enabled the settlers to keep a few animals and, in some cases, to use this as the basis for expansion. Livestock farming differs from grain production in its flexibility and in the vital importance of commercial expertise – knowing when to buy and sell.

The commercial side of communities on the commons and wastes is less well explored. David Brown illuminated the remarkable concentration of pedlars in the Staffordshire hamlets of Flash, on the remote Derbyshire border, and Hollinsclough in the eighteenth and early nineteenth centuries. His discussion of No Man's Heath, where Warwickshire, Leicestershire, Staffordshire and Derbyshire met, showed how that settlement provided a range of skills and services.[50] As with the livestock trades, buying and selling, not self-sufficiency or subsistence, were implicit in these heathland communities. Their position on parish and county borders thwarted government attempts to license, control and tax them.

What of Little Londons? They remain elusive and their small size has allowed them to remain so. Links with the livestock trade, particularly droving, seem likely and would help to explain their proliferation. As London and other towns grew, the numbers of flocks and herds coming from afar increased enormously. Those flocks and herds

---

49 See here the papers by David Brown, 'Relationship between local elites and central government'; 'Reassessing the influence of the aristocratic improver: the example of the fifth Duke of Bedford (1765–1802)', *Agricultural History Review*, 47 (1999), pp. 182–95; 'The rise of industrial society and the end of the self-contained village, 1760–1900?', in C. Dyer (ed.), *The self-contained village? The social history of rural communities, 1250–1900* (Hatfield, 2006), pp. 114–37.

50 David Brown, 'The autobiography of a pedlar: John Lomas of Hollinsclough, Staffordshire (1747–1823)', *Midland History*, 21 (1996), pp. 156–66; David Brown, 'Relationship between local elites and central government'.

needed fodder and water at every overnight stop, and every potential stopping place, where short-term grazing in fields and commons had to be bought from local people, had only limited resources. New routes and pastures had to be found. The rough pastures, commons and woodland on parish edges were easier to rent for short periods than land on more closely managed farms whose leases frequently included clauses forbidding subletting. They could be most easily skirted if the land was far from main settlements. The drovers were also trading as they went, so it was natural for their stopping points to become contact points for deals. This much is plausible from the little evidence we have. Beyond that we move into the realm of historical speculation. Is it too much of a leap to see Little Londons as centres for the 'grey' economy of the countryside, for backchannel deals, for trade that was barely legal, or blatantly illegal, such as poached game, the venison trade and smuggled goods?

Chapter 10

Personal names and settlement in the south Yorkshire Pennines[*]

George Redmonds

This short paper has been written with David Hey very much in my mind. He and I walked hundreds of miles in Yorkshire and north Derbyshire and our main aim was always to spend time in the hamlets and farmsteads that were familiar to us through our shared interests in family history, surname research, the Pennine landscape, the ancient pattern of highways and vernacular architecture. There was great satisfaction in visiting such atmospheric places as Barnside in Hepworth and Upper Oldfield in Honley, both with buildings dating from the seventeenth century or earlier, and for which the place-name evidence can be traced to the thirteenth century.

In our conversations we each had something to contribute (Figure 10.1). My particular interest was the early history and meaning of place-names, many of which I considered had been glossed over in the available works of reference, particularly in Smith's volumes on Yorkshire for the English Place-name Society.[1] Today I shall often speak critically of those volumes so I should acknowledge at the start the tremendous debt we all owe to the pioneering scholars who set themselves the monumental task of compiling and editing the county place-name society volumes. Without their research there would be no starting point. A.H. Smith was a pioneer in the subject. I was first alerted to the limitations of Smith's work by Stephen Moorhouse, in the ground-breaking archaeological survey of West Yorkshire published almost 40 years ago.[2]

If one of my aims on this occasion is to offer new evidence for minor place-names and to show how much still needs to be done in that particular field of research, the more significant point is to make a plea for a change in attitude by place-name scholars, a request to look again at which names are classed as important and to argue for a different emphasis in methodology. The place-names that originated in the

---

[*] George Redmonds was anxious that his contribution to the memorial conference for David Hey should be included in any volume that might subsequently appear. Accordingly he sent the editor his paper a few days after the conference. As may be seen, it was unfootnoted. Sadly Dr Redmonds died a few weeks after the conference on 10 August 2018. We publish his paper as delivered with a few editorial alterations and a minimum of notes.

1   A.H. Smith, *The place-names of the North Riding of Yorkshire*, English Place-name Society, 5 (Cambridge, 1928); A.H. Smith, *The place-names of the East Riding of Yorkshire and York*, English Place-name Society, 14 (Cambridge, 1937); A.H. Smith, *The place-names of the West Riding of Yorkshire*, 8 vols, English Place-name Society, 30–37 (Cambridge, 1961–3).

2   M.L. Faull and S.A. Moorhouse (eds), *West Yorkshire. An archaeological survey to A. D. 1500*, 3 vols and map portfolio (Wakefield, 1981).

Figure 10.1. David Hey and George Redmonds, 2015. Photograph courtesy of Pat Hey.

Old English period, and that includes a significant number not recorded in Domesday Book, are properly the concern of scholars who have a thorough understanding of the languages used by the native population and successive waves of settlers, and if we do not possess those skills we are dependent on the opinions expressed by those who do. The fact that most such names pre-date by several centuries the first examples noted emphasises the difficulties faced by those experts.

On the other hand, the vast majority of place-names in any English township were coined in the post-Conquest years, and their meanings can often be found in contemporary documentation. The task of explaining those names demands some linguistic knowledge, of course, but perhaps they can best be interpreted by scholars working in different fields, historians and linguists using a multi-disciplinary approach. Indeed, since the information we have in the volumes of the English Place-name Society is often inaccurate or misleading, it is likely to be local studies that will solve the problems of identification and meaning. That will be to the benefit of many of Yorkshire's so-called minor names.

The local historian has a role to play even where the major names are concerned. The place-name Bradley will serve as an illustration of how difficult it can be for a person who is not familiar with an area to provide us with accurate information. The index to Smith's volumes on Yorkshire lists 14 Bradleys. One of these is Bradley in Huddersfield and another is Bradley Mills in Dalton, a mile or so away, on the opposite side of the river Colne.

The two earliest pieces of evidence offered by Smith for the Dalton place-name are *molendina de Bradeley* in 1195–1215 and an unqualified *Bradelay* in 1269. Unfortunately, these are both incorrectly identified. The former is a reference to the corn mill lower down the valley at Colne Bridge, a locality within the vill of Bradley which at that time belonged to Fountains Abbey. The Domesday vill of Bradley was organised as a grange estate by the abbey and it subsequently lost its independence, perhaps as a result of depopulation, but it survived as a territory and became a hamlet division within Huddersfield. This corn mill had therefore nothing to do with Bradley Mills in Dalton. The context of the reference of 1269 is to 'the field of Bradelay in the territory of Deneby' – that is, Denby Grange, a Byland Abbey property that had no connection with either Dalton or Huddersfield. The 'field of Bradelay' is not mentioned by Smith under Denby and is not indexed independently.

Bradley Mills is actually in Kirkheaton parish, which adjoins Huddersfield. It marks the site of a former fulling mill: Walter Bradley was the miller there in 1688 and Henry Bradley in 1716, and it was this family's association with the mill that was responsible for the place-name. When Joseph Atkinson was operating the mill in 1755 it was referred to as Bradley Miln and the canal map of 1778 has Bradley Mill clearly marked. In this part of Yorkshire it was not unusual for a tenant's name to be given to a fulling mill; examples include Sunderland Mill in Mytholm Bridge and Swallow Mill in Whitley. Hinchliffe Mill in Holmfirth takes its name from a former tenant and is not a medieval settlement, as implied by Smith.

It is, of course, confusing for those who are not familiar with the area to have Bradley in Huddersfield and Bradley Mills in Dalton as near neighbours, but Smith's problems were not confined to Bradley Mills: he noted that the Huddersfield hamlet of Bradley was sometimes referred to as Nether Bradley and considered that this served to distinguish it from its neighbour Bradley Mills. In fact, the distinction was with Over Bradley in Stainland, four and a half miles away. It may seem unusual for two places so far apart to be differentiated in this way but the explanation is likely to be that the Savile family had interests in both places and needed to distinguish between them. Similarly, also in the Huddersfield area, Westheaton was a name given in some manorial accounts to Kirkheaton and it was contrasted with Eastheaton, which was Hanging Heaton in Dewsbury parish. Such prefixes may have been a scribal convenience, never in general use as place-names.

The two Bradleys on the lower Colne were not the only problem that Smith had with this place-name, for he saw Bradley Brook in Slaithwaite, which was also in Huddersfield parish, as distinct from both Bradley Mills and Nether Bradley. However, he offered the same etymology – 'broad clearing' – quite unaware that the quoted spelling, found on the Jefferys' map of 1771–2, was a dialect form of Brideley Brook, a name that occurs regularly in the Dartmouth estate records, the earliest reference pre-dating 1216. The Slaithwaite stream was named after either an early clearance or the 'de Brideley' family who then lived in the township. Their surname survived into the nineteenth century, but not in the Colne Valley, and the evidence suggests that in other parts of Yorkshire it was eventually absorbed by the more prolific surname Bradley.

More generally, Smith and those who helped him were quite often careless when it came to identifying where such names belonged. Another of the 14 Bradleys indexed was 'Bradley Gate', listed under Huddersfield, with its etymology supported by an example noted in a thirteenth-century deed. The 'gate' was said to be from

Scandinavian *gata*, a road. On checking the deed we find that the reference was to 'Bradleygate … within the vill of Staynland'. Again the context confirms the mistaken identification. There is a locality known as Bradley Gate in Huddersfield, but it has not been noted earlier than 1521 and the spelling on that occasion was 'Bradley Yatte', not a road, therefore, but a gate, from Old English *geat*.

If we now move to the subject of so-called minor names it soon becomes evident that a lack of early data caused Smith to offer mistaken etymologies for scores of settlement sites, and his suggested meanings were seldom advanced cautiously. In the Fulstone place-name Deershaw, which he first noted in 1637, the prefix was assumed to be a reference to the animal, whereas the early spelling 'Derneschaghe' indicates that the settlement took its name from the river Dearne, which had its source close by. This was recorded as a by-name in 1316, which adds more than 300 years to the place-name's history. Similarly, the prefix of Deerstones in Hazlewood, a Bolton Priory estate, was taken to refer to deer, an interpretation that is impossible given spellings such as Digherstones from 1303. The connection is surely with the surname of Nicholas Diheres, a tenant named in 1296–8.

Faced with the same lack of early examples, Smith repeatedly misleads us. Liley Hall in Mirfield will make that point. For his explanation of this place-name he relied on the modern spelling, noted in 1589. It was, he said, 'probably flax clearing … with a common loss of -*n*- as in Lillands'. There are earlier references from when Richard Thurgarland was in possession of 'the capital messuage called Lyley', but these spellings would not have altered Smith's understanding of the name. However, when we examine the pedigree of the Thurgarlands it is clear that the property had passed to them from a family called Liley, specifically via Beatrix, who was the sole heiress of William Liley of Liley Place in 1493. The house was evidently named after the family so the problem is therefore the meaning of the surname. This is found regularly as 'de Lile', latinised as de Insula, and examples occur in and around Mirfield from the twelfth century. The modern spelling was recorded as early as 1433, no doubt influenced by the names of neighbouring townships such as Emley and Farnley. In Glover's Visitation of 1612 George Thurgarland claimed descent from William de Insula of Lyle. The surname Liley survives in the neighbourhood.

It seems sometimes as though an Old English origin had to be found. For Dunford House in Methley Smith had only the 1592 spelling 'Dunsforth house or place'. His suggested etymology was the Old English personal name *Dun(n)* plus 'ford', a river crossing, and yet in the same records where the spelling of 1592 occurred is a reference to a tenant named Roger de Dunsford in 1341. This man almost certainly owed his name to the village of Dunsforth near Boroughbridge, and 'Dunsforth house' is likely to mark the site of his original residence.

The origin of Scarhouse in Golcar is evidence that moves of that distance were formerly not uncommon. The hillside location of the hamlet in this case seems to point to Scandinavian *sker* 'a scar' or 'rocky cliff' as the meaning, but when Thomas Haghe was the tenant in the period 1430–60 he was regularly said to be of Skyrehous or of Skyres in Golcar, and the connection here is with a family called 'de Skyres'. They are first mentioned in 1315 and the source of their distinctive surname was almost certainly Skiers Hall near Wombwell, where a family with that name had been living from the early thirteenth century. The Saviles had interests in both regions and Robert del Skyres of Wombwell sued John Savile of Golcar in 1356 for dispossessing him of certain lands. The change in Golcar from Skirehouse to Scarhouse was aided by the hillside location but it reflects the local pronunciation, as did Bradley from Brideley.

Place-names with a surname as the first element were particularly frequent in the hill country. The irony is that many of these were surnames that had a place-name origin close by. That is most obvious in the case of Meltham House in Fulstone, which dates from when a family named Meltham moved into Holmfirth, probably towards the end of the fourteenth century. Less obviously, Mear House, Flush House, Holme House and Dam House were settlements established by families named Mear, Flush, Holme and Dam, all of whom owed their surnames to localities in the same territory. In each case Smith's evidence was late and he took the origins to be topographic. It is not just that his examples are late and his explanations often incorrect: the real problem is the readers' inference that the moorland hamlets had their origins in the sixteenth or seventeenth centuries when in reality they were almost all in existence before 1350. It is most obvious when the surname in question became extinct early in its history, often as a result of the Black Death. The extraordinary number of new place-names is almost certainly the result of a phase of intensive clearance carried out from *c.*1307, well documented in the published volumes of the Wakefield court rolls.[3]

The story of the Wooldale hamlet of Choppards in Wooldale is typical. It has a dramatic location and its few houses mark the upward limit of the cultivated land, on the boundary with the moor. The name is listed by Smith, who quoted several examples, the earliest of 1647, but he offered no suggestion as to a possible meaning. However, it is clear from the published court rolls that this was literally Chopard's place or house: Robert Chobard or Chopard was a Wakefield manor tenant from the early fourteenth century, apparently moving the 15 or so miles south-west from Wakefield into Holmfirth. References include: 1297, Robert Chobard, Wakefield; 1313–33, Robert Chobard or Chopard, Wooldale; 1352, Robert Chopard … a party in a plea of debt, Holmfirth court. In 1313 Chobard took possession of '14 acres with buildings' in Cartworth and three years later paid 2s for further land in Longley, a territory in Wooldale. The Robert mentioned in 1352 may have been a son of the original tenant, but no later examples of the surname have yet been found. It was probably French in origin. In 1502 John Hyncheclyff was the tenant of *Choppards* and its subsequent history is well documented.

The settlement was therefore established more than three centuries earlier than the Smith reference suggests, and a score or more of similar place-names tell much the same story. Directly comparable are Totties, also in Wooldale, and Ozzings in Shelley. In this latter case the hamlet can be shown to have been where a family called Osan was living from the early fifteenth century, when it was recorded as Osanplace. In fact Osan was a Shelley surname from the late thirteenth century, unusual at first glance but almost certainly derived from Osanna, a first name given to girls who were born on a Palm Sunday. Living in the township in the 1250s was John the son of

---

3 W.P. Baildon *et al.* (eds), *Court rolls of the manor of Wakefield*, Yorkshire Archaeological Society Record Series, 29, 36, 57, 78, 109 (Leeds, 1901–45); Yorkshire Archaeological and Historical Society, Wakefield Court Rolls series (19 vols, 1974–).

Osanna of Shelley. Smith dealt with this place-name under the headword Ox Ings, a misreading of Ozings' on the Jefferys' map of 1771–2. He interpreted this reference literally and justified that interpretation by saying that Middle English 'x' often became [z] in north-country dialects.

Similar developments – that is, from a personal name, via a surname or by-name, to a place-name – are not uncommon. They explain Gregory in Whitley and Mocock Place in Austonley, both from *c*.1300. More interesting perhaps is Ebsonhouse in Fulstone. Smith identified this with a place-name Hobsonhouse, dated 1551, which he linked with George and William Hobson, assuming that the vowel had been incorrectly transcribed. The court rolls show that George and William Hobson lived in Stanley near Wakefield, in the same manor but 14 or 15 miles from Fulstone. In fact we can trace the origin of Ebsonhouse to a certain Herbert of Butterley, who was living in Fulstone in 1275, probably in the hamlet of Butterley. He is recorded as taking nine and a half acres of new land in 1286 but may have died soon afterwards. Herbert was a very uncommon first name at that time and his descendants, Richard, Robert and Thomas, all had the by-name 'son of Herbert'. The pet form of Herbert was 'Hebbe' and in 1313 Richard son of Hebbe was in possession of 12½ acres in Fulstone, 'with buildings'. In 1332 Herbert's grandson Thomas inherited the 'dwelling house' and was referred to as Thomas, son of Richard, son of Hebbe. There can be no doubt I think that the dwelling was 'Hebbeson house'. In 1350 the property passed to Alice, the daughter and heir of Thomas Hebson, and it must be concluded that the surname Hebbeson became extinct locally when Thomas's widow Agnes remarried in 1351.

Smith made no mention of the hamlet that we know as Larks House. It lies to the east of Meal Hill Lane in Hepworth, a group of stone-built houses apparently of no great antiquity. The name is shown on the Ordnance Survey map of 1854 and seven families were living there at the time of the 1851 census. The clue to a much longer history can be found in the baptismal register of Holmfirth Chapel. During the 1790s the distinctive first name of Gamaliel Battye is the vital evidence that links the modern spelling Larks House to *Louks House*, a form of the name on record from 1550 when a clothier called George Castill was granted permission 'to enjoy a messuage called *Lowekeshowse*, and 25 acres of land' in the graveship of Holme.

No direct earlier reference to the place-name has yet been found, but Loukes as a Hepworth surname is on record from the mid-fourteenth century. More significantly, in 1339 a messuage in *Heppeworth* was granted to Cecily, the daughter of *John de Louk*, and this seems certain to be about the time that Loukes House was named. The court rolls have entries that indicate quite clearly that 'Louk' was a first name or baptismal name, a short or pet form of Louecock or Lovecock, a first name of Old French origin, no doubt a nickname of sorts from the French word 'wolf'. There is a possible candidate in the Hepworth area: 1275 *Lovekoc de WIvedale*; 1316 'John of *Loukes* of *WIvedale*'. However, the pet form was not used on every occasion, and an entry for 1332 catches the name en route to becoming hereditary while offering an earlier date for the dwelling that would become Loukes House: 1332 'Alice daughter of *Richard Loucokson* surrenders a messuage … in Hepworth'. The surname Loukes or Lowkes survived in Holmfirth into the 1420s and is found subsequently in other parts of Wakefield manor and south Yorkshire, but it never became numerous.

On occasion Smith suggested meanings based on very late evidence and took no account of the local topography. For Holme in Slaithwaite he had a single map reference of 1843. The place-name is now represented by small clusters of houses at Lower and Upper Holme, and Smith derived these names from Old Norse *holmr*, a water meadow. Both hamlets are high on the hills to the west of present-day Slaithwaite. Further to the west is Slaithwaite Hall, which marks the site of the original settlement. Spellings from *c.*1200, which include *Houwom*, are evidence that Holme in this instance can be compared with Holme on the Wolds, meaning 'on the hills', from Scandinavian *i haugum*, the dative plural of *haugr*.

Of particular importance to the local historian is the information we have relating to the status of Holme, described in deeds of 1363 as *la vill de Howom juxta Slaghtwayt*. Even earlier, in *c.*1200, land was said to lie in the *campis de Houm*, so it existed as a 'town' with its own arable land for several centuries: it continued to be described in sixteenth-century wills as *Haume in the half township of Slaithwaite* and retained hamlet status for a while. However, it was not mentioned independently in Langdale's topographical dictionary or in Baines's trade directory, both published in 1822. The first examples of the present spelling are recorded from the late sixteenth century.

An intriguing side to the history of 'Holme' is that it gave rise to a surname in Slaithwaite that has a linguistic history similar to the place-name. The (*de*) *Hawme* family remained in that part of the Colne Valley from 1332 into the 1600s, at which time their surname started to be confused with Holmes, notably just over the watershed in Elland parish. The original spelling was not recorded in the West Riding Hearth Tax of 1672 and I have found no later examples. It is not necessarily extinct for it is possible that some families now called Holme or Holmes descend from the Slaithwaite family.

We can be alerted to these minor settlement names by the suffixes 'house' and 'place', or simply the possessive 's'. These were once very common in some parishes. In Methley, for example, more than 30 dwellings had 'place' as a suffix between 1367 and 1642. However straightforward many of these might seem, it is local information that can solve the meaning. Ward Place in Cartworth, for example, for which Smith had spellings from 1709, was said to be 'doubtless the surname Ward'. I feel certain he was wrong and am confident that the first element was originally Wade not Ward. Ward is not a local name, whereas the Wade family resided in Cartworth from the fourteenth century until *c.*1580: Wade Place was originally where they lived and it survived as a Cartworth place-name into the seventeenth century: e.g. 1578 John Crosland of Wadeplace; 1639 John Charlesworth of Wadeplace. I have not found an alias of the place-name to confirm that development but the two surnames could certainly be confused: in 1767 we have Nathaniel Ward otherwise Wade.

One of David Hey's late publications was an article published in 2013 in *Northern History*.[4] In it he used family names and minor place-names to tell the story of Thurlstone's medieval landscape. In many ways it was a record of walks we had done together in all weathers over the previous 20 years or so and it contains one paragraph in particular that reflects how comfortable he was by then when discussing minor settlement names. My story concerns the unusual farm name Illions. Throughout his life he had passed the farm and been puzzled by its obscure

---

4   David Hey, 'Townfields, royds and shaws: the medieval landscape of a south Pennine township', *Northern History*, 50 (2013), pp. 216–38.

name: it is listed by Smith with a reference from 1565 but unexplained. A deed in the Savile family papers in Nottingham records the grant of a messuage next to Smallshaw to Robert Illian and his wife in 1359. The location is exact and the farm still bears the family's name. Further research showed that Ylian as a personal name is found in the area from *c.*1200. From Peter McClure and Oliver Padel came confirmation that Illion was an uncommon Breton first name. David derived a great deal of satisfaction from solving its origin.

Index

The counties employed in the index are 'historic' English counties, i.e. those existing before the local government reorganization of 1974.